NICARAGUA

NICARAGUA

LIVING IN THE SHADOW OF THE EAGLE

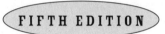

FIFTH EDITION

THOMAS W. WALKER
AND
CHRISTINE J. WADE

**WESTVIEW
PRESS**

A Member of the Perseus Books Group

Westview Press was founded in 1975 in Boulder, Colorado, by notable publisher and intellectual Fred Praeger. Westview Press continues to publish scholarly titles and high-quality undergraduate- and graduate-level textbooks in core social science disciplines. With books developed, written, and edited with the needs of serious nonfiction readers, professors, and students in mind, Westview Press honors its long history of publishing books that matter.

Published by Westview Press,
A Member of the Perseus Books Group

Find us on the World Wide Web at www.westviewpress.com.

The drawing in the lower portion of the cover was produced especially for the fourth edition by the late Leóncio Sáenz of Nicaragua. During the revolutionary period Sáenz was a frequent artistic contributor to *Nicaráuac, Pensamiento Própio*, and other Nicaraguan publications. In addition, his works hung in the outer office of President Daniel Ortega and were featured in exhibitions around the world.

Every effort has been made to secure required permissions to use all images, maps, and other art included in this volume.

Westview Press books are available at special discounts for bulk purchases in the United States by corporations, institutions, and other organizations. For more information, please contact the Special Markets Department at the Perseus Books Group, 2300 Chestnut Street, Suite 200, Philadelphia, PA 19103, or call (800) 810-4145, ext. 5000, or e-mail special.markets @perseusbooks.com.

Designed by Trish Wilkinson
Set in 11 point Minion Pro

Library of Congress Cataloging-in-Publication Data

Walker, Thomas W., 1940–
    Nicaragua : living in the shadow of the eagle / Thomas W. Walker and Christine J. Wade. — 5th ed.
        p.   cm.
    Includes bibliographical references and index.
    ISBN 978-0-8133-4387-7 (hardcover : alk. paper) — ISBN 978-0-8133-4526-0 (e-book) 1. Nicaragua—History. 2. Nicaragua—Relations—United States. 3. United States—Relations—Nicaragua. 4. Nicaragua—Politics and government. I. Wade, Christine J. II. Title.
F1526.W175 2011
972.85—dc22   2010045676

10 9 8 7 6 5 4 3 2 1

Contents

■ Preface

When, in 2002, coauthor Walker first decided to change the subtitle of the fourth edition of this book from *The Land of Sandino* to *Living in the Shadow of the Eagle*, there was some concern that the subtitle should more appropriately stress some outstanding characteristic inherent in Nicaragua. Stressing the influence of Augusto César Sandino—as in the original title—had been a way of doing that. However, Walker defended his proposal for the new title with an analogy: If one is describing a Japanese bonsai tree, is it best to focus mainly on the inherent characteristics of the species being discussed? Wouldn't it be better to emphasize the external factors affecting the morphology of that organism—indeed, that affect the nature of all bonsai trees regardless of species? The unusual aspect of a bonsai is not its species but rather the environmental stress to which humans have deliberately subjected it in order to achieve a different beauty.

The bonsai analogy, of course, is not perfect. In some senses, a plant can be made more graceful and interesting by stressing it. However, when a nation-state is subjected to the prolonged external interference of a regional hegemon—no matter how well intentioned—its social, economic, and political systems are often hurt and deformed. The result is not usually beautiful.

Nicaragua shares with most Latin American countries a centuries-old experience of U.S. intervention and interference. But few countries have been so extensively and repeatedly intervened in as Nicaragua. This edition, like earlier ones, shows how U.S. interference inexorably led to the Sandinista Revolution of the late twentieth century. First, after the country's formal independence in the nineteenth century, England and the United States squabbled over control of Nicaragua. At one point in the 1850s, U.S. filibuster William Walker actually took over the country and made himself president long enough to be recognized by Washington. Later, U.S. Marines occupied Nicaragua for most of the period from 1912 to 1933. Then, the U.S.-appointed head of the U.S.-created "Nicaraguan" National Guard, Anastasio Somoza García, created a dynastic dictatorship that was passed on to two of his sons and lasted until 1979. During this time, the Somozas' corrupt National Guard came to hold the distinction of being the most heavily U.S.-trained military establishment in Latin America. Finally, on July 19, 1979, a massive national uprising coordinated by the Sandinista National Liberation Front (FSLN) overthrew West Point–educated dictator Anastasio Somoza Debayle—often referred to as "the Last Marine."

We also detail the history and nature of the subsequent nationalist government led by the FSLN (1979–1990). The government's quite moderate social, economic, political, and international policies are carefully described. So, too, are the efforts by the U.S. government to bring this nationalistic experiment to an end. We show how U.S. programs of economic strangulation, low-intensity warfare, and disinformation were ultimately successful in so undermining the Sandinista experiment that it was voted out of power by a cowed and desperate electorate in the second of two free elections held during the period.

The updated annotated bibliography includes the scores of books published about the country since 1990. Most chapters now include sections on the nature and impact of the U.S.-orchestrated conservative restoration (1990–2007) and return of Daniel Ortega (2007 onward). We see how the three administrations in this period—those of Violeta Chamorro, Arnoldo Alemán, and Enrique Bolaños—owed their existence, in large part, to heavy-handed U.S. involvement in the 1990, 1996, and 2001 elections. Once "in power," these leaders were then pressured to implement economic and social policies approved of by Washington. The result of the new social and economic policies—enforced by the International Monetary Fund, the World Bank, and the Inter-American Development Bank (in which the United States has controlling interests)—was a reversal of the old Sandinista "logic of the majority." Instead, the new administrations pursued neoliberal economic policies, which, though they eventually brought growth to the economy, created such a regressive distribution of income that Nicaragua's place among the nations of the world on the United Nations Development Program's Human Development Index (measuring social as well as economic factors) dropped from 60th at the time of Chamorro's inauguration to 116th ten years later.

By the early twenty-first century, Nicaragua had come nearly full circle. True, it was more democratic than it had been before the overthrow of the Somozas. So too, however, were most Latin American countries at that point; unlike during the cold war, formal democracy was now a part of the U.S. formula for Latin America. Of greater importance to the common citizen, however, was the fact that Nicaragua was once again as fully under U.S. control as it had been in the days of the Somozas. U.S.-approved economic and social policies were being implemented and—though they resulted in modest growth—were causing poverty and maldistribution of income to be as great as they had been in the dark days of the Somozas.

In 2006, U.S. officials tried once again to influence the outcome of the presidential elections. However, by that time, the dismal social performance of the three post-Sandinista governments and a split in the forces that had brought them to power allowed Sandinista leader Daniel Ortega to return to the presidency. Though Washington had no choice but to formally accept the results of these internationally certified elections, it would, as we will show, continue to meddle in the affairs of that tiny country. Thus, considering Nicaragua's recent history in light of its past, we feel very justified in having changed the subtitle of the book to the more realistic, if less upbeat, *Living in the Shadow of the Eagle*. For Nicaragua, there long has been—and probably always will be—an "eagle" on the northern horizon.

Acknowledgments

The authors would like to express their gratitude to a number of individuals, groups, and institutions who helped in producing the various editions of this book. First, thanks are due the Nicaraguan people and several governments for their kind hospitality and extensive cooperation. We are also grateful to the editors of *Caribbean Review, Current History*, Houghton Mifflin and Company, and Scholarly Resources Inc., for their kind permission to use occasional phrases, sentences, and paragraphs that appeared in earlier Walker publications for which they hold the copyrights. The logistical support of Alice McGrath, Milagros Lanzas, and Gabriela Chavarría in various tasks related to later editions is gratefully acknowledged. For kindly reading and commenting on parts of the manuscript, thanks are due Alejandro Bendaña, Judy Butler, Eduardo Cavazos, Ricardo Chavarría, Joseph Collins, Kenneth P. Erickson, Peter Kemmerle, Reynold Nesiba, Francisco Pérez, Janet Polzer, Susan E. Ramírez-Horton, Charles Roberts, Charles Stansifer, Eric Wagner, Anne U. Walker, and Sergio Zeledón. We would also like to thank Karl Yambert and the staff at Westview Press for their commitment to this project.

Thomas Walker is particularly indebted to the Department of Political Science, the College of Arts and Sciences, the Center for International Studies, and the Office of Research and Sponsored Programs at Ohio University for the financial support that enabled him to make trips to Nicaragua following the liberation. Walker also thanks Chris Wade for joining him as coauthor—thus injecting new vigor, insight, and cheer into this project as he nears full retirement. Finally, he is very grateful to his wife,

Anne, and children, Joe, Carlos, James, and Emilie, for their understanding and support beyond the call of duty especially during the work on the first few editions.

Christine Wade would like to thank Washington College for financial support that enabled her to conduct research in Nicaragua in 2009. She is especially grateful to Judy Butler, Gabriela Chavarría, Milagros Lanzas, Scott Palmer, and Dan Premo for their kindness and support. She would also like to thank her husband, Greg, for his love and encouragement. Finally, she is indebted to her dear friend and coauthor Tom Walker for providing her with so many wonderful opportunities and quite a few laughs along the way.

Thomas W. Walker and Christine J. Wade

Acronyms and Abbreviations

ALBA	Bolivarian Alliance for the Peoples of Our America
ALN	Nicaraguan Liberal Alliance
AMNLAE	Luisa Amanda Espinosa Association of Nicaraguan Women
AMPRONAC	Association of Women Confronting the National Problem
ANS	Sandinista Children's Association
APRE	Alliance for the Republic
ASTC	Sandinista Association of Cultural Workers
ATC	Rural Workers' Association
BCLs	Light Hunter Battalions
BLIs	Irregular Warfare Battalions
CAFTA	Central American Free Trade Agreement
CDC	Civil Defense Committee
CDRS	Ramiro Sacasa Democratic Coordinating Committee
CDS	Sandinista Defense Committee
CEB	Christian Base Community
CENI	Central Bank's Negotiable Investment Certificate
CEPAD	Evangelical Committee for Developmental Aid
CONDECA	Central American Defense Council
COPPPAL	Permanent Conference of Political Parties of Latin America
CORDENIC	Commission on the Recovery and Development of Nicaragua

COSEP	Superior Council of Private Enterprise
CPC	Citizens Power Councils
CSE	Supreme Electoral Council
CST	Sandinista Workers' Central
CTN	(Social Christian) Confederation of Workers of Nicaragua
CUS	Confederation of Labor Unity
DN	Sandinista National Directorate
ENABAS	National Foodstuffs Enterprise
EPS	Sandinista Popular Army
FAD	Democratic Armed Forces
FAO	Broad Opposition Front
FARC	Revolutionary Armed Forces of Colombia
FDN	Nicaraguan Democratic Forces
FIR	International Reconstruction Fund (Nicaragua)
FPR	Revolutionary Patriotic Front
FMLN	Farabundo Martí National Liberation Front
FSLN	Sandinista National Liberation Front
FSMN	Nicaraguan Teachers' Union Federation
GPP	Prolonged Popular War (faction)
IDB	Inter-American Development Bank
IMF	International Monetary Fund
INCAE	Central American Institute of Business Administration
INPRHU	Institute for Human Promotion
INSSBI	Nicaraguan Social Security and Welfare Institute
JGRN	Governing Junta of National Reconstruction
JMRs	Municipal Juntas for Reconstruction
JS-19	19th of July Sandinista Youth
MAP-ML	Marxist-Leninist Popular Action Movement
MDN	Nicaraguan Democratic Movement
MINVAH	Ministry of Housing and Human Settlements
MPS	Sandinista Popular Militias
MRS	Sandinista Renovation Movement
MUR	United Revolutionary Movement
OAS	Organization of American States
PC	Conservative party

PCD	Democratic Conservative party
PCN	Nicaraguan Communist party
PETRONIC	Petroleum of Nicaragua
PLC	Constitutional Liberal party
PLI	Independent Liberal party
PPSC	Popular Social Christian party
PRI	Institutional Revolutionary party (Mexico)
PS	Sandinista Police
PSCN or PSC	Nicaraguan Social Christian party
PSD	Social Democratic party
PSN	Nicaraguan Socialist party
PUCA	Central American Unity party
RAAN	North Atlantic Autonomous Region
SI	Socialist International
SSTV	Sandinista Television System
TP	Proletarian Tendency
TPAs	Popular Anti-Somocista Tribunals
UNAG	National Union of (Small) Farmers and Ranchers
UNO	National Opposition Union or (beginning in 1990) National Organized Union
UPANIC	Union of Nicaraguan Farmers
USAID	U.S. Agency for International Development
WHISC	Western Hemisphere Institute for Security Cooperation

I am an anti-imperialist. I am opposed
to having the eagle put its talons on any other Land.

—MARK TWAIN
OCTOBER 15, 1900

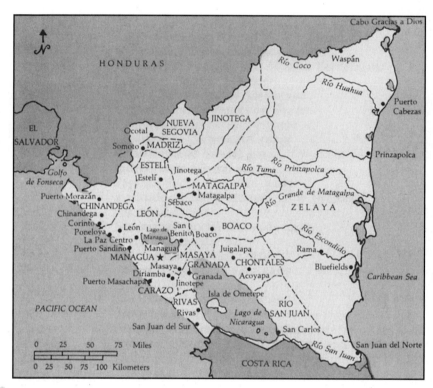

Nicaragua

1
Introduction

Located at the geographic center of Central America, with Honduras to the north and Costa Rica to the south, Nicaragua is the largest country in the region. Even so, its 57,143 square miles (148,000 square kilometers) of surface is only about that of Illinois (57,914 square miles), and its population of about 5.9 million actually made it slightly less populous than Missouri (5.98 million) in 2010. Nevertheless, Nicaragua is an extremely interesting and unique country with an importance that, at least for a while, far exceeded its size. Although there have been many revolts and coups d'état in Latin America, Nicaragua is one of only a handful of Latin American countries to have experienced a real social revolution, by which we mean a rapid process of change in social and economic as well as political structures.

The physical characteristics of Nicaragua have long drawn the attention and captured the imagination of outsiders. The country has abundant and rich agricultural lands, considerable potential for geothermal and hydroelectric energy, important timber and mineral resources, and conveniently located waterways that make Nicaragua an ideal site for an interoceanic canal.

Though located entirely within the tropics, this small country varies from one region to another in temperature and other climatic characteristics. Altitude, mountainous land barriers, and the differing meteorological influences of the Caribbean and the Pacific Ocean are the determining factors. As throughout the tropics, altitude rather than season determines temperature. On the lowlands of the Pacific and Caribbean coasts, temperatures usually are quite high. In the central mountain ranges—or Cordilleras—that

1

transverse the country from northwest to southeast, the climate is temperate. The mountains also influence Nicaraguan weather by acting as a natural barrier between the predominantly humid environment of the Caribbean and the seasonally dry patterns of the Pacific.

As a result of these factors, Nicaragua can be divided conceptually into three distinct regions: the Caribbean lowlands, the central highlands, and the western lowlands. Occupying nearly half of the country, the Caribbean lowlands are composed of hot, humid tropical rain forests, swamps, and savannahs. As the most appropriate type of agricultural activity in such an environment involves the primitive slash-and-burn technique, this vast region has never been able to support a large human population—at present less than 8 percent of the national total lives there.

Due to the more moderate and seasonal nature of rainfall in the central highlands and western lowlands, these regions are more inviting for commercial agriculture and human habitation. The temperate climate and rich soils of the highlands make an ideal environment for coffee cultivation. Indeed, some of the best coffee in the world comes from the highland department of Matagalpa. The western lowlands are appropriate for such crops as cotton, rice, and sugar. A chain of volcanoes running through the western lowlands from northwest to southeast enriches the soil of the region through frequent dustings of volcanic ash. The principal cities and most of the population of Nicaragua are in the western lowlands.

Another important physical factor is the position of certain large lakes and rivers. Even in the colonial period, explorers and settlers knew that interoceanic travel across Nicaragua was possible via water routes, taking advantage of the San Juan River, Lake Nicaragua, and Lake Managua. The amount of overland travel required to complete the journey was small. As a result, Nicaraguan waterways were regularly used as commercial routes for transisthmian travel during the nearly three centuries of colonial rule. And in the nineteenth and twentieth centuries, the country's obvious potential as a canal site made Nicaragua the object of frequent foreign intrigue and intervention.

Nicaragua is blessed not only in natural resources and environment but also in certain demographic, social, and cultural characteristics. First, unlike some Latin American countries, it is not overpopulated. Indeed, although it has an abundance of arable land, Nicaragua's population is relatively small. Second, the people are relatively homogeneous and culturally integrated. There are no major racial, ethnic, linguistic, or religious divisions. Practically all Nicaraguans are Catholic, speak Spanish, and share a common cultural heritage. The majority are mestizo, a mixture of Spanish and Indian. And though there are some "pure" whites, Indians, and blacks, little racial prejudice exists. Finally, Nicaraguans are a congenial, outgoing people with every reason to be proud of things *nica*, such as their distinctive cookery, music, dialect, literary heritage, and sense of humor.

Ironically, in spite of its human and natural potential, Nicaragua is a poor country, and the majority of the people have endured great oppression throughout history. Even in the late 1970s the annual gross national product (GNP) per capita was only a little over US$800. Moreover, this statistic obscures the fact that income in Nicaragua was so unevenly distributed that 50 percent of the people probably had an annual disposable income of only $200. The average citizen lived in inadequate housing, ate poorly, and prior to the 1979 revolution, had little access to education, health care, or other public services. In 1979 the estimated life expectancy at birth for the average Nicaraguan was fifty-three years—ten years less than the average for Central America and eighteen years less than the average for the Latin American nation with the greatest longevity, Cuba.[1]

The roots of Nicaragua's problem lie in a phenomenon that many social scientists refer to as *dependency*. Most countries in the world are dependent to one degree or another on other countries. Interdependence does not necessarily imply dependency. Dependency refers to a specific situation in which the economy of a weak country is externally oriented and the government is controlled by national and/or international elites or classes that benefit from this economic relationship. Whereas the dominant elites in an industrial country usually have an interest in maintaining a healthy society and, therefore, a citizenry capable of consuming at high levels, the rulers of a dependent society have no such interest because their markets are largely external. For them, the common citizen is important not as a potential consumer but rather as a source of cheap and easily exploitable labor. In such societies the means of production and income tend increasingly to be concentrated in a few hands. Though impressive growth in the GNP often occurs, significant benefits almost never "trickle down" to the people, no matter how long the process goes on and no matter how much development takes place.[2]

Except briefly during the Sandinista Revolution (1979–1990), Nicaragua has been an extreme case of this common phenomenon. From the days of the Spanish conquest in the sixteenth century, the Nicaraguan economy had always been externally oriented, and the people who exercised power had been the beneficiaries of this relationship. First, hundreds of thousands of Indians were exported as slaves. Later, when that "resource" was used up, the elites exported timber, beef, and hides. During the late nineteenth century, coffee became an important product on the world market. In the twentieth century, especially after the Second World War, the country developed a diversified repertoire of exports ranging from cotton, coffee, and sugar to beef and gold. Throughout Nicaraguan history, a small elite controlled most of the means of production and garnered most of the benefits. The country's rulers—whether openly dictatorial or ostensibly democratic—almost always governed on behalf of the privileged few.

Paralleling this history of domestic exploitation—and frequently an essential ingredient of it—was a history of foreign intervention and control. During the colonial period, the Spanish faced sporadic challenges from the British government and English pirates for control of Nicaraguan territory. In the middle of the nineteenth century, the country was actually ruled by a U.S. citizen for a brief period. In the twentieth century, the U.S. government imposed its dominion over Nicaragua first by direct armed intervention (from 1912 to 1925 and from 1926 to 1933), later through the client dictatorships of the Somoza family (from 1936 to 1979), and finally through subservient conservative democracies (from 1990 to 2007).

Yet if dependency, exploitation, and mass deprivation constitute recurrent themes in Nicaraguan history, so, too, do the ideas of nationalism and popular resistance. Nicaraguan history and folklore are replete with nationalist heroes and martyrs: the Indian *cacique* ("chief"), Diriangén, who fought against the Spanish at the outset of the colonial period; Andrés Castro, who took a stand against the forces of the North American filibuster-president, William Walker, in the mid-nineteenth century; the liberal dictator José Santos Zelaya, who defied British and U.S. imperial designs at the turn of the century; Benjamín Zeledón and Augusto César Sandino, who fought the U.S. occupiers in the early twentieth century; and Carlos Fonseca Amador, a cofounder of the Sandinista Front of National Liberation (FSLN), who died in the guerrilla struggle against the Somoza dictatorship in 1976.

By their actions, these men preserved and reinforced in the Nicaraguan people a stubborn strain of irrepressibility and national pride. Finally, catalyzed into action early in 1978 by the brutal assassination of a prominent and beloved opposition newspaper editor, Nicaraguans of all classes rose up against the dictatorship of Anastasio Somoza Debayle and the system he represented. Eighteen months later, at a cost of approximately 50,000 dead, the Nicaraguan revolution had triumphed. A brutal and selfish dictator had been overthrown, and a revolutionary government representing the aspirations of countless generations of Nicaraguans had finally come to power.

The Nicaraguan people were aware of the historic significance of their victory. In spite of the tremendous cost of the war, the mood in the country in July 1979 was one of near universal ecstasy. On July 20, the largest crowd ever assembled in Central America greeted the new government in the central plaza. A few days later, one young woman, after detailing the loss of various family members, exclaimed, "That [the death and destruction] doesn't matter. The revolution triumphed! I feel as if I had just been born! Like a little baby with a whole life ahead of me!"

In a sense, the people of Nicaragua *had* just been born. Almost immediately the new government took steps to reverse the centuries-old patterns of elite control and dominance. A substantial segment of the economy was nationalized, exports were put under strict government control, a massive literacy campaign was launched, and new ideas in health, housing, and public education were generated and put into practice. However, these changes alarmed conservative politicians and policy makers in Washington, who, two years later, began to sponsor a counterrevolutionary war and implement other destabilizing policies in a broad program of "low-intensity conflict" against Nicaragua. These efforts eventually caused so much death, destruction, and economic hardship that paradoxically, in 1990, in the second of two free national elections held by the revolutionary government, a Nicaraguan population desperately craving peace and an end to its economic woes voted into office a conservative government openly sponsored by the United States. Under heavy U.S. pressure, the new government then moved quickly to dismantle changes made during the revolution.

This book deals with the history of the Nicaraguan people and their social, economic, and political reality, past and present. It also examines the programs and policies—domestic and foreign—of the revolutionary government. The themes of elite exploitation, foreign manipulation, national resistance, revolutionary redirection, and counterrevolutionary resurgence receive special attention. We hope this approach will help the reader not only to appreciate the origins of the revolution and the various programs that the revolutionary government implemented but also to understand the social polarization, bitterness, opportunism, and cynicism that set in during the period that followed the end of that unusual experiment.

NOTES

1. *1979 World Population Data Sheet* (Washington, D.C.: Population Reference Bureau, 1979).

2. For a good discussion of dependency, see Ronald H. Chilcote and Joel C. Edelstein, "Alternative Perspectives of Development and Underdevelopment in Latin America," in their edited work *Latin America: The Struggle with Dependency and Beyond* (New York: John Wiley and Sons, 1974), pp. 1–87.

2

Early History

The Pre-Columbian Period to the Mid-1930s

The history of Nicaragua is among the most turbulent and interesting in all of the Americas. If, on the one hand, it features incredible elite exploitation, mass suffering, and foreign interference, it also includes a significant element of popular resistance, national pride, and human nobility.

THE PRE-COLUMBIAN PERIOD

Even before the arrival of the Spaniards in the sixteenth century, the territory that we now call Nicaragua apparently was not a land of human tranquility. A demographic outpost of various Meso- and South American Indian groups, Nicaragua was an ethnically complex region. The most obvious dissimilarities were between the various indigenous tribes related to South American peoples who lived in the rain forests and savannahs to the east of the Central Cordillera and the Meso-American groups that inhabited the more hospitable western regions. The former, though primarily hunters and gatherers, also engaged in slash-and-burn agriculture, as do some of their descendants today. The more culturally sophisticated inhabitants of the western regions, on the other hand, were sedentary agriculturalists who raised corn, beans, and vegetables and lived in established towns with populations sometimes numbering in the tens of thousands. The western tribes spoke a variety of Meso-American languages reflecting

several distinct waves of settlement from what is today Mexico and northern Central America. Though the western Indians rarely had anything to
do with their more primitive counterparts across the mountains, contact
and conflict among the tribes of the west were common. Warfare, slavery,
and involuntary tribute by the weak to the strong were among the basic
ingredients of pre-Columbian life in the west. In a sense, then, many of
the traits that characterized colonial rule existed long before the first *conquistadores* set foot in the land.

THE COLONIAL PERIOD: 1522–1822

The Spanish conquest of Nicaragua was an extension of the colonization
of Panama, which began in 1508. Plagued by internal conflict, disease, and
Panama's inhospitable natural environment, the Spaniards were not in a
position to expand their control to the immediate north for well over a decade. It was only in 1522 that Gil González, commanding a small band of
explorers under contract to the Spanish crown, finally set foot in Nicaragua. The purpose of his expedition—like that of other *conquistadores*—
was to convert souls and to obtain gold and other riches from the native
population. Considering that he managed to convert close to 30,000 Indians, carry off nearly 90,000 pesos worth of gold, and discover what
appeared to be a water link between the Caribbean and the Pacific, González's venture into Nicaragua was a clear success.

It was not without its anxious moments, however. Though at first submissive, some Indians eventually decided to resist the bearded strangers.
One of these was the legendary chief Diriangén, from the region around
what is today the city of Granada. Several days after an initial meeting with
González, in which he promised to bring his people to the Spaniard for
conversion, Diriangén returned to attack the outsiders with several thousand warriors, causing them to retreat overland to the Pacific Ocean. To
make matters worse, before they reached the safety of their Pacific fleet,
González and his men were also set upon by warriors under the command
of another chief, Nicarao. It was 1524 before the Spanish, under Francisco
Hernández de Córdoba, returned to Nicaragua and imposed their control
over the region.

The early years of the colonial period had a profound and lasting impact on the nature of Nicaraguan society and politics. The most important

and tragic result of the conquest was demographic—the near total destruction of the large Indian population of the region. Incredible as it seems, it appears that Spanish chroniclers and early historians may have been fairly accurate when they reported that an original native population of around a million was reduced to tens of thousands within a few decades of the arrival of Gil González.[1] This incredible depopulation was the result of several factors. The outright killing of natives in battle, probably accounting for the demise of a few thousand, was the least significant factor. Death by exposure to diseases brought to the New World by the Spaniards was much more important. The fact that Indians had little natural immunity to such common ailments as measles and influenza resulted in an immediate and dramatic reduction in their numbers throughout the Americas. It is likely that hundreds of thousands of Nicaraguan Indians perished of disease within a few decades.

Slavery was a third important factor that reduced Nicaragua's native population. Claims by writers of those times that 400,000 to 500,000 natives were gathered and exported into bondage during the first two decades of the colonial period seem to stand up to close scholarly investigation. The archives of the times show that there were enough slave ships of sufficient capacity making frequent enough trips to have accomplished this exportation.[2] The demand for slaves throughout the Spanish colonies—and especially in Peru in the 1530s—was very high. Though the Spanish themselves captured some slaves, many more were turned over to them by "friendly" Indian chiefs as a form of obligatory tribute. The life expectancy of these unfortunate souls was short. Many—sometimes 50 percent or more—died during the sea journey from Nicaragua to their intended destination. Most of the rest perished in slavery within a few years. As a result, supply never caught up with demand and, although the Spanish crown tried unsuccessfully to stop this lucrative trafficking in human life, the slave boom came to an end only when the resource was all but depleted. By the 1540s the Indian population of western Nicaragua appears to have plummeted to between 30,000 and 40,000—and it declined gradually for several decades thereafter.

The result of this demographic holocaust is that Nicaragua today, instead of being a predominantly Indian country, is essentially mestizo in racial type and almost exclusively Spanish in language and other aspects of culture. Though most of the cities and towns of the country bear Indian names reflecting the culture of their founders, few of the people who walk their streets today are aware of what the names mean or who the original inhabitants were.

Another legacy of the colonial period—this one primarily political—was the rivalry between the principal cities of León, to the northwest of Lake Managua, and Granada, on the northern shore of Lake Nicaragua. Though both were founded by Francisco Hernández de Córdoba in 1524, they differed from each other in important cultural, social, and economic characteristics. As it was originally felt that Granada would be the political capital of the colony, the more "aristocratic" *conquistadores* chose to settle there. Spanish soldiers of lower rank and social status were packed off to León to defend the colony against incursions and claims by other Spanish adventurers from the north. As it turned out, however, León, not Granada, became the administrative center of the country, and Granada found itself forced to submit to the rule of a series of corrupt administrators based in what it considered a culturally inferior city. To make matters worse, there were significant differences in the economic interests of the two cities. The wealth of the self-styled aristocrats in Granada was based largely on cattle and on trade with the Caribbean via Lake Nicaragua and the San Juan River. Though cattle also were important in the region around León, many of the Leonese were also involved in such middle-class occupations as shipbuilding, the procurement and sale of pine products, and government service. International trade in León was oriented almost entirely toward the Pacific. The Catholic Church hierarchy, though stationed in the administrative center in León, sympathized with the aristocrats in Granada. Mutual jealousy and suspicion between the Leonese and Granadinos festered in a controlled form until independence allowed it to boil over into open warfare.

Curiously, the most flamboyant and prosperous years of the colonial period in Nicaragua were the first few decades, the time of the conquest and the slave trade. Once the Indian population had been depleted, the colony became an underpopulated backwater. Indeed, there was actually a severe manpower shortage, which forced some gold mines to close and caused landowners increasingly to switch from labor-intensive crop production to cattle raising. The economic foundation of this now underdeveloped colony was adequate to support the lifestyle of the landowning aristocrats in Granada and the merchants of León, but insufficient to provide for general prosperity.

To make matters worse, from the mid-seventeenth century on, the debilitated colony was frequently plagued by pirate attacks. As a result, trade via both the Caribbean and the Pacific was restricted and at times interrupted. By the mid-eighteenth century, the British, who were openly supportive of the pirates, became so bold as to occupy and fortify parts of the Caribbean coast. They maintained some claim over that region for well over a century.

INDEPENDENCE

The end of colonial rule in Central America simply added to the woes of the common Nicaraguan, for it meant the removal of the one external force that had kept the elites of León and Granada from sending their people into open warfare against each other. Mutual resentment between the two cities had flared up in 1811, a decade before the expulsion of the Spanish. When León, after first leading Granada into an insurrection against the crown, reversed its position and supported the royal authorities, it left the Granadinos in miserable isolation to receive the brunt of Spanish revenge. Nicaragua won its independence in stages: first as a part of the Mexican empire of Agustín de Iturbide in 1822, then as a member of the Central American Federation in 1823, and finally as an individual sovereign state in 1838. Throughout this period, the Leonese, who eventually came to call themselves Liberals, and the Granadinos, who championed the Conservative cause, squabbled and fought with each other over the control of their country. After 1838, the chaos and interregional warfare intensified. Presidents came and went as one group or the other imposed temporary control.

With Spain out of the way, other foreign powers began to interfere in Nicaraguan affairs, with the objective of dominating the interoceanic transit potential of the infant country. The British had long maintained a presence on the east coast. In the eighteenth century they had actually set up a form of protectorate over the Miskito Indians in that region. In the 1840s U.S. expansion to the Pacific coast of North America and the discovery of gold in California stimulated intense U.S. interest in Nicaragua as the site for an interoceanic transit route. Therefore, when the British moved to consolidate their control over the Miskito Coast by seizing the mouth of the San Juan River, the United States became alarmed and protested vigorously to the British. In 1850 the two countries attempted to diffuse the potential for conflict by signing the Clayton-Bulwer Treaty, in which both sides forswore any unilateral attempt to colonize Central America or to dominate any transisthmian transit route.

THE WALKER AFFAIR

The treaty, however, failed to bring peace to Nicaragua. By the mid-1850s the two emerging themes of Nicaraguan political life—foreign interference and interregional warfare—converged to produce an important turning point and one of the most bizarre episodes in Central American history: the Walker affair. In spite of the Clayton-Bulwer Treaty, the clearly conflicting interests of Britain and the United States in the area had kept tension between the two countries at a high level. Both countries frequently took sides in Nicaraguan domestic politics—the British tending to support the Conservatives, and the Americans, the Liberals. Finally, in 1854, the Liberals, who were at the time losing in a struggle to unseat the Conservatives, turned for help to a San Francisco–based soldier of fortune named William Walker.[3]

Though often depicted as a simple villain, Walker was an extremely interesting and complex individual. The son of a pioneer family from Tennessee, he graduated from college and earned a medical degree while still in his teens. He then pursued a law degree, practiced that profession for a short while, turned to journalism, and finally became a soldier of fortune— all before he had reached his mid-thirties. In some senses he was an idealist. As a journalist he championed the cause of abolition, and like many people of that era, he was a firm believer in manifest destiny—the imperialist expansion of Yankee ideals, by force if necessary, beyond the boundaries of the United States.

In accordance with his pact with the Liberals, Walker sailed in June 1855 from California to Nicaragua with a small band of armed Californians. After some initial military setbacks, he and his Liberal allies took Granada in October and set up a coalition government under a Conservative, Patricio Rivas. Almost from the start, the real power in the government was Walker himself, who rapidly began to implement a series of Liberal developmentalist ideas that included the encouragement of foreign investment and the increased exploitation of Nicaraguan resources. In July 1856, Walker formally took over the presidency.

Initially Walker seemed to have at least the tacit support of the U.S. government. His entrance into the Nicaraguan civil war met with no serious resistance from Washington, which was quick to recognize the puppet government of Patricio Rivas. However, the British and the governments of the other Central American countries were appalled by this bald-faced Yankee attempt to create a U.S. outpost on the Central American isthmus. And many Nicaraguans of both parties became increasingly alarmed at the foreign takeover of their country. This was especially true in 1856 when Walker, the dictator-president, legalized slavery and declared English to be the official language. As a result, it was not long before the onset of a war in which Nicaraguans of both parties and, at one time or another, troops from all of the Central American republics (armed and backed financially by England, certain South American countries, and a variety of public and private interests in the United States) fought against the hated foreigners. In the spring of 1857, the U.S. government intervened to arrange a truce and to allow Walker to surrender and leave Nicaragua. (Walker returned to Central America in yet another filibustering attempt in 1860, but he was captured by the British and turned over to the Hondurans, who quickly tried him and put him before a firing squad.) So important is the war against Walker in Nicaraguan patriotic lore that the independence day that *nicas* celebrate on September 14 is a commemoration of a decisive battle at San Jacinto against Walker and his U.S. troops.

THE CONSERVATIVE PERIOD: 1857–1893

For more than three decades following the defeat of Walker, the country enjoyed relative peace and stability. True, several thousand Indians lost their lives in 1881 in the tragic War of the Comuneros—a rebellion aimed at halting the takeover of their ancestral lands by wealthy coffee growers. But the elites of Nicaragua were temporarily at peace during this period. As a result of their association with the U.S. filibuster, the Liberals had been discredited. The Conservatives, therefore, were able to rule, without interruption and with only sporadic and halfhearted resistance from their traditional adversaries, from 1857 to 1893. A new constitution was adopted in 1857. Thereafter, "elected" Conservative presidents succeeded each other at regular four-year intervals, breaking the old tradition of *continuismo* (an individual's self-perpetuation in power). The country was also blessed in this period with a relative lull in foreign interference, which came as a result of the completion in 1855 of a transisthmian railroad in Panama that temporarily took the pressure off Nicaragua as a focal point of interoceanic transit. And finally, during these decades, Managua, which had become the capital in 1852, grew and prospered as a result of a coffee boom in that area.

ZELAYA AND ZELEDÓN

Conservative rule, however, was not to last. In 1893 the Liberals, under the leadership of José Santos Zelaya, joined dissident Conservatives in ousting the Conservative government of Roberto Sacasa. Three months later, they overthrew the dissident Conservative whom they had initially placed in power and replaced him with Zelaya himself. For the next sixteen years Zelaya was not only the dictator of Nicaragua but also one of the most important figures in Central American regional politics.

Zelaya was a controversial and unjustly maligned figure. He is commonly described in U.S. textbooks on Central and Latin American history as a corrupt, brutal, cruel, greedy, egocentric, warmongering tyrant. In 1909 President William Howard Taft denounced him as "a blot on the history of Nicaragua." Careful examination of the facts, however, reveals that this depiction has much less to do with the reality of Zelaya's rule than with official U.S. frustration and resentment over the Liberal dictator's stubborn defense of national and Central American interests in the face of burgeoning U.S. interference in the region's affairs following the Spanish-American War.[4]

Zelaya would be described more accurately as a relatively benevolent, modernizing, authoritarian nationalist. Born in Managua in 1853, the son of a Liberal coffee planter, he was educated at the Instituto de Oriente in Granada. At sixteen he was sent to France for further studies, and there he became imbued with the positivist philosophies of Auguste Comte and Herbert Spencer. When he returned to his homeland at nineteen, he immediately entered politics. Subsequently, as the young mayor of Managua, he set up a lending library and stocked it with the works of the French philosophers.

There is no doubt that, as dictator of Nicaragua, Zelaya used whatever means necessary to keep himself in power. Democracy did not exist; freedom of the press was often curtailed. It is also true that Zelaya was certainly no great social reformer. But there is little evidence of his alleged cruelty. His constitution of 1893 abolished the death penalty, and he apparently made a practice of granting amnesty, after a decent interval, to captured opposition insurgents.

What is more important, Zelaya initiated many reforms in Nicaragua. In the first place, he worked to secularize Nicaraguan society; his constitution separated church and state and guaranteed freedom of religion and free secular education, and he financed the opening of new schools and the training of Nicaraguans abroad. By the end of his rule, the government was devoting approximately 10 percent of the budget to education.

Like other Latin American positivist leaders of the time, he made a significant effort to modernize the economy. His government surveyed and opened new lands for the expansion of the coffee industry. It also fostered the collection and storage of information by setting up the National Archives and Museum, reorganizing the General Statistics Office, and conducting a national census. In addition, his government invested in the physical infrastructure of communication by purchasing steamships and building roads and telegraph lines. As a result of these modernizing efforts, there was, during the Zelaya period, a rapid increase in the production of such export commodities as coffee, bananas, timber, and gold.

In foreign affairs, Zelaya worked to defend Nicaraguan interests and to promote Central American reunification. More effective in the former than in the latter, he is best known for his success in getting the British to withdraw once and for all from the Miskito Coast. Although they had essentially agreed to withdraw in the 1860 Treaty of Managua, they had not done so. In 1894, Zelaya sent troops to the city of Bluefields, accepted the Miskito king's dubiously valid petition for incorporation, and expelled the protesting British consul from the territory. The British responded with a blockade of Nicaragua's Pacific port, but the United States—anxious to enforce the Monroe Doctrine—pressured them to back down and to accept full Nicaraguan sovereignty over the disputed area.

Zelaya's efforts at promoting Central American reunification, though unsuccessful, were significant. Capitalizing on a region-wide resurgence of Central American nationalism, stimulated in part by his own success in confronting the British on the Miskito Coast, Zelaya convened the Conference of Amapala in 1895, in which Nicaragua, Honduras, and El Salvador agreed to form a confederation called the *República Mayor* (the Greater Republic). A diplomatic representative was dispatched to the United States and received by President Grover Cleveland, and a constitution for this larger political entity was written in 1898. Unfortunately, before it could go into effect, the incumbent government of El Salvador was overthrown and the new government withdrew from the union. The confederation subsequently collapsed.

Much is made in some accounts of the apparent fact that Zelaya was a disrupter of the peace in Central America. He did, indeed, invade neighboring Honduras on two occasions. However, it is equally true that he preferred to let the *República Mayor* collapse rather than send troops to El Salvador to hold it together by force. In addition, he settled boundary disputes with both of Nicaragua's neighbors through arbitration rather than by force. In the case of the boundary dispute with Honduras, he peacefully accepted a settlement that went against Nicaragua's claims.

Zelaya's downfall in 1909 was largely the result of a mounting conflict with the United States. It is important to remember that in that country at the turn of the century, "imperialism" was not a dirty word. The Spanish-American War had given the United States a colonial empire, and many Americans felt that their country had a legitimate colonial role to play in Central America. Zelaya's assertion as a regional leader and champion of Central American unity was, at least in part, a response to this threat—a response Washington resented. Zelaya also had the audacity to refuse to grant the United States canal-building rights that would have included U.S. sovereignty over certain Nicaraguan territory. As a result, the United States became involved in engineering Panamanian "independence" from Colombia and in 1903 signed the treaty it wanted with the new government it had helped create. A few years later, the Americans became alarmed at rumors that Zelaya was negotiating with the British and the Japanese to build a second—and potentially competitive—canal through Nicaragua.

The upshot of these and other sources of friction between the United States and Zelaya was that Washington eventually let it be known that it would look kindly on a Conservative overthrow of Zelaya. In 1909, when the revolt finally took place in Bluefields, Zelaya's forces made the tactical mistake of executing two confessed U.S. mercenaries. The United States used this incident as an excuse to sever diplomatic relations and to send troops to Bluefields to ensure against the defeat of the Conservatives. Though he held on for a few more months, Zelaya was ultimately forced to accept the inevitable, to resign, and to spend the rest of his life in exile.

Before his resignation, Zelaya attempted to save the situation for his party by appointing a highly respected Liberal from León, Dr. José Madriz, to succeed him. The U.S. government, however, was determined that the Zelayista Liberals relinquish control. Washington refused to recognize the new government, and early in 1910, when Madriz's troops succeeded in routing the rebel forces in an attempted thrust to the west and drove them back to Bluefields, the commander of U.S. forces in that town forbade government troops from attacking rebel positions. In the face of such foreign interference, it was impossible for the Liberals to win, much less to govern. On August 20, 1910, the Madriz government collapsed and was replaced by a puppet, pro-U.S. regime supported by the Conservatives and some opportunistic Liberal *caudillos* (strongmen).

For the next two years (1910–1912), the economic and political situation deteriorated rapidly. The rebellion had disrupted the planting of crops and disturbed other sectors of the economy, and although the Madriz government had left the national treasury with a favorable balance, the new government squandered this resource almost immediately and began wildly printing paper money. Washington arranged private bank loans to its new client regime, but much of the loan money almost immediately went into the pockets of corrupt politicians. It was necessary to renegotiate loans and to allow the United States to become involved in the supervision of customs collection and the management of payment of the foreign debt.

The abysmal situation into which the country had fallen offended the national pride of many Nicaraguans, among them a young Zelayista Liberal, Benjamín Zeledón. A teacher, newspaperman, and lawyer, Zeledón had served Zelaya's government as a district judge in the newly liberated Caribbean territories, as an officer in the war with Honduras in 1907, as Nicaragua's representative to the Central American Court of Justice, and finally, at the age of thirty, as minister of defense. Under the Madriz government, he had continued as minister of defense and been elevated to the rank of general of the armies. In July 1912, when a group of dissident Conservatives rebelled against puppet president Adolfo Díaz, Zeledón and a group of Liberals joined in the uprising to rid Nicaragua of "the traitors to the Fatherland."

At first it appeared that the insurgents might win. Zeledón and his Liberal followers seized León and several other cities and cut communications to Managua. However, in the words of one U.S. observer of the time, "the

U.S. could hardly permit the overthrow of the Conservative authorities. [If the rebels won] all of the efforts of the State Department to place Nicaragua on her feet politically and financially would have been useless, and the interests of the New York bankers . . . would be seriously imperiled."[5] Therefore, under the old pretext of protecting U.S. lives and property, U.S. Marines were sent into Nicaragua. Though resistance by dissident Conservatives was quickly overcome, Zeledón not only rejected U.S. demands that he, too, surrender but also warned the U.S. commander that he, his superiors, and the "powerful nation" to which he belonged would bear the "tremendous responsibility and eternal infamy that History will attribute to you for having employed your arms against the weak who have been struggling for the reconquest of the sacred rights of [their] Fatherland."[6]

Badly outnumbered by the combined U.S. and Nicaraguan government forces, Zeledón's troops were besieged and defeated, and he was captured by Nicaraguan troops. Though the United States was in a position to save Zeledón's life, Major Smedley D. Butler, in a telegram to his superiors, suggested that "through some inaction on our part someone might hang him."[7] Butler's advice was apparently taken, for, on the following day, the Conservative government announced that Zeledón had died in battle. Before the young patriot's body was buried, it was dragged through the little hamlet of Niquinohomo. There, by historical coincidence, a short, skinny, seventeen-year-old boy was among those who witnessed government troops kicking the lifeless form. This seemingly insignificant teenager—who later commented that the scene had made his "blood boil with rage"—was Augusto César Sandino.

THE U.S. OCCUPATION, THE NATIONAL GUARD, AND SANDINO

For most of the following two decades, Nicaragua was subjected to direct foreign military intervention. U.S. troops were stationed there from 1912 to 1925 and again from 1926 to 1933, an intervention apparently motivated by a variety of concerns. Relatively unimportant, though not negligible, was the desire to protect U.S. investments. The involvement of U.S. bankers in Nicaragua has been mentioned. There was also a sincere, if naive, belief in some circles that U.S. involvement could somehow help bring democracy to the country. The most important motivations, however, seem to have been geopolitical. U.S. decision makers felt it imperative to maintain a stable pro-U.S. government in Nicaragua, a country that, in addition to being an ideal site for a second transisthmian waterway, was located in the center of the U.S. sphere of influence in Central America.

During the first occupation, from 1912 to 1925, the United States ran Nicaraguan affairs through a series of Conservative presidents—Adolfo Díaz, Emiliano Chamorro, and Diego Manuel Chamorro. The relationship was symbiotic. The United States needed the Conservatives, and the Conservatives—who had neither the military strength nor the popular backing to maintain themselves in power—needed the United States. The Liberals were well aware that any attempt to regain power by means of an uprising would simply mean another unequal contest with the forces Zeledón faced in 1912, so an uneasy quiet prevailed.

The most notable product of the period was the Bryan-Chamorro Treaty, signed in 1914 and ratified in 1916. By the terms of this document the United States acquired exclusive rights, in perpetuity, to build a canal in Nicaragua, a renewable ninety-nine-year lease to the Great and Little Corn Islands in the Caribbean, and a renewable ninety-nine-year option to establish a naval base in the Gulf of Fonseca. In return, Nicaragua was to receive payment of $3 million. In reality, however, the U.S. officials who ran Nicaraguan financial affairs channeled much of that paltry sum into payments to foreign creditors. The aspects of the treaty dealing with the Corn Islands and the Gulf of Fonseca were hotly contested by El Salvador and Costa Rica, and the Central American Court of Justice decided in their favor. Though the United States had originally played a principal role in the creation of the court, it now chose to ignore its decision and, in so doing, contributed significantly to its collapse a few years later.

By the mid-1920s, U.S. decision makers had convinced themselves that the Conservatives were ready to carry on without the presence of U.S. troops. They were wrong. Within a few months of the first U.S. withdrawal in August 1925, conflicts flared up among the ruling Conservatives, and in 1926 the Liberals seized the initiative and staged a rebellion. The inevitable outcome was that the Conservatives were forced to turn again to Washington for salvation, and U.S. troops returned to Nicaragua.

During the second occupation, Washington showed greater skill and imagination in manipulating Nicaraguan affairs. It arranged a truce between the Liberals and the Conservatives that, among other things, provided for a U.S.-supervised election in 1928. Though José María Moncada, the candidate of the majority Liberal party, won that contest, the United States was prepared to live with a Liberal president because, in the words of one scholar, the North Americans "controlled his regime from a number of points: the American Embassy; the Marines . . . ; the Guardia Nacional, with its United States Army Officers; the High Commissioner of Customs; the Director of the Railway; and the National Bank."[8] Under the circumstances, it no longer mattered whether the chief executive was a Liberal or a Conservative. Increasingly secure in this fact, the Americans in 1932 oversaw yet another election won by yet another Liberal—this time, Juan B. Sacasa, ironically the same person who had led the Liberal uprising of 1926 that brought about the second occupation.

The importance of this period (1927–1933) lies much less in the individuals who happened to occupy the presidency than in the fact that, during these six years, forces were being shaped that were to have a powerful and paradoxical impact on Nicaragua for at least the next half century. This was the time of the germination of the Somoza dictatorship, which was to rule Nicaragua for over four decades, and of the reinvigoration of a revolutionary nationalist tradition that would ultimately overthrow that dictatorship in favor of a radically new system.

The revolutionary tradition was dramatically resuscitated by Augusto César Sandino, who led a long guerrilla war against U.S. and government forces during the second occupation of his country. Sandino was a fascinating person. Born in 1895 of a common-law union between a moderately well-to-do landowner and an Indian woman, he was accepted by his father and nurtured philosophically in the high principles that were supposed to form the basis of Liberal practice. He worked for his father until he was twenty-five, when he fled Nicaragua after a fight in which he wounded a man who had insulted his mother. He eventually ended up in Tampico, Mexico, working for Standard Oil of Indiana. There he absorbed some of the ideals of the Mexican Revolution—in particular the emphasis on the dignity of the Indian. In 1926 he returned to Nicaragua and found employment in a U.S.-owned gold mine. When the Liberal insurrection broke out that year, he organized a fighting unit and joined the insurgents. In 1927, after the rest of the Liberals had agreed to the U.S.-sponsored peace settlement, he chose to continue the battle against the puppet Conservative government. This decision inevitably brought him into conflict with U.S. troops and quickly turned his partisan crusade into a war of national liberation.

Though he wrote and spoke eloquently and profusely, Sandino was a man of action rather than a theorist. He did have certain ideas and opinions about the future of Nicaraguan politics and society. For instance, he advocated the formation of a popularly based political party and endorsed the idea of organizing land into peasant cooperatives. But more than anything else, he was a nationalist and an anti-imperialist. Quite simply, he found the U.S. occupation and domination of his country to be offensive and unacceptable. "The sovereignty and liberty of a people," he said, "are not to be discussed, but rather, defended with weapons in hand."[9]

In his struggle against the U.S. occupiers and their military allies, Sandino often used some of the brutal methods endemic to factional warfare in the rugged Segovias region where he was based. He was not above subjecting captured government and U.S. troops and their civilian allies to ritual mutilation before death.[10] In his own words, "Liberty is won not with flowers but with bullets, and for this reason we have been compelled to utilize the *cortes de chaleco, chumbo, y blumer*." (The "blumer" cut, for instance, involved severing the hands and lower legs of the captive and letting him bleed to death.)[11] The purpose was to chasten the enemy and allied civilians. To his credit, though, and unlike his adversaries, Sandino also instituted a strict code against rape as an instrument of intimidation.[12]

At the same time and much more important, Sandino developed an effective set of guerrilla tactics through a process of trial and error. At first he used conventional military tactics, sending large groups of men into combat against an entrenched and well-equipped enemy. As a result, his troops initially took heavy casualties without inflicting serious damage. Learning from this mistake, he quickly developed the more classic guerrilla strategies of harassment and hit-and-run. In addition, he cultivated the support of the peasants in the regions in which he operated. They, in turn, served as an early warning communication network and as ad hoc soldiers during specific guerrilla actions.

For their part, the U.S. occupiers also played a very rough game. Upon his arrival in Nicaragua in 1928, one Marine wrote to his fiancée that "we got instructions to bring him [Sandino] in but not as a prisoner. . . . I wish I'd meet him. I'd bring him in the way they want him."[13] And U.S. forces used tactics that would become familiar during the Vietnam War—the aerial bombardment of "hostile" towns and hamlets, the creation of what amounted to "free fire zones" in rural areas, and the forced resettlement of peasants to what, later in the century, would be called "protective hamlets."[14]

All this, of course, only solidified civilian support for Sandino. There were fluctuations in guerrilla activity and strength, but when the United States finally withdrew in January 1933, Sandino was still "as great a threat . . . as he had been at any previous point in his career."[15]

Ironically, the threat Sandino posed dissolved almost immediately after the Americans left. Because his major condition for peace had been the departure of the Marines, Sandino signed a preliminary peace agreement, in February 1933, with the Sacasa government. Calling for a cessation of hostilities and a partial disarmament of the guerrillas, the document also guaranteed amnesty for Sandino's men and a degree of autonomy for those Sandinistas who wished to settle in the territory along the Río Coco. In 1934 there were further peace negotiations. In the long run, however, Sandino was deceived, captured, and executed. But his daring stand against the foreign occupiers had been an example and had legitimized a set of tactics that were to be successfully employed by the Sandinista Front of National Liberation in overthrowing a U.S.-client dictatorship almost a half century later.

The other force that came into its own during the second U.S. occupation and had a profound impact on the future of the country was the National Guard of Nicaragua. Washington had long felt that what Nicaragua really needed was an apolitical constabulary that could maintain stability and create a healthy environment for political and economic development. Although a halfhearted attempt to create such a force had been made toward the end of the first occupation, the concept was not effectively implemented until the late 1920s. By then the United States was becoming increasingly tired of directly running Nicaragua's internal affairs. And, of course, there was the desire to "Nicaraguanize," if you will, the war against Sandino. Top priority, therefore, was placed on recruiting, training, arming, and equipping the Guard. In the haste of the moment, safeguards aimed at maintaining the apolitical character of the Guard were set aside. As the Marines were leaving, command of this new "national" army passed from the Americans to a congenial, ambitious, English-speaking Nicaraguan politician, Anastasio Somoza García. Less than four years later, an elitist dictatorial system based on a symbiotic relationship between the now corrupted and thoroughly politicized National Guard and the Somoza family had come into being. This system was to plunder, degrade, and bring agony to the Nicaraguan people for more than four decades.

NOTES

1. For an excellent, scholarly examination of the early depopulation of Nicaragua, see David Richard Radell, "Native Depopulation and the Slave Trade: 1527–1578," in his *An Historical Geography of Western Nicaragua: The Spheres of Influence of León, Granada, and Managua, 1519–1965* (Ph.D. dissertation, University of California, Berkeley, 1969), pp. 66–80.

2. Ibid., pp. 70–80.

3. No known relation of coauthor Walker.

4. For an excellent reexamination of Zelaya, see Charles L. Stansifer, "José Santos Zelaya: A New Look at Nicaragua's Liberal Dictator," *Revista/Review Interamericana*, vol. 7, no. 3 (Fall 1977), pp. 468–485. The interpretation and much of the information in my short treatment of Zelaya is drawn from this fine source.

5. Dana G. Munro, *The Five Republics of Central America* (New York: Russel & Russel, 1967), p. 243.

6. A handwritten letter from Zeledón to Colonel J. H. Pendleton, Masaya, October 3, 1912. Xerox copy courtesy of Zeledón's grandson, Sergio Zeledón.

7. Major Smedley D. Butler as quoted in Richard Millett, *The Guardians of the Dynasty: A History of the U.S.-Created Guardia Nacional de Nicaragua and the Somoza Family* (Maryknoll, N.Y.: Orbis Books, 1977), p. 32.

8. Ralph Lee Woodward Jr., *Central America: A Nation Divided* (New York: Oxford University Press, 1976), p. 200.

9. Though this is one of the best-known sayings from Sandino, we do not have the original citation.

10. Michael J. Schroeder, "Horse Thieves, to Rebels, to Dogs: Political Gang Violence and the State in the Western Segovias, Nicaragua, in the Time of Sandino, 1926–1934," *Journal of Latin American Studies*, vol. 28, no. 2 (May 1996), pp. 427–428.

11. Ibid., p. 428.

12. Ibid.

13. Emil G. Thomas, Letter to Fiancée, April 1, 1928, p. 7, from a collection of the Thomas Letters in the Archives at the Ohio University Alden Library, Athens, Ohio.

14. Michael J. Schroeder, "The Sandino Rebellion Revisited: Civil War, Imperialism, Popular Nationalism, and State Formation Muddied Up Together in the

Segovias of Nicaragua, 1926–34," in *Close Encounters of Empire: Writing the Cultural History of U.S.-Latin American Relations*, ed. Gilbert M. Joseph, Catherine C. LeGrand, and Ricardo D. Salvatore (Durham, N.C., and London: Duke University Press, 1998), pp. 208–268.

15. Millett, *Guardians of the Dynasty*, p. 98.

3

Recent History, Part 1

The Somoza Era and the Sandinista Revolution

In the Latin American context, Nicaraguan history since 1933 is unusual in at least two respects. First, though many other countries have suffered dictatorial rule, Nicaragua's forty-two-and-a-half-year subjugation to the Somozas was unique not only in its duration but also in its dynastic character. Nowhere else in Latin America has dictatorial power passed successively through the hands of three members of the same family. Second, Nicaragua is one of only a handful of Latin American countries to have seriously attempted social revolution.

THE RISE OF ANASTASIO SOMOZA GARCÍA: 1933–1937

The founder of the Somoza dynasty, Anastasio Somoza García, was a complex and interesting individual. Born on February 1, 1898, the son of a moderately well-to-do coffee grower, "Tacho" Somoza was just short of thirty-five years old when the departing Marines turned over to him the command of the National Guard. His early ascent to this pivotal position of power was no mere accident. Intelligent, outgoing, persuasive, and ambitious, he was an unusual young man. He received his early education at the Instituto Nacional de Oriente and went on for a degree at the Pierce School of Business Administration in Philadelphia, where he perfected his English and met and married Salvadora Debayle, a member of one of Nicaragua's important aristocratic families. Upon his return to Nicaragua, he joined the Liberal revolt in 1926. Though he and his troops were ingloriously routed, he subsequently worked his way up in Liberal party politics, eventually serving as minister of war and minister of foreign relations. A beguiling, gregarious young man with an excellent command of English, he got along well with the U.S. occupiers and was involved in the creation of the National Guard.

In the years immediately following the departure of the Marines, Somoza worked efficiently to consolidate his control over the Guard. In the wake of real or apparent anti-Somoza conspiracies, he purged various officers who might have stood in his way. Also, on February 21, 1934, he gave his subordinates permission to capture and murder Augusto César Sandino. In doing so, he not only eliminated a potential political rival but also endeared himself to many of the guardsmen, who harbored an intense hatred of the nationalist hero who had frustrated them for so long. Sandino's execution was followed by a mop-up operation in which hundreds of men, women, and children living in the semiautonomous region previously set aside for the former guerrillas were slaughtered. Finally, he encouraged guardsmen at all levels to engage in various forms of corruption and exploitative activities, thus isolating them from the people and making them increasingly dependent on their leader.

By 1936, Somoza was sufficiently sure of his control of the Guard—and hence Nicaraguan politics—to overthrow the elected president, Juan B. Sacasa, and stage an "election" in which he was the inevitable winner. His inauguration on January 1, 1937, confirmed a fact that had long been apparent: In the wake of the U.S. occupation, the National Guard and its chief had become the real rulers of Nicaragua.

THE RULE OF ANASTASIO SOMOZA GARCÍA: 1937–1956

Somoza García was the dictator of Nicaragua for the next nineteen years. Occasionally, for the sake of appearance, he ruled through puppets, but for most of the period, he chose to occupy the presidency directly. In these years he developed an effective style of rule that was to characterize the Somoza dynasty until the late 1960s. The Somoza formula was really rather

A sinister embrace: Anastasio Somozo García (left) and Augusto C. Sandino (right) a few days before Somoza's National Guard carried out the assassination of Sandino in 1934. (Photo courtesy of *Barricada*)

simple: maintain the support of the Guard, cultivate the Americans, and co-opt important domestic power contenders.

The Guard's loyalty was assured by keeping direct command in the family and by continuing the practice of psychologically isolating the guardsmen from the people by encouraging them to be corrupt and exploitative. Accordingly, gambling, prostitution, smuggling, and other forms of vice were run directly by guardsmen. In addition, citizens soon learned that in order to engage in any of a variety of activities—legal or not—it was necessary to pay bribes or kickbacks to Guard officers or soldiers. In effect, rather than being a professional national police and military force, the Guard was a sort of mafia in uniform, which served simultaneously as the personal bodyguards of the Somoza family.

Somoza also proved to be very adept in manipulating the Americans. Though Washington did occasionally react negatively to his designs to perpetuate himself indefinitely in power, the beguiling dictator was always able in the end to mollify U.S. decision makers. In addition to personal charm, he relied heavily on political obsequiousness in maintaining U.S. support. His regime consistently backed U.S. foreign policy. Washington's enemies were automatically Somoza's enemies, be they the Axis powers in the late 1930s and early 1940s or the Communists thereafter. The United States was allowed to establish military bases in Nicaragua during the Second World War and to use the country as a training area for the CIA-organized counterrevolution against Guatemalan president Jacobo Arbenz in 1954. Somoza even offered to send guardsmen to fight in Korea. In return, Somoza was lavishly entertained at the White House and received lend-lease funds to modernize the National Guard.

The dictator was also clever in his handling of domestic power groups. After the murder of Sandino and his followers, he adopted a more relaxed policy toward the opposition. Human rights and basic freedoms—for the privileged at least—were more generally respected. Whenever possible, the Conservative leadership was bought off—the most notable example being the famous "pact of the generals" in which the Conservative chiefs agreed to put up a candidate to lose in the rigged election of 1951 in return for personal benefits and minority participation in the government.

In addition, Somoza pursued developmentalist economic policies that emphasized growth in exports and the creation of economic infrastructure and public agencies such as the Central Bank, the Institute of National Development, and the National Housing Institute. Although the unequally distributed growth produced by this developmentalism did little for the common citizen, it did benefit Somoza significantly. In addition to providing opportunities to expand his originally meager fortune to around $50 million by 1956, it also created vehicles for employing and rewarding the faithful.

The rule of Anastasio Somoza García came to an abrupt and unexpected end in 1956 as the dictator was campaigning for "election" to a fourth term as president. On September 20, a young poet named Rigoberto López Pérez infiltrated a reception honoring the dictator and pumped five bullets point-blank into Somoza's corpulent hulk. In a letter he had sent to his mother, with instructions that it be opened only in the event of his death, López explained, "What I have done is a duty that any Nicaraguan who truly loves his country should have done a long time ago."[1]

If López, who was immediately shot by Somoza's bodyguards, thought his *ajusticiamiento* (bringing to justice) of the dictator would rid his country of Somoza rule, he was sadly mistaken. Although he died a few days later (in spite of the very best emergency medical assistance the Eisenhower administration could provide), Somoza already had taken steps to ensure a smooth transition of rule within his immediate family. His sons, Anastasio and Luís, had been educated in the United States, the former at West Point and the latter at Louisiana State University, the University of California, and the University of Maryland. The more politically oriented Luís, president of the Congress at the time of his father's death, was constitutionally empowered to fill the presidency in the case of an unexpected vacancy. His more militarily inclined brother, Anastasio, had been head of the National Guard since 1955. When their father was killed, Luís automatically assumed the presidency, while his brother used the National Guard to seize and imprison all civilian politicians who might have taken steps to impede the dynastic succession. In 1957, Luís was formally "elected" to a term that would expire in 1963.

LUÍS SOMOZA AND THE PUPPETS: 1957–1967

The decade 1957–1967 bore the mark of Luís Somoza Debayle, a man who seemed to enjoy "democratic" politics and appeared to be committed to the modernization and technical and economic development of his country. The older and wiser of the two Somoza sons, Luís was convinced that in order to preserve the system and protect the family's interests, the Somozas would have to lower their political and economic profile. His ideas and principles fitted neatly with the underlying philosophy and stated objectives of the U.S.-sponsored Alliance for Progress, which was being inaugurated with great fanfare in those years. Many of the programs Luís promoted in Nicaragua—public housing and education, social security, agrarian reform—coincided with the reform projects of the Alliance for Progress.

In politics, Luís attempted to modernize the Liberal party, encouraging dissident Liberals to return to the fold and new civilian leaders to emerge. In 1959 he even had the constitution amended to prevent any member of his family—in particular his intemperate and ambitious younger brother, Anastasio—from running for president in 1963. From the end of his term until his death from a heart attack in 1967, Luís ruled through puppet presidents, René Schick Gutiérrez and Lorenzo Guerrero.

In spite of appearances, however, all was not well during this period. Alliance for Progress developmentalism, while creating jobs for an expanded bureaucracy and providing opportunities for the further enrichment of the privileged, had little positive impact on the lives of the impoverished majority of Nicaraguans, and "democracy" was a facade. Elections were rigged, and the National Guard, as always, provided a firm guarantee that there could be no real reform in the political system.

Not surprising, therefore, were a number of attempts to overthrow the system through armed revolt. Some of these attempts were made by younger members of the traditional parties, one was led by a surviving member of Sandino's army, and—from 1961 on—a number of operations were carried out by a new guerrilla organization, the Sandinista National Liberation Front (FSLN). In response to these "subversive" activities, the dictatorship resorted to the frequent use of the state of siege, and Washington helped increase the National Guard's counterinsurgency capabilities.

Though there is no doubt that Luís Somoza disapproved strongly of his younger brother's ambition to run for president in 1967, it is equally clear that there was little he could have done to block it. Anastasio was, after all, the commander of the National Guard. Therefore, in June 1967—after a blatantly rigged election—Anastasio Somoza Debayle became the third member of his family to rule Nicaragua. Luís's death a few months earlier and the bloody suppression of a mass protest rally shortly before the election symbolized the end of an era of cosmetic liberalization and the return to a cruder and harsher style of dictatorship.

ANASTASIO SOMOZA DEBAYLE'S FIRST TERM: 1967–1972

Anastasio differed from his older brother in several important respects. First, whereas Luís had attempted to build up a civilian power base in a rejuvenated Liberal party, Anastasio felt much more comfortable relying simply on military power. As chief of the Guard, he relied on the old tradition of encouraging corruption and protecting officers from prosecution for crimes committed against civilians. In addition, whereas Luís and the puppets had surrounded themselves with a group of highly trained developmentalist technicians (*los minifaldas*, the miniskirts), Anastasio soon began replacing these skilled administrators with essentially unqualified cronies and political allies, many of whom were Guard officers Somoza wanted to pay off or co-opt. Finally, whereas Luís had felt that, for the sake of image, the family should consolidate rather than expand its already vast fortune, his younger brother exercised no such restraint in using public office for personal enrichment. The result of all this was that by 1970 Somoza's legitimacy and civilian power base were evaporating rapidly, and the government was becoming increasingly corrupt and inefficient.

According to the constitution, Anastasio was to step down from the presidency when his term expired in 1971. The dictator, however, was not bothered by such technicalities. Once in office he quickly amended the constitution to allow himself an additional year. Then, in 1971, with the advice and encouragement of U.S. Ambassador Turner Shelton, he arranged a pact with the leader of the Conservative party, Fernando Agüero, whereby he would step down temporarily and hand power over to a triumvirate composed of two Liberals and one Conservative (Agüero, of course), who would rule while a new constitution was written and an election for president was held. The transfer of power, which took place in 1972, was more apparent than real, as Somoza retained control of the Guard. The inevitable result was that, in 1974, Somoza was "elected" to another term of office that was formally scheduled to last until 1981.

THE BEGINNING OF THE END: 1972–1977

The half decade following the naming of the triumvirate in 1972 was a time of mounting troubles for the Somoza regime. Most of the responsibility for the growing systemic crisis lay in the excesses and poor judgment of the dictator himself. Somoza's first major demonstration of intemperance came in the wake of the Christmas earthquake of 1972, which cost the lives of more than 10,000 people and leveled six hundred blocks in the heart of Managua. Somoza might have chosen to play the role of concerned statesman and patriotic leader by dipping into the family fortune (which, even then, probably exceeded $300 million) in order to help his distressed countrymen. Instead, he chose to turn the national disaster to short-term personal advantage. While allowing the National Guard to plunder and sell international relief materials and to participate in looting the devastated commercial sector, Somoza and his associates used their control of the government to channel international relief funds into their own pockets. Much of what they did was technically legal—the self-awarding of government contracts and the purchasing of land, industries, and so on that they knew would figure lucratively in the reconstruction—but little of it was ethically or morally uplifting.

It was at this point that open expressions of popular discontent with the Somoza regime began to surface. Although the triumvirate was technically in power when the quake struck, Somoza lost no time using the emergency as an excuse to push that body aside and proclaim himself head of the National Emergency Committee. There were many high-sounding statements about the challenge and patriotic task of reconstruction, but it soon became apparent that his corrupt and incompetent government was actually a major obstacle to recovery. The promised reconstruction of the heart of the city never took place. Popular demand for the building of a new marketplace to replace the one that had been destroyed went unheeded. Emergency housing funds channeled to Nicaragua by the U.S. Agency for International Development (USAID) went disproportionately into the construction of luxury housing for National Guard officers, while the homeless poor were asked to content themselves with hastily constructed wooden shacks. Reconstruction plans for the city's roads, drainage system, and public transportation were grossly mishandled. As a result, there was a series of strikes and demonstrations as the citizens became increasingly angry and politically mobilized.

It was at this point, too, that Somoza lost much of the support that he had formerly enjoyed from Nicaragua's economic elite. Many independent businessmen resented the way he had muscled his way into the construction and banking sectors. And most were angry at being asked to pay new emergency taxes at a time when Somoza—who normally exempted himself from taxes—was using his position to engorge himself on international relief funds. As a result, from 1973 on, more and more young people with impressive elite backgrounds joined the ranks of the Sandinista National Liberation Front, and some sectors of the business community began giving the FSLN their financial support.

The second wave of excess followed a spectacularly successful guerrilla operation in December 1974. At that time, a unit of the FSLN held a group of elite Managua partygoers hostage until the government met a series of demands, including the payment of a large ransom, the publication and broadcast over national radio of a lengthy communiqué, and the transportation of fourteen imprisoned FSLN members and themselves to Cuba.[2] Enraged by this affront to his personal dignity, Somoza imposed martial law and sent his National Guard into the countryside to root out the "terrorists." In supposed pursuit of that objective, the Guard engaged in extensive pillage, arbitrary imprisonment, torture, rape, and summary execution of hundreds of peasants.

Unfortunately for Somoza, many of the atrocities were committed in areas where Catholic missionaries happened to be stationed. As a result, the priests and brothers could—and did—send detailed information about these rights violations to their superiors. The Catholic Church hierarchy—already displeased with Somoza's decision in the early 1970s to extend his term of office beyond its original legal limit—first demanded an explanation from the dictator and then denounced the Guard's rights violations before the world.

Somoza's flagrant disregard for human rights earned him considerable international notoriety. His excesses became the subject of hearings of the U.S. House of Representatives Committee on International Relations[3] and a lengthy Amnesty International investigation.[4] In all, by the middle of the decade, Somoza stood out as one of the worst human rights violators in the Western Hemisphere.

The year 1977 was a time of mounting crisis for the Somoza regime. That winter, the Catholic Bishops' Conference of Nicaragua devoted its New Year's message to a ringing denunciation of the regime's violations of human rights; the U.S.-based International Commission of Jurists expressed concern over the military trial of 111 individuals accused of working with the guerrillas; and Jimmy Carter, who had advocated in his campaign that the United States begin promoting human rights internationally, was inaugurated as president of the United States. Throughout 1977, the Carter administration pressed President Somoza to improve his human rights image. James Theberge, a right-wing, cold war warrior, was replaced as U.S. ambassador to Nicaragua by the more humane and congenial Mauricio Solaún, and military and humanitarian aid was used as a prod in dealing with the client regime. In response to the changing mood in Washington, Somoza early that year ordered the National Guard to stop terrorizing the peasantry. In September, he lifted the state of siege and reinstated freedom of the printed press.

Somoza's problems had been compounded in July, when the obese, hard-drinking dictator suffered a near fatal heart attack—his second—and had to be transported to the Miami Heart Institute, where he spent the next one and a half months. This episode stimulated Nicaraguans of all political stripes to consider anew their country's political future. Even Somoza's aides, convinced that he would not return from Miami, began looting the treasury and plotting openly over the succession. As a result, when the dictator did recover, he was faced, upon his return to Nicaragua, with very serious problems within his own political household. Over the next three months he purged many of his former top advisers, including Cornelio Hüeck, president of the National Congress and national secretary of his own Liberal party.

By the last quarter of 1977, the Somoza regime was in deep trouble. Many Nicaraguans were frustrated and disappointed that nature had not been allowed to accomplish a second *ajusticiamiento* the previous summer. With the lifting of the state of siege and the reinstatement of freedom of the press, they could vent their feelings. Newspapers such as Pedro Joaquín Chamorro's *La Prensa* were free to cover opposition activities and discuss in vivid detail the past and present corruption and rights violations of the Somoza regime. In a single week that coauthor Walker spent in Nicaragua early in December, *La Prensa* ran articles on opposition meetings, a successful guerrilla action in the north, the fate of "missing" peasants in guerrilla areas, Somoza's relationship with a blood-plasma exporting firm (Plasmaféresis de Nicaragua), and the apparent embezzlement of USAID funds by Nicaraguan Housing Bank officials. As a result, the regime's popular image dropped to an all-time low, and Managua was alive with gossip and speculation about the impending fall of the dictator.

This situation undoubtedly emboldened the opposition. In October, FSLN guerrillas attacked National Guard outposts in several cities and towns, and a group of prominent citizens—professionals, businessmen, and clergy who subsequently became known as The Twelve—denounced the dictatorship and called for a national solution, which would include FSLN in any post-Somoza government. While several opposition groups spoke of a dialogue with Somoza, many, if not most, Nicaraguans felt, as The Twelve did, that

> there can be no dialogue with Somoza . . . because he is the principal obstacle to all rational understanding. . . . Through the long and dark history of *Somocismo,* dialogues with the dictatorship have only served to strengthen it . . . and in this crucial moment for Nicaragua, in which the dictatorship is isolated and weakened, the expediency of dialogue is the only political recourse that remains for *Somocismo.*[5]

Even that expediency was to evaporate shortly thereafter in the reaction to the assassination of Pedro Joaquín Chamorro.

THE WAR OF LIBERATION: 1978–1979

On January 10, 1978, as he was driving to work across the ruins of old Managua, newspaper editor Pedro Joaquín Chamorro died in a hail of buckshot fired at close range by a team of professional assassins. This dramatic assassination was the final catalyst for a war that culminated in the complete overthrow of the Somoza system eighteen months later. Though this struggle is often referred to as a civil war, many Nicaraguans are quick to point out that the term does not fit because it implies armed conflict between two major national factions. The Nicaraguan war, they maintain, was actually a "war of liberation" in which an externally created dictatorial system supported almost exclusively by a foreign-trained personal army was overthrown through the concerted effort of virtually all major groups and classes in the country. Somoza, they say, was simply "the last marine."

The assassination of Chamorro—a humane and internationally renowned journalist who, little over three months before, had received Columbia University's María Moors Cabot Prize for "distinguished journalistic contributions to the advancement of inter-American understanding"— enraged the Nicaraguan people. Though it is possible that Somoza may not have been directly responsible for the crime, few of his countrymen took that possibility seriously. Immediately after the assassination, angry crowds surged through the streets of Managua burning Somoza-owned buildings and shouting anti-Somoza slogans. Later, when it became apparent that the official investigation of the murder was to be a cover-up, the chambers of commerce and industry led the country in an unprecedented general strike that lasted for more than two weeks with 80 to 90 percent effectiveness. Strikes of this sort had almost always proven fatal to Latin American dictatorships; but it was not so in the case of Anastasio Somoza, for he had the firm support of a thoroughly corrupt military establishment that simply could not afford to risk a change of government. When it became clear that it was hurting the Nicaraguan people more than their well-protected dictator, the strike was called off.

The fact that the strike was over, however, did not mean that Somoza's troubles had ended. To the contrary, Nicaraguans of all classes had experienced the thrill and surge of pride that came with defying the dictator and were, therefore, in no mood to let things slip back to normal. For the next several months, acts against the regime came in various forms. There were daring and quite successful FSLN attacks on National Guard headquarters in several cities, mass demonstrations, labor and student strikes, and—a new factor—civil uprisings in urban areas.

The events of February in Monimbó—an Indian neighborhood in Masaya—were a preview of what was to happen in most Nicaraguan cities that September, when poorly armed civilians rose up against the dictatorship only to be brutally pounded into submission. Fighting in Monimbó broke out between the local inhabitants and the Guard on February 10, the one-month anniversary of the Chamorro assassination, and again on February 21, the forty-fourth anniversary of Sandino's assassination. On the second occasion, the inhabitants set up barricades, hoisted banners declaring Monimbó to be a free territory, and held the Guard back for almost a week with a pathetic assortment of weapons consisting of homemade bombs, .22-caliber rifles, pistols, machetes, axes, rocks, and clubs. Before it could declare Monimbó "secure" on February 28, the regime had to use a force of six hundred heavily armed men backed by two tanks, three armored cars, five .50-caliber machine guns, two helicopter gunships, and two light planes.[6] In the process, the neighborhood was devastated and many dozens, perhaps hundreds, of civilians were either killed outright or arrested and never seen again.

Meanwhile, Somoza was defiantly reiterating his intention to stay in power until the expiration of his term of office in 1981. Swearing that he would never resign before that time, he sputtered angrily at one point, "They will have to kill me first. . . . I shall never quit power like Fulgencio Batista in Cuba or Pérez Jiménéz in Venezuela. I'll leave only like Rafael Leonidas Trujillo of the Dominican Republic. . . . That is, dead."[7] In a calmer mood on another occasion he commented, "I'm a hard nut. . . . They elected me for a term and they've got to stand me."[8]

The Nicaraguan people, however, were not about to stand Somoza for another two years, much less wait until 1981 to participate in yet another rigged election—the "solution" that the United States, at that time, was promoting. Acts of passive resistance and violent opposition continued. July was a particularly active month. On July 5, The Twelve returned from exile, in defiance of the dictator's wishes, and were greeted as heroes by huge crowds at the airport and throughout the country. On July 19, "over 90% of the businesses in Managua and 70% of those in the country as a whole" answered the Broad Opposition Front's (FAO) call for a one-day, show-of-strength general strike.[9] And on July 21, Fernando Chamorro, an automobile sales executive, carried out a daring, one-man rocket attack on *El Bunker*—Somoza's fortified, subterranean office and living quarters—where Somoza was holding a cabinet meeting.

The situation finally came to a head in August. Early that month, the Nicaraguan people heard to their astonishment that Jimmy Carter had sent Somoza a private, but subsequently leaked, letter late in July congratulating him for his promises to improve the human rights situation in Nicaragua. Exasperated by this news and determined to recapture the initiative, the FSLN decided to set in motion plans for its most spectacular guerrilla action to date, the seizure of the National Legislative Palace in the heart of old Managua. According to Edén Pastora, the "Commander Zero" who led the operation, the FSLN had been outraged by Carter's letter. "How could he praise Somoza while our people were being massacred by the dictatorship? It was clear it meant support for Somoza, and we were determined to show Carter that Nicaraguans are ready to fight Somoza, the cancer of our country. We decided, therefore, to launch the people's struggle."[10]

Operation Pigpen, which began on August 22, was as successful as it was daring. Dressed as the elite Guard of Somoza's son, Anastasio III, twenty-five young FSLN guerrillas, most of whom had never set foot in the National Palace, drove up in front, announced that "the chief" was coming, brushed past regular security personnel, and took command of the whole building in a matter of minutes. Before most of them even realized what was happening, more than 1,500 legislators, bureaucrats, and others conducting business in the palace were hostages of the FSLN. It was another humiliating defeat for Somoza. After fewer than forty-eight hours of bargaining, the FSLN commandos extracted a list of stinging concessions from the dictator, including $500,000 in ransom, space in the press and airtime on radio for an anti-Somoza communiqué, government capitulation to the demands of striking health workers, and guarantee of safe passage out of the country for fifty-nine political prisoners and the guerrillas. The governments of Panama and Venezuela vied with each other for the honor of providing the FSLN commandos with air transportation and asylum. And thousands of Nicaraguans cheered the new national heroes on the way to the airport as they departed.

The success of the FSLN palace operation triggered massive acts of defiance by Nicaraguan society as a whole. On August 25, the Broad Opposition Front (composed, at that time, of most of Nicaragua's political parties and organizations) demanded Somoza's resignation and declared another nationwide strike, which paralyzed the country for almost a month. Simultaneously, Monimbó-style civil uprisings occurred in cities throughout the country, including Masaya, Matagalpa, Managua, Chinandega, León, Jinotepe, Diriamba, and Estelí. Once again, young people armed only with an assortment of pistols, hunting rifles, shotguns, homemade bombs, and the moral support of their elders erected paving-block barricades and battled elite units of Somoza's National Guard. Several towns—including León, the traditional stronghold of Somoza's Liberal party—held out for a week or more against terrible odds.

The outcome, however, was inevitable. Somoza and his hated National Guard knew that they were in a struggle for their very lives. The Guard, therefore, fought with unusual ferocity and vengeance, leveling large sections of several cities and taking the lives of between 3,000 and 5,000 people. The dictator's own son and heir apparent, Harvard-educated Anastasio Somoza Portocarrero, led the ground operations. After first "softening up" insurgent cities and neighborhoods with aerial strafing and bombardment, government troops moved in to "mop up." As most of the active insurgents usually had withdrawn by the time the troops took the cities, the mop-up operations frequently involved the mass summary execution of noncombatants—in particular those males who had the misfortune of being of fighting age.[11]

The events of August and September 1978 caused Nicaraguans on both sides to do some hard thinking. For his part, Somoza apparently began to realize that his dictatorial system might be doomed. In the next ten months, he and his associates worked feverishly to liquidate assets and transfer money abroad. At the same time, however, Somoza displayed an outward determination to hold on and to crush the "Communist . . . jerks." He announced plans to double the size of the Guard and bragged openly that, in spite of a U.S. arms freeze, he was having little trouble getting the arms and ammunition he wanted on the open market (mainly from Israel and Argentina).

Somoza was also quite clever in manipulating the United States in his efforts during this period to buy time. The September uprisings had caused the Carter administration, at least temporarily, to feel that Somoza might not be able to survive until 1981. This feeling was accompanied by a growing sense of alarm that Nicaragua might turn into "another Cuba."[12] The dictator played very effectively upon these cold war fears. His lobbyists in Washington argued passionately that Somoza was a loyal ally of the United States, about to be overthrown by Cuban-backed Communists. And from

October to January, Somoza himself toyed with a U.S.-led mediation team from the Organization of American States (OAS) while it attempted to negotiate a transition agreement between Somoza and the small handful of traditional politicians who were still willing to make deals with the dictator. Dangling the idea of a national plebiscite before the OAS team and his traditional "opponents," Somoza did not kill the mediation process until January 1979, when he apparently was sufficiently confident of his own military strength that he no longer needed such charades.

Ironically, even though the Carter administration reacted with anger to Somoza's treachery by reducing its diplomatic presence in Managua and by finally withdrawing its small team of military attachés, the Americans, too, apparently felt that Somoza had weathered the storm. In May 1979, the administration once again aided the dictator by reversing an earlier position and allowing a $66 million International Monetary Fund (IMF) loan for Nicaragua to be approved without U.S. opposition.

Meanwhile, the Nicaraguan people had also learned some valuable lessons from the events of August and September 1978. It was clear that neither general strikes nor poorly armed mass uprisings would drive Somoza from office. The dictator and his Guard had demonstrated their willingness to slaughter and destroy in order to preserve their position. The next uprising, therefore, would have to be led by a larger, well-trained, well-armed guerrilla force. Accordingly, for the next eight months, the Sandinista National Liberation Front worked to prepare itself for a massive final offensive. The recruitment and training of young men and women—primarily students from urban areas—went on at a frenetic pace as the regular FSLN army expanded from several hundred to several thousand. Members of the opposition—particularly The Twelve—traveled throughout the world explaining the Sandinista cause and soliciting donations. Money received from various governments in Latin America, the Social Democratic parties of Western Europe, and solidarity groups in the United States and elsewhere was used to purchase modern, light, Western-made weapons on the international arms market. In March 1979, the FSLN, which formerly had been divided into three factions, finally coalesced under one nine-man directorate and issued a joint declaration of objectives. The stage was set for the final offensive.

After a false start in Estelí in April, the real final offensive was declared early in June 1979. Paving-block barricades were erected in poor neighborhoods throughout the country, and National Guard outposts were overcome one by one as the dictator's control of the country shrank. In mid-June a broad-based government-in-exile was announced by the FSLN. Alarmed by the near certainty of a popular victory, the United States tried various schemes to block such an outcome, including a request to the OAS that a peacekeeping military force be sent to Managua. When this proposal for armed intervention was unanimously rejected, the Carter administration finally began to deal directly with the provisional government. Using various threats and promises, it tried unsuccessfully to force the FSLN to agree to preserve the National Guard—albeit in an altered form—and to include "moderates," such as members of the Guard and Somoza's party, in the government. When the FSLN refused, Washington finally accepted the inevitable and arranged for the departure of Somoza to Miami on July 17. A day later, the provisional government took the oath of office in a ceremony held in León, and on July 19, the FSLN entered Managua and accepted the surrender of most of what was left of the National Guard. Ecstatic crowds tore the statues of Anastasio Senior and Luís Somoza from their pedestals and dragged the broken pieces triumphantly through the streets. On July 20, the provisional government entered the capital and appeared in the main plaza to receive the acclaim of a jubilant and grateful people. The Sandinista insurrection had won unconditionally.

THE CONFLUENCE OF GRASSROOTS MOVEMENTS

The overthrow of the Somoza dictatorship had been a product, in large part, of the confluence of two grassroots movements, both having their origins in the 1960s. One of these was Marxist, the other Catholic. The older of the two, the FSLN, was founded in July 1961 by Carlos Fonseca, Silvio Mayorga, and Tomás Borge, former members of the local pro-Soviet Nicaraguan Socialist party (PSN). For these young Nicaraguans, this old communist party was too Stalinist in organization and too subservient to the Soviet policy of "peaceful coexistence," which in Latin America often meant the docile acceptance of pro-U.S. dictatorships. The founders of the FSLN were determined to create an authentically Nicaraguan revolutionary movement, based on the tactics and sociopolitical objectives of Augusto César Sandino.

For a long time the young rebels were not very successful. At first they attempted to replicate Sandino's tactic of creating a rural guerrilla *foco* (nu-

Fighting at the barricades. Ironically, the *adoquín* paving blocks used to construct the barricades were made in the dictator's own factory. (Photo courtesy of *Barricada*)

cleus) from which to harass the government. In 1967, this tactic led to the disaster of Pancasán, an area in the north in which most of the FSLN's best cadres were surrounded in their *foco* and killed by the National Guard. From then until 1974, the surviving Sandinistas reverted to a strategy of "accumulation of force in silence," temporarily abandoning guerrilla activities and working instead to organize peasants and the urban poor. In 1974, they returned to guerrilla activities, carrying out the successful Managua kidnap-ransom operation mentioned earlier.

The next year, harassed by an enraged Anastasio Somoza, the FSLN split into three "tendencies" in a dispute over strategies. The Prolonged Popular War (GPP) faction was most inclined to follow the SLN's original rural *foco* strategy. The Proletarian Tendency (TP) stressed the need to work with and mobilize the urban worker. Neither the GPP nor the TP felt that the time was ripe for an all-out insurrection. In contrast, the *Terceristas* (Third Force) advocated immediate urban and rural insurrection and a tactical alliance with all anti-Somoza forces, including the bourgeoisie. In the long run, Operation Pigpen and the September 1978 uprisings legitimized the strategy of the *Terceristas*. By March 1979, the three factions had formally reunited in preparation for the final offensive.

The Triumph—July 19, 1979.
(Photo courtesy of *Barricada*)

Meanwhile, a very important Catholic effort at mass mobilization was also being waged in the 1970s. Its roots lay in the second Latin American Bishops' Conference held at Medellín, Colombia, in 1968. There the bishops had produced a document condemning the structural inequities of most Latin American social, economic, and political systems and calling for the clergy to make a "preferential option for the poor." Persons of the cloth were urged to organize Christian Base Communities (CEBs), in which Christ's liberating message would be discussed and the poor, who would be told that they, too, were made in the image of God, would be assisted in becoming socially and politically aware and encouraged to demand social justice. To assist the clergy in spreading the "social gospel" and in creating the CEBs, community leaders would be trained as lay Delegates of the Word.

Soon these directives were being implemented throughout Latin America—even in Nicaragua, where much of the clergy, until the late 1960s, had earned a reputation for being quite conservative. The activities of the lay delegates and the CEBs led to the creation and formation of other grassroots organizations which mobilized labor, peasants, students, and women. By the mid-1970s, the Somoza regime, which had come to feel threatened by these "subversive" activities, began to strike back, attacking CEBs and, in some cases, murdering lay delegates. This violence radicalized many young Catholics and led some of them to join, or cooperate with, the FSLN.

By 1978, the progressive Catholics and the FSLN were essentially working in tandem in expanding the grassroots organizations and preparing for the final insurrection. The Triumph of July 1979, then, was the product of a joint effort. Accordingly, the revolutionary system that would replace the Somoza dictatorship would be influenced as much by its Catholic humanist roots as by the peculiarly nationalist brand of Marxism of the original founders of the FSLN.

THE SANDINISTAS IN POWER

The new system was inevitably controversial both at home and abroad. Though ardently nationalist and, in many cases, deeply religious, most Sandinistas were also openly Marxist or Marxist-Leninist in that they found the writings of Marx and Lenin useful in understanding and explaining the history and current condition of Latin America. Consequently, they were automatically viewed with suspicion by Nicaragua's middle- and upper-class minority—who feared the immediate imposition of a Soviet-style state and economy—and by foreign policy makers in Washington—who were worried about the specter of a "second Cuba." Internally, these fears led to a rapid class polarization, rumor mongering, and a notable lack of cooperation in the reconstruction effort on the part of the private sector. Internationally, especially after the election of Ronald Reagan in the United States, these perceptions produced a multifaceted program to destroy the Sandinista Revolution, including a campaign of propaganda and disinformation depicting the government of Nicaragua as a grim, totalitarian Communist regime and an instrument of Soviet expansionism in the Americas.[13] Although most of these allegations were either completely groundless or very nearly so, the U.S. mass media and opposition politicians (perhaps fearing to appear "naive," "liberal," or "biased") rarely challenged the carefully cultivated "conventional wisdom." Reagan's tactics for dealing with the Sandinistas could be criticized but not the administration's picture of the Nicaraguan regime itself.

For U.S. scholars who did research in Nicaragua during this period, the discrepancy between what was heard in the United States and what was seen in Nicaragua proved stark and frustrating.[14] Far from being a coterie of wild-eyed ideologues, the Sandinistas behaved in a pragmatic and, indeed, moderate fashion throughout the nearly eleven years they were in power. Although they were forced increasingly to rely on the Socialist Bloc for trade and aid, they did not impose a Soviet-style state or a Communist, or even Socialist, economic system. They succeeded in carrying out innovative and highly successful social programs without inordinately straining the national budget. And contrary to the "conventional wisdom," their performance in the area of human rights—though not flawless—would rank Nicaragua at least in the top third of Latin American states.[15]

The Sandinistas enjoyed a number of political assets at the time of their victory, but their power was not limitless. Their greatest asset was the fact that their victory had been unconditional. The old National Guard had been defeated and disbanded. The new armed forces were explicitly Sandinista—that is, revolutionary and popularly oriented. What is more, the mass organizations created in the struggle to overthrow the dictator gave the FSLN a grassroots base that dwarfed the organized support of all potential rivals. Finally, the new government enjoyed broad international support. Nevertheless, the country's new leaders were well aware that their revolutionary administration faced certain geopolitical and economic constraints. The Soviet Union had made it clear that it was not willing to underwrite a "second Cuba." Hard currency would not be forthcoming from that source, nor would military support in the event of a U.S. invasion. Furthermore, unlike Cuba, Nicaragua was not an island. Its long borders were highly vulnerable to paramilitary penetration, and any attempt to impose a dogmatic Marxist-Leninist system certainly would have generated a mass exodus of population. Finally, the Catholic Church in Nicaragua was so important and Catholics had played such a crucial role in the War of Liberation that the Sandinistas were neither inclined nor well situated to attack the Catholic traditions of their country. For these reasons, it ought not to surprise us that the Sandinistas, in fact, attempted to govern in a pragmatic, nonideological fashion.

Sandinista rule was marked by a high degree of consistency and continuity throughout—owing at least in part to the fact that the overall political trajectory of the revolution was set during these years by the same nine-person Sandinista Directorate (DN). Decisions made by DN were based on consensus or near consensus. Reportedly, important decisions were never made on a 5-to-4 vote. This inherently conservative style of revolutionary stewardship meant that domestic and international policy, though adaptive in detail, remained consistent in overall characteristics and goals. During the entire period, the Sandinistas promoted (1) a mixed economy with heavy participation by the private sector, (2) political pluralism featuring interclass dialogue and efforts to institutionalize input and feedback from all sectors, (3) ambitious social programs, based in large part on grassroots voluntarism, and (4) the maintenance of diplomatic and economic relations with as many nations as possible regardless of ideology.

However, in spite of such overarching continuity, it is possible to divide the years of Sandinista rule into four subperiods that were clearly conditioned by the country's international environment. The first, which lasted until the election of Ronald Reagan in November 1980, was a time of euphoria and optimism. The second, spanning the nearly two years from that election to the spring of 1982, was a period of growing awareness of, and concern with, the hostile intentions of the new administration in Washington. In the third, during the almost three years that elapsed from the spring of 1982 through the inauguration of elected president Daniel Ortega in January 1985, the revolutionary system rose to the challenge of withstanding an unprecedentedly massive surrogate invasion, direct CIA sabotage, and economic strangulation while at the same time institutionalizing itself and even augmenting its already wide base of grassroots support. However, in the fourth period, the final five years of the Sandinista government, the death, destruction, and economic collapse brought on primarily by the Contra War and other U.S.-orchestrated programs of destabilization eventually caused such desperation among the Nicaraguan people that a majority voted in 1990 for a U.S.-sponsored opposition coalition capable, it was hoped, of ending the paramilitary and economic torment of Nicaragua.

The first year was the quiet before the storm. Jimmy Carter was still president of the United States. Though not pleased with the Sandinista victory, his administration had decided to make the best of it, offering economic aid with strings attached in the hopes of manipulating the Sandinistas in a direction acceptable to conservative Washington. During this period, the FSLN consolidated the revolution politically by promoting the growth of grassroots organizations, reorganizing the Sandinista armed forces, and reequipping them with standardized military matériel. Much of the latter was obtained from the Socialist Bloc; the United States had earlier refused an arms purchase request by the Sandinistas. Nevertheless, the Sandinista Army was quite small (15,000–18,000 soldiers), and the civilian militia—little more than an association of patriotic marching units—barely constituted even a credible addition to the country's defensive force.

In economic affairs, the Sandinistas decided to honor Somoza's foreign debt in order to maintain Nicaraguan creditworthiness in Western financial circles. Lengthy negotiations with the international banking community led to concessionary terms for repayment. Public loans and aid poured in from a wide variety of countries. And although the government immediately confiscated properties owned by the Somozas and their accomplices, it respected the rest of the private sector and even offered it substantial financial assistance.

In line with the decision to preserve a large private sector, the revolutionaries also created an interim government in which all groups and classes in society, including the privileged minority, could have a voice. The plural executive (Governing Junta of National Reconstruction), created shortly before the victory, included wealthy conservatives as well as Sandinistas. The interim legislative body (Council of State) gave corporative representation to most parties and organizations of significance in Nicaraguan society. This was also a time of ambitious social programs—most notably the 1980 Literacy Crusade, which lowered the national illiteracy rate from 51 percent to 13 percent at relatively low cost to the government owing to its ability to mobilize massive voluntary participation.

The period was not without tension, however. Class polarization had set in almost immediately. Many in the minority privileged classes were certain that totalitarian communism was just around the corner. Accordingly, some fled immediately to Miami, while others first illegally decapitalized their industries, transferred money abroad, and then fled. Moreover, a crisis of sorts occurred early in 1980, when conservatives on the Junta resigned in a pique over the fact that the organizations representing their class had been given representation on the new Council of State that was only slightly more than equivalent to the minority percentage that they represented in the population as a whole. At the same time, the independent daily, *La Prensa*, was taken over by a conservative wing of the Chamorro family, and from then on it was to take a highly critical position, playing to the fears of the privileged classes.

On balance, however, these were not bad times. Other conservatives were found to replace those who had resigned from the Junta. Human rights in general were respected. And *La Prensa* was allowed to make scurrilous and frequently false attacks on the system with virtual impunity. Former Somoza military personnel and accomplices were subjected to legal investigation and trial rather than execution. Indeed, the death penalty itself was immediately abolished.

The second period, one of growing concern and apprehension, began in the fall of 1980 with the election of Ronald Reagan. That summer the Republican party platform had "deplor[ed] the Marxist-Sandinista takeover of Nicaragua" and had promised to end all aid to that country. Campaign aides to Reagan had advised using on Nicaragua the full gamut of techniques (e.g., economic destabilization, surrogate invasion) employed by the United States in the past to destroy Latin American regimes of which Washington did not approve. In fact, the new administration wasted little time in implementing these suggestions. Early in 1981, U.S. economic assistance to Nicaragua was terminated, and the administration began to allow anti-Sandinista paramilitary training camps to operate openly in Florida, California, and the Southwest.[16] That December, President Reagan signed a directive authorizing the CIA to spend $19.8 million to create an exile paramilitary force in Honduras to harass Nicaragua.[17] Although some counterrevolutionary (*contra*) attacks occurred as early as 1981, such activity increased markedly in 1982, as bridges, oil-refining facilities, and other crucial infrastructure, in addition to civilian and military personnel, were targeted. That same year, too, the United States used its central position in the World Bank and the Inter-American Development Bank (IDB) to cut off the flow of badly needed multilateral loans to Nicaragua.

This growing external threat was clearly reflected in Nicaragua in increased class polarization, greater emphasis on austerity and defense, and some—albeit still relatively mild—government infringements on human rights. The acceleration of class polarization began almost immediately after the Reagan victory. By 1980, many in the privileged classes apparently saw even less need than before to accommodate themselves to the new revolutionary system. Within days of Reagan's victory, representatives of the Superior Council of Private Enterprise (COSEP) walked out of the Council of State. On November 17, Jorge Salazar, vice president of COSEP and head of the Union of Nicaraguan Farmers (UPANIC), was killed in a shoot-out with state security forces while allegedly meeting with gunrunners in preparation for armed counterrevolutionary activities. Even though the government televised highly damaging evidence against him, Salazar immediately became a martyr for the privileged classes.

From then on, tension mounted steadily as the conservative Catholic Church hierarchy, the opposition microparties, COSEP, and *La Prensa*—all working in obvious coordination with the U.S. Embassy—showed less and less inclination to engage in constructive dialogue and an ever greater tendency to obstruct and confront. This behavior, in turn, generated resentment by the masses. In March 1981, for instance, Sandinista Defense Committees (CDSs) "in effect challenged the authority of the Ministry of the Interior by [staging demonstrations] blocking plans by the opposition MDN [Nicaraguan Democratic Movement] to hold a political rally [at Nandaime] that had been presented by the government as proof that pluralism was still viable in Nicaragua."[18]

In addition, an increased emphasis was placed on military preparedness. The Sandinista Army was almost immediately expanded to around 24,000 persons, the level at which it would stay until 1983. Recruitment and training for members of the militia were stepped up markedly, and obsolete Czech BZ-52 ten-shot rifles were imported to arm them. Socialist Bloc tanks, anti-aircraft equipment, helicopters, and troop transport vehicles were also imported. Moreover, there was talk of obtaining Soviet MiG fighter jets. This buildup, however, was clearly defensive, as noted in a staff report of the House Committee on Intelligence, when, in September 1982, it chastised the U.S. intelligence community for making dramatic public statements about Nicaragua's offensive intentions and capabilities while, at the same time, secretly briefing high-level administration officials to the contrary.[19] Meanwhile, there was a general belt-tightening as the importation of nonessential goods was restricted and salaries were held down.

All of the government social programs were continued. Indeed, in 1981, over 70,000 young people participated in a voluntary primary health crusade. But overall, the people of Nicaragua were beginning to feel the negative effects of the Reagan assault on their country.

Finally, as is true in all states in time of war or threat of war, certain human rights were gradually infringed upon in the name of national security. Late in 1981, in response to *contra* activity in the region, the government ordered the involuntary evacuation of over 10,000 Miskito Indians from isolated communities along the Río Coco. Although careful investigations into this matter indicate that the evacuation itself was carried out in a humane fashion, some isolated incidents occurred during subsequent security activities on the Miskito Coast in which individual commanders or soldiers disobeyed orders to respect the lives of prisoners and were apparently responsible for the execution or permanent "disappearance" of up to 150 individuals.[20] Also apparent was a deterioration in the right to due process for political prisoners in general and on the Miskito Coast in particular. Finally, on a half-dozen occasions, *La Prensa* was closed for two-day periods. This action was taken under the terms of a press law decreed by the original Junta (of which, ironically, *La Prensa* owner Violeta Chamorro had been part)—a law calling for such action in the event that an organ of the media was found to have disseminated material that was not only false *but also* destabilizing. However, even with these shutdowns, *La Prensa* continued to operate freely and in bitter opposition to the government more than 95 percent of the time. Moreover, at no point during this period did human rights infringements in Nicaragua even remotely approach the wholesale abuses prevalent in a number of other Latin American countries. In fact, late in 1982, the U.S. ambassador to Nicaragua, Anthony Quainton (a Reagan appointee), admitted candidly to a group of which coauthor Walker was a part that the human rights situation there was better than in El Salvador or Guatemala—ironically, two countries that Washington was then trying to portray as having made great strides in this respect.

The third period, from early 1982 through the beginning of 1985, might aptly be labeled "weathering the storm." The "storm," in this case, was the Reagan administration's massive and multifaceted campaign to destabilize and overthrow the Sandinista government, which, by the onset of this period, was "covert" in name only. The CIA-coordinated recruitment, training, arming, and disgorging of *contras* into Nicaragua had escalated rapidly from the force of 500 originally envisioned in the CIA finding of late 1981 to over 15,000 by 1984 (a proportionately equivalent invasion of the United States would have numbered over 1.28 million). Direct involvement by CIA personnel was also evident in the destruction of Nicaraguan oil-storage facilities late in 1983 and the mining of Nicaraguan harbors early in 1984. Furthermore, ever larger numbers of U.S. military personnel participated in nearly continuous, highly menacing joint military maneuvers in Honduras and in naval "exercises" off both Nicaraguan coasts.

Accompanying these military and paramilitary efforts was an escalating program of economic strangulation. Washington continued to block approval of Nicaraguan loan requests before the World Bank and the IDB.

U.S. trade with Nicaragua was drastically curtailed. In October 1982, Standard Fruit Company suddenly pulled its banana-buying operation out of Nicaragua in spite of the fact that, just the year before, it had reached a very concessionary agreement with the Nicaraguan government. In May 1983, the Nicaraguan quota for exporting sugar to the United States was cut by 90 percent. And Washington made an effort, albeit an only partially successful one, to get other countries to stop trading with Nicaragua.

These activities had a clear impact on Nicaragua, though not always one that U.S. policy makers would have desired. In economic matters the country was hurt, but by no means brought to its knees. Although the economy grew steadily under Sandinista rule (except in 1982, when a severe flood occurred, followed by drought), problems inherited from Somoza, combined with a sharp decline in the world prices of Nicaragua's export commodities and the enormous direct and indirect cost of the Contra War, meant that by this third period Nicaragua was having increasing problems in servicing its debt. Accordingly, Venezuela ceased (1983) and Mexico drastically curtailed (1984) supplies of oil to the country. As a result, by 1984 and 1985 the Sandinistas were forced to turn to the Soviet Union for most of their petroleum needs. The scarcity of foreign exchange also meant severe shortages of imported goods and of products manufactured in Nicaragua from imported materials or with imported machinery. Of course, such shortages also triggered rampant inflation and spiraling wage demands, which could not be satisfied given the tremendous diversion of government revenues into defense.

Social services were also negatively affected. As increased emphasis was placed on defense, government spending on health, education, housing, food subsidies, and so on, had to be cut back. Further, it is clear that the *contras* were deliberately targeting the social service infrastructure. Many government employees in health, education, and cooperatives were kidnapped, tortured, and killed; schools, clinics, day-care centers, and grain-storage facilities were destroyed. However, if all of this activity was designed to so damage the living standards of most Nicaraguans that they would become angry with their government and ultimately overturn it, someone had badly miscalculated. Although the human condition did decline during this period, support for the government actually appears to have grown—as measured by levels of membership in pro-Sandinista grassroots organizations.[21] In the aftermath of the Triumph (1979–1980), membership reached a peak of about 250,000 to 300,000 persons. Thereafter, it declined for a couple of years—as a result, perhaps, of apathy or a sense of lack of fulfill-ment of unrealistically high expectations for the revolution. However, by late 1982, grassroots membership had begun to climb again, and by 1984, it had doubled or tripled over the previous high-water mark. By then, around half of all Nicaraguans age sixteen or older were members in voluntary sup-port organizations.[22] Clearly the intervening variable was the Contra War, the effects of which really began to hit home late in 1982. Simply put, Nica-raguans had come together to support their government in this time of na-tional emergency and foreign threat.

The same period also witnessed a significant buildup in the military. Nicaragua stepped up its purchase of military hardware such as helicopters, propeller-driven aircraft, artillery, antiaircraft equipment, troop trans-ports, and light weaponry—mainly from the Socialist Bloc (the United States had applied pressure to dissuade other potential suppliers, such as France). By 1983 or 1984, the Sandinista Army, which had held constant at around 24,000 strong since 1981, increased to over 40,000; in addition, late in 1983 a military draft was instituted. At the same time, the Sandinista Militia—a lightly trained body of over 60,000 civilian volunteers who had previously been armed with liberated Somoza-era weaponry and obsolete Czech BZ-52 rifles—was largely reequipped with Socialist Bloc AK-47 au-tomatic rifles. This increased preparedness (combined with the fact that in Nicaragua itself, the *contras* had little political support) paid off. The *con-tras* proved incapable of achieving even their most minimal objective of seizing and holding a Nicaraguan population center that could be declared the seat of a new government.

At first, the political response of the Sandinistas to the external threat was predictably defensive. In the spring of 1982, following *contra* attacks on important Nicaraguan infrastructure and the disclosure in the U.S. media of President Reagan's earlier authorization of funding for CIA-sponsored paramilitary operations against their country, the government declared a state of prewar emergency under which certain civil and politi-cal rights were temporarily suspended. Some measures (such as the short-term preventive detention of suspected "subversives") had actually begun during the previous period; others (such as precensorship of the printed media) were new. The implementation of these measures was relatively mild. The short-term preventive detention measure affected only a few hundred persons at any one time. And *La Prensa*, though now heavily censored, at least continued to function. (In U.S. ally El Salvador, the only real opposition papers had long since been driven completely out of business through the murder or exile of their owners.)

Another new political measure, decreed in July 1982, was the massive decentralization of government. Under it, the country was divided into six "Regions" and three "Special Zones" for all governmental functions. The main purpose of this reform was to avoid the stifling effects of centralized bureaucratic control by creating institutions for local decision making and public policy implementation; another important objective was to institute a system of government that could continue functioning even if communications were badly disrupted or if Managua were occupied by enemy troops.

Eventually, however, as more and more Nicaraguans rallied around their government, the Sandinistas came to show renewed confidence in the people and to take a more relaxed approach to domestic politics. Late in 1983, the government actually passed out many tens of thousands of automatic weapons to civilians so that they could help defend their families, farms, villages, and neighborhoods. Meanwhile, the government, in consultation with all political parties and groups that chose to enter into dialogue, had been working to create a mechanism to implement the Sandinistas' oft-repeated promise to hold general elections. Eventually, in September 1983, and with considerable opposition input, a political parties law was hammered out and enacted. Three months later the government announced that the elections would be held in 1984. Early in 1984, November 4 was set as the exact date, and in March, an electoral law modeled after "key components of the French, Italian, Austrian, and Swedish electoral systems" was enacted.[23] The Reagan administration denounced the Nicaraguan election in advance as a "Soviet-style farce" and then, with the U.S. media, portrayed businessman Arturo Cruz (at that time a highly paid CIA "asset") as the only viable opposition candidate. Cruz (whom in fact the United States had not intended to run) then played the role of a potential but reluctant candidate who ultimately, with great fanfare, decided not to enter the race on the grounds that the conditions for a free election did not exist.[24] Just before the election, the United States pressured another candidate to withdraw at the last moment. Nevertheless, the election did take place as scheduled, and though either ignored or panned by the U.S. media, it was certified as being a meaningful, clean, and relatively competitive election (given the difficult circumstances under which it was held) by a number of observer delegations representing Western European parliaments and governments, the U.S.-based Latin American Studies

Association (LASA), and so on.[25] Although voting was not obligatory, 75 percent of those registered (93.7 percent of the voting-age population had registered) cast ballots. Although three parties each to the right and the left of the FSLN appeared on the ballot, the Sandinistas captured 63 percent of the vote. That gave the presidency and vice presidency to Daniel Ortega and Sergio Ramírez, and sixty-one of the ninety-six seats in the new National (Constituent) Assembly to the FSLN.

The fourth and longest major subperiod of Sandinista rule was the time of decline from 1985 to 1990. This is not to say that there were no successes during that period but rather that the most important characteristic of those years was an essentially externally generated economic collapse and consequent internal political destabilization.

The January 1985 inauguration of Daniel Ortega, Nicaragua's first democratically elected president, should have been a cause for celebration. It was not; there were too many signs of trouble in the making. First, the previous November, the Reagan administration had skillfully obscured the nature of the election. In the United States, news of the election had been immediately drowned in intensive media coverage of deftly timed Reagan administration disinformation "leaks" that Soviet-built MiG jets were en route by ship to Nicaragua. Though groundless, these allegations raised to a fever pitch U.S. paranoia over the "Nicaraguan menace." Most of the thin election coverage that did take place in major U.S. media ignored the judgment of the disinterested international observer teams, choosing instead to echo Washington's distorted depiction. The lone major exception was the *Christian Science Monitor*, which timidly noted that the international observers had judged the Nicaraguan election as better than that conducted earlier that year in the U.S. client state of El Salvador.[26] But even that newspaper, perhaps not comfortable with possibly being seen as "out on a limb," would soon forget its initial evaluation.

The behavior of the Reagan administration early in 1985 made it clear that Washington had no intention of coexisting with Sandinista Nicaragua. Bilateral talks being conducted between U.S. and Nicaraguan diplomats during the run-up to the U.S. election of 1984 were unilaterally broken off by the United States at the beginning of the new year. In February, Reagan admitted that it was the objective of his administration to dismantle the Sandinista power structure unless the Sandinistas decided to cry "uncle."[27] This admission was followed in May by a complete embargo of U.S.-Nicaraguan trade.

For the next half decade, the Sandinistas tried to make the best of a bad, often impossible, situation. Though there were many setbacks, there were also some notable successes. First, during 1985 and 1986, the newly elected National Assembly worked to produce a constitution. In January 1987, after considerable legislative debate and domestic and international consultation, an original and simply worded democratic constitution was promulgated.[28] At the same time, after considerable negotiation and compromise, an innovative arrangement for the autonomy of Atlantic coast peoples was agreed to, and for all practical purposes, peace in that part of the country was achieved. In addition, parties and election laws were written in 1988 and amended in 1989 in order to carry out the constitutional mandate of a national election in 1990. Another major achievement was the containment of the *contras*. After 1982, the *contra* presence in Nicaragua had escalated rapidly to a high of around 15,000 troops by the mid-1980s. According to the U.S. Pentagon, approximately ten regular soldiers are normally required to contain one guerrilla fighter. Though Nicaragua (with a regular army that peaked at just over 80,000 troops) was never able to achieve anywhere near that ratio, its leaders adopted tactics that made up for the deficiency. Reportedly taking much of their strategy directly from U.S. Army counterinsurgency manuals and practices,[29] they created Irregular Warfare Battalions (BLIs) and Light Hunter Battalions (BCLs), which could take the war to the enemy under very difficult conditions. The leaders also accelerated agrarian reform, at least in part to solidify support in rural areas. They continued to pass out large numbers of AK-47 and AK-M assault rifles to civilians in threatened regions. Finally, the government extended the policy, begun in 1983, of granting amnesty to anyone willing to desert the *contras*. As a result, by the spring of 1988, their disintegrating and demoralized enemy had begun to sue for peace. From then on, though the United States would continue to maintain the *contras* as an irritant and potential threat to the Sandinistas and a stimulus for Nicaragua to continue high levels of military expenditures it could not afford, the U.S. surrogates would never again constitute a serious military problem.[30]

A final achievement of the 1985–1990 period was the maintenance of a relatively laudable record in the area of human rights.[31] Though there were scattered exceptions, respect for the "integrity of person"—the citizen's right not to be tortured, raped, murdered, or otherwise physically abused by agents of the government—was generally maintained throughout the period. [32] Social and economic rights were promoted as well as any government could do under the circumstances. And civil and political rights—which under international law may be restricted in times of external threat and national emergency—were only moderately and occasionally infringed upon. Indeed, Nicaragua's record in this latter category compared favorably with that of the United States and England in time of war and was much better than that of the contemporary U.S. client regimes of Guatemala and El Salvador.

However, these successes were ultimately overshadowed by the economically and politically destabilizing impact of continued U.S. economic and surrogate military aggression. Causing direct and indirect damage of over $9 billion to an export-oriented economy that in the best of years exported only a little more than $700 million, the U.S. campaign against Nicaragua achieved dramatic results.[33] The economy, which had grown in the first four years of the revolution and had leveled off in 1984 and 1985, began to plummet thereafter. According to a UN report, the annual inflation rate had reached 33,602 percent by 1988,[34] while real per capita income was sharply reduced. That year, and even more so in 1989, the government was forced to implement harsh austerity measures that, though they reduced inflation in 1989 to 1,690 percent,[35] threw thousands of government employees out of work. Significantly, all of these events were taking place just before the 1990 election.

During the same period, various exigencies created by the war, combined with economic hard times, also impacted negatively on the grassroots movement that had been the base of the Sandinista Revolution. Instead of being used primarily as devices to promote the sectoral interests they were supposed to be representing, the grassroots organizations were asked by the FSLN and the state to perform tasks important to the preservation of the revolution as a whole. Because some of these tasks were onerous—for instance, requests that neighborhood committees assist in the recruiting of draftees and that union leaders urge patience in the face of falling standards of living—or at the very least drained resources from the pursuit to meet more immediately felt needs, they tended to delegitimize the mass organizations. What is more, the increasingly desperate economic situation made it even more difficult for ordinary citizens to devote time to anything but the fulfillment of personal and family needs. All of this caused membership in grassroots organizations to decline gradually in 1985 and 1986 and then to plummet in 1987 and 1988.

The war itself also brought great suffering and therefore took a heavy political toll. According to internal government statistics that coauthor

Walker obtained from the outgoing government in January 1990, the death toll for the entire Contra War (1980–1989) was 30,865.[36] This included 21,900 *contras* and 8,965 individuals categorized by the government as "our people"—approximately 4,860 government troops and 4,105 others, mainly civilians. Calculating roughly that the population of Nicaragua, which grew from 2.5 million to 3.8 million in the period 1979–1989, averaged about 3.3 million during the war years, the over 30,000 dead represented 0.9 percent of the population. An equivalent loss for the United States would have been 2.25 million or over thirty-eight times the U.S. death toll in the entire Vietnam War. The war also produced 20,064 wounded, many of them so permanently disabled that they would be wards of the state for the rest of their lives.

Thus, by the 1990 elections, the Nicaraguan electorate was thoroughly tired of war. Continued hostile U.S. rhetoric toward the Sandinistas and sharply escalated *contra* activity in Nicaragua in the four months leading up to the 1990 elections convinced many Nicaraguans that the war, and hence the suffering, would not be terminated unless the Sandinistas lost on February 25.[37]

Washington's awareness of its success in destabilizing Nicaragua in the second half of the 1980s would seem to explain why the U.S. attitude toward elections in Nicaragua changed from 1984 to 1989–1990. In 1984, prior to the major impact of the destabilization, it was clear that the Sandinistas would win a free election against any conceivable opposition. In fact, a U.S. Embassy representative conceded to the Latin American Studies Association observer team that he thought they would take 70 percent of the vote in such an election. (As it turned out, he was off by less than 7 percentage points.) He added, "Who else has ever brought so much to the Nicaraguan people in so short a period of time?"[38] And as an unnamed senior Reagan administration official commented to a *New York Times* reporter just prior to the election, if someone like Arturo Cruz were to run and lose, "the Sandinistas could *justifiably* claim that the elections were legitimate, making it much harder for the United States to oppose the Nicaraguan Government" (emphasis added).[39] Thus the U.S. strategy in 1984 was to promote the opposition's abstention so that it would be possible to delegitimize the inevitable outcome.

Five years later, however, after Nicaragua had dropped to the unenviable status of being the poorest country in the Western Hemisphere, and with the Nicaraguan people now desperately tired of war and deprivation, a U.S. strategy of promoting a unified opposition electoral coalition made good sense. Thus, while repeatedly and disingenuously criticizing Nicaragua's election laws as "stacked" in the Sandinistas' favor, stressing every minor irregularity that took place, and expressing grave doubts that a free election was possible (apparent rhetorical insurance in the event of a Sandinista victory), Washington used millions of covert dollars and promised overt funding[40] to weld a united opposition (National Opposition Union, UNO) out of fourteen disparate microparties and to promote the electoral success of its candidates. Leaving nothing to chance, the United States, said one State Department official at the time, decided to "micromanage the opposition."[41] And while accelerating the Contra War and repeatedly expressing hostility toward the Sandinistas, administration spokespersons from President George H. W. Bush on down made numerous statements not only endorsing UNO's presidential candidate, Doña Violeta Barrios de Chamorro, but indicating that the economic blockade and U.S. support for the *contras* would end if she won.

Actually, U.S. bureaucratic inertia prevented much of the nearly $8 million in overt U.S. funding from getting to Nicaragua before the election. The money that did get there began to arrive around the turn of the year, far too late to have much impact on the outcome. In addition, whereas the FSLN ran a glitzy modern campaign with tracking polls, targeted appeals, and huge rallies, UNO appeared to be handicapped by an inarticulate presidential candidate, open internal bickering, limited campaign outreach, and smaller rallies. As it turned out, however, the entire campaign period was probably essentially irrelevant. The voters of Nicaragua had a stark choice: Vote for the FSLN, which, though it promised to defend national sovereignty and promote social justice, was apparently powerless to end the war and the economic blockade; or vote for UNO, which, though its candidates and leaders had a very questionable record on the issues of sovereignty and social justice, appeared almost certain to be able to end the military and economic aggression.

The UNO victory was clear cut. Chamorro won about 55 percent of the valid presidential votes compared to Daniel Ortega's 41 percent. Of the ninety-two seats in the National Assembly, UNO captured fifty-one, the FSLN won thirty-nine, and two independent parties, the Social Christian party (PSC) and the United Revolutionary Movement (MUR), took one apiece.

Burnt by the experience of having had the Reagan administration and the U.S. press dismiss the 1984 election as a "farce," the Sandinistas had made sure that the 1990 election would be even more heavily observed. As it turned out, their second election was "one of the most intensely observed in history."[42] The United Nations, which had never before observed an election in the Western Hemisphere, and a Carter Center/Organization of American States team (to name just two of the observer entities) both employed a scientific technique for the stratified sampling of local vote counts that enabled them to project the outcome to within 1 percent of the final count less than three hours after the polls closed. By 9:30 p.m., Ortega and Chamorro were given these projections.

Though it was clear to many impartial observers that the Nicaraguan people had voted, as the Sandinistas would repeatedly argue, with a "gun held to their heads,"[43] Daniel Ortega delivered a moving and dignified concession speech early the following morning. Later that day, he went to Chamorro's house, embraced and congratulated her, and promised to support her in her new role. Significantly, there were almost no celebrations by UNO voters and activists. Though Nicaraguans normally mark anything worth celebrating with the chatter of firecrackers and the boom of rockets, Managua was strangely silent in the aftermath of the UNO "triumph." After some bargaining over the nature of the transition, Violeta Barrios de Chamorro was inaugurated on schedule on April 25, 1990.

NOTES

1. Rigoberto López Pérez as quoted in Mayo Antonio Sánchez, *Nicaragua Año Cero* (Mexico City: Editorial Diana, 1979), p. 96.

2. For an FSLN account of this action and a transcript of the communiqué, see Comando Juan José Quezada, *Frente Sandinista: Diciembre Victorioso* (Mexico City: Editorial Diogenes, S.A., 1976).

3. U.S. Congress, House Committee on International Relations, Subcommittee on International Organizations, *Human Rights in Nicaragua, Guatemala and El Salvador: Implications for U.S. Policy,* hearings, June 8–9, 1976 (Washington, D.C.: U.S. Government Printing Office, 1976).

4. Findings summarized in *Amnesty International Report, 1977* (London: Amnesty International Publications, 1977), pp. 150–153.

5. *Apuntes para el Estudio de la Realidad Nacional*, no. 1 (June 1978), p. 9.

6. Ibid., p. 22.

7. "Somoza Rules Out Early Departure," *Central America Report*, vol. 5, no. 12 (March 20, 1978), p. 95.

8. "The Twelve: Nicaragua's Unlikely Band of Somoza Foes," *Washington Post,* July 23, 1978.

9. "Nicaragua Strike," *Central America Report,* vol. 5, no. 29 (July 24, 1978), p. 231.

10. "Rocking Nicaragua: The Rebels' Own Story," *Washington Post,* September 3, 1978, p. C-1.

11. Organization of American States, Inter-American Commission on Human Rights, *Report on the Situation of Human Rights in Nicaragua* (Washington, D.C.: General Secretariat of the OAS, 1978).

12. For more detailed analysis of U.S. policy making in this period, see William LeoGrande, "The Revolution in Nicaragua: Another Cuba?" *Foreign Affairs,* vol. 58, no. 1 (Fall 1979), pp. 28–50; and Richard R. Fagen, "Dateline Nicaragua: The End of an Affair," *Foreign Policy,* no. 36 (Fall 1979), pp. 178–191.

13. For some specific examples of the use of disinformation against Nicaragua, see Thomas W. Walker, "The Nicaraguan-U.S. Friction: The First Four Years, 1979–1983," in *The Central American Crisis,* ed. Kenneth M. Coleman and George C. Herring (Wilmington, Del.: Scholarly Resources, 1985), pp. 181–186.

14. Coauthor Walker had the privilege of working with several dozen such scholars while editing *Nicaragua in Revolution* (New York: Praeger, 1982); *Nicaragua: The First Five Years* (New York: Praeger, 1985); *Reagan Versus the Sandinistas: The Undeclared War on Nicaragua* (Boulder, Colo.: Westview Press, 1987); and *Revolution and Counterrevolution in Nicaragua: A Comprehensive Overview* (Boulder, Colo.: Westview Press, 1991).

15. Throughout its period of rule, the revolutionary government invited human rights monitoring organizations such as the Organization of American States, Inter-American Commission on Human Rights, Amnesty International, and Americas Watch to examine its human rights performance. Readers interested in Nicaragua's human rights performance should examine the numerous reports that they issued; also see Michael Linfield, "Human Rights," in Walker, ed., *Revolution and Counterrevolution in Nicaragua.*

16. The story of the *contra* training camps first became public via Eddie Adams, "Exiles Rehearse for the Day They Hope Will Come," *Parade Magazine,* March 15, 1981, pp. 4–6.

17. "U.S. Plans Covert Operations to Disrupt Nicaraguan Economy," *Washington Post,* March 10, 1982, and "U.S. Said to Plan 2 C.I.A. Actions in Latin Region," *New York Times,* March 14, 1982.

18. Jack Child, "National Security," in James D. Rudolph, ed., *Nicaragua: A Country Study* (Washington, D.C.: U.S. Government Printing Office, 1982), p. 202.

19. See note 18 in Chapter 8.

20. Organization of American States, Inter-American Commission on Human Rights, *Report on the Situation of Human Rights of a Segment of the Nicaraguan Population of Miskito Origin* (Washington, D.C.: OAS, 1984).

21. Our estimates of grassroots organization memberships are rough. They are based on conversations that coauthor Walker held during ten visits to Nicaragua with individuals working in mass mobilization, and on Luís H. Serra, "The Sandinista Mass Organizations," in *Nicaragua in Revolution,* Walker, ed., pp. 95–114, and Luís H. Serra, "The Grass-Roots Organizations," in *Nicaragua: The First Five Years,* Walker, ed., pp. 65–89.

22. Interestingly, this estimate is essentially corroborated by an in-house U.S. Embassy estimate for late 1984, which places grassroots membership at 700,000–800,000. This information was revealed by an official in the U.S. Embassy to a group of which coauthor Walker was a part on June 25, 1985.

23. Latin American Studies Association (LASA), *The Electoral Process in Nicaragua: Domestic and International Influences, Report of the Latin American Studies Association Delegation to Observe the Nicaraguan General Election of November 4, 1984* (Austin, Texas: LASA, 1984), p. 29.

24. Cruz, who later went on to serve the CIA briefly as one of the "civilian heads" of the *contras,* eventually came to regret his covert work as a foreign agent. At a conference on Nicaragua at Sonoma State University on April 22, 1989, coauthor Walker confronted fellow speaker Cruz with the description of Cruz's 1984 activities as given earlier in this chapter. Remarkably, instead of denying the charges, Cruz delivered an impassioned mea culpa, in which he described his work for the CIA as one of the two major "sins" he had committed against the Nicaraguan people (the other being his earlier association with the revolutionary government).

25. LASA, *The Electoral Process*; Thom Kerstiens and Piet Nelissen (official Dutch Government Observers), "Report on the Elections in Nicaragua, 4 November 1984" (photocopy); Irish Inter-Party Parliamentary Delegation, *The Elections in Nicaragua, November 1984* (Dublin: Irish Parliament, 1984); Parliamentary Human Rights Group, "Report of a British Parliamentary Delegation to Nicaragua to Observe the Presidential and National Assembly Elections, 4 November 1984" (photocopy); and Willy Brandt and Thorvald Stoltenberg, "Statement [on the Nicaraguan elections in behalf of the Socialist International]," Bonn, November 7, 1984.

26. Dennis Volman, "Nicaragua Vote Seen as Better Than Salvador's," *Christian Science Monitor,* November 5, 1984, pp. 13, 14.

27. "After Reagan's 'Uncle' Policy, Managua Announces 'Flexibility,'" *Latin American Weekly Report,* March 1, 1985, p. 1.

28. See Kenneth Mijeski, ed., *The Nicaraguan Constitution of 1987: English Translation and Commentary* (Athens, Ohio: Monographs in International Studies, Latin American Series, no. 17, 1991).

29. Col. Alden M. Cunningham, "The Sandinista Military: Current Capacities, Future Roles and Missions," a paper prepared for the conference "Nicaragua: Prospects for a Democratic Outcome," sponsored by the Orkand Corporation (under contract with the CIA), October 12, 1988, Washington, D.C., p. 6.

30. For a more complete discussion of the role of the armed forces, see Thomas W. Walker, "The Armed Forces," in Walker, ed., *Revolution and Counterrevolution in Nicaragua.*

31. For a reasoned and well-documented examination of this matter by a Harvard-trained lawyer who did an internship in Nicaragua at the time, see Michael Linfield, "Human Rights," in Walker, ed., *Revolution and Counterrevolution in Nicaragua.*

32. Throughout most of the war, human rights organizations certified that violations of the right of integrity of person that were occasionally committed by Nicaraguan security forces in the field appeared to have taken place randomly and against the instructions of the central government. Only for a short period in the late 1980s did one reputable human rights organization feel it had detected "a *pattern* of killings of *contra* supporters and *contra* collaborators" (emphasis added). In stark contrast to the endemic and patterned killing of many tens of thousands of people in the U.S. client states of Guatemala and El Salvador, this pattern, though reprehensible, reportedly involved two severe beatings, fourteen disappearances, and seventy-four murders. See Americas Watch, "The Killings in Northern Nicaragua" (New York: Americas Watch, October 1989).

33. Economic costs are from the Nicaraguan case against the United States at the International Court of Justice. The total claim was for $17.8 billion. The lower figure used in the text was obtained after deducting "damages to development and sovereignty, compensation for the dead and wounded, and 'moral damages.'" For a breakdown of these economic costs, see Kent Norsworthy and Tom Barry, *Nicaragua: A Country Guide* (Albuquerque, N.M.: Inter-Hemispheric Education Resource Center, 1990), p. 59.

34. [United Nations] Comisión Económica para América Latina y el Caribe, "Balance Preliminar de la Economía de América Latina y el Caribe, 1990," *Notas Sobre la Economía y el Desarrollo,* no. 500/501 (December 1990), p. 27.

35. Ibid.

36. These and the statistics in the rest of the paragraph are from eight pages of charts provided to coauthor Walker by the Nicaraguan Ministry of the Presidency in January 1990.

37. Coauthor Walker was in a particularly good position to attest to this up-surge in *contra* activity; as a member of the Latin American Studies Association Commission to Observe the 1990 Nicaraguan Election, Walker was specifically assigned to observe and investigate the campaign and election in the war zones of northern Nicaragua in late 1989 and early 1990.

38. As quoted in Michael E. Conroy, "The Political Economy of the Nicaraguan Elections," a paper prepared for presentation at the "Coloquio sobre las Crísis Económicas del Siglo XX," Universidad Complutense de Madrid, April 15, 1990, p. 1. A member of the LASA observer team, Conroy was present at the interview of that official.

39. Phillip Taubman, "U.S. Role in Nicaragua Vote Disputed," *New York Times,* October 21, 1984, p. 12.

40. Latin American Studies Association Commission to Observe the 1990 Nic-araguan Election, *Electoral Democracy Under International Pressure* (Pittsburgh: LASA, March 15, 1990), pp. 24–26.

41. An unidentified State Department official as quoted in "Chamorro Takes a Chance," *Time*, May 7, 1990.

42. LASA Commission, *Electoral Democracy*, p. 31.

43. See, for instance, "Editorial: The Ungovernable Nicaragua," *Barricada Inter-nacional*, December 1, 1990, p. 3.

4

Recent History, Part 2

The Conservative* Restoration and the Return of Daniel Ortega

In the two decades following the 1990 electoral defeat of the Sandinistas, many if not most of the much acclaimed *logros* (achievements) of the revolution, both social and institutional, would be reversed—some slowly, some almost immediately. Strikingly insensitive to the welfare of the poor majority, the three conservative governments in power until 2007 worked from the start to implement policies that undermined the social gains the poor majority had enjoyed since 1979 in health care, education, housing, land tenure, and so on. And starting a bit later, the two dominant rival *caudillos* of the period, Arnoldo Alemán and Daniel Ortega, would make a series of self-serving pacts that would subvert and corrupt the very institutions of the rule of law and democracy so carefully created in the 1980s under governments in which Ortega, ironically, had played a central role.

---

*The terms "conservative" and "liberal" as used in Nicaragua and, indeed, most of Latin America, may be confusing to the U.S. reader. Both are based in nineteenth-century history (Chapter 2) and both describe parties (Liberal and Conservative), persons, and phenomena the U.S. reader today would see as conservative. Hence, in this and subsequent chapters, "conservative" (lowercase "c") is used in the generic sense to describe all three administrations in power from 1990 to 2007, even though two bore the Liberal (uppercase "l") label.

THE CHAMORRO YEARS: 1990–1997

The Chamorro years are difficult to evaluate.[1] On the one hand, the new administration was truly reactionary in social and economic matters, and the poor majority suffered noticeably.[2] On the other hand, Violeta Chamorro's administration succeeded in taming inflation and, after several years, achieving modest economic growth. What is most laudable, however, is that President Chamorro was a peacemaker who believed that binding up the political wounds of the Nicaraguan family was essential for both successful governance in the short run and democratic consolidation in the future.

Economic and Social Policy

It would be unfair to say that the Chamorro administration introduced economic neoliberalism to Nicaragua. In fact, the Sandinistas had implemented harsh economic stabilization measures in the late 1980s in response to the hyperinflation caused mainly by spending on the Contra War. However, the new administration embraced neoliberalism with enthusiasm and intensified its implementation. Government properties were privatized, government expenditures were cut, budgets were balanced, and tariff barriers were lowered.

Though these policies curbed inflation and eventually resulted in slight economic growth, they inevitably pummeled the poor majority. The downsizing of government, the cutbacks in social services, the privatization of state enterprises, and the credit emphasis on agro-export rather than peasant production of domestic foodstuffs combined to exacerbate the misery of ordinary Nicaraguans. Unemployment, underemployment, drug addiction, crime rates, homelessness (especially among children), and domestic violence all soared.

Further aggravating the grim social picture, the demobilization of the *contras* and the bulk of the national armed forces threw tens of thousands of young men—with little training or experience in anything except violence—into the streets. Though the Chamorro administration promised ex-combatants land and resettlement benefits in the peace agreements of 1990, it ultimately fell far short of fully meeting these commitments. Sporadically throughout the 1990s, rearmed *contras* (*recontras*), ex-Sandinista

The vanquished and the victor: On April 25, 1990, Violeta Chamorro receives the presidential sash from Daniel Ortega. (Photo courtesy of *Barricada*)

military (*recompas*), and mixed units of both (*revueltos*) engaged in re-newed guerrilla activity or banditry in rural areas.[3] Though organized armed conflict declined after the mid-1990s, such cases continued even into the late 1990s.[4]

Politics and Government

Given that in its two recent wars—the War of Liberation (1978–1979) and the Contra War (1981–1990)—Nicaragua had lost almost 3 percent of its population, it is not surprising that the period of the Chamorro adminis-tration was marked by intense political invective and conflict that some-times turned violent. Indeed, what is really surprising is that this period also saw considerable progress toward national reconciliation and demo-cratic consolidation and that there were almost no assassinations of high-level political actors.

Grassroots organizations—representing the poor majority of Nicara-guans—played a significant role in the politics of this period. The Rural Workers' Association, the National Union of Farmers and Ranchers, and mixed *contra/compa* groups of ex-combatants were involved in the negoti-ations regarding the privatization of state farms, successfully insisting that some of the land be deeded to former workers and ex-combatants. The Na-tional Workers Front did the same in the privatization of urban state-owned properties. At other times, when the government was unresponsive, these and other groups staged marches, demonstrations, and strikes to force government respect for the interests of ordinary people.

Meanwhile, the Chamorro administration steadfastly eschewed pres-sure from the United States (from 1990 through 1993) and right-wing members of UNO to engage in a vengeful "desandinization" program. In-stead, the administration wisely allowed Sandinista General Humberto Ortega to remain at the head of the military. Assured in this way that there would not be an anti-Sandinista bloodbath, the FSLN accepted the demo-bilization of the army from more than 80,000 to less than 15,000 troops. In addition, the Chamorro government, the FSLN leadership, and a wide spectrum of politicians engaged in frequent bargaining, negotiating, and pact making. This ultimately resulted in a majority consensus in the Na-tional Assembly, which made possible the promulgation of a new Military Code (1994), increasing civilian control over the military; some revisions

Fran's S

4213

Saturday, January 20, 2018

Fran, J S
4213

of the 1987 constitution (1995), including prohibiting reelection of the president and curbing the powers of that office; and the passage of Property Stability Law 209 (1996), which created a framework for dealing with property disputes arising out of the revolutionary period. Clean elections for the second autonomous government on the Atlantic coast in 1994 also seemed to bode well for a successful consolidation of democracy.

However, all may not have been as well as it seemed. Many in the UNO coalition that had brought Violeta Chamorro to power in 1990 were alienated by her attempts at pact making, especially her gestures of reconciliation toward the Sandinistas. Many of their leaders had won positions as mayors in Nicaragua's largest cities. Nurtured by USAID funds destined exclusively for municipalities that had voted the Sandinistas out, these individuals engaged in public works and neopopulist politics that won them wide popular support. Under their leadership, the old Liberal party—the majority party of Nicaragua until it became corrupted by the Somozas—was resuscitated as various splinter Liberal parties were fused under the banner of the Liberal Alliance. The Liberals did well in the Atlantic coast elections of 1994, and they would win the national elections of 1996.

The 1996 Election

As an official observer at the 1984 and 1990 elections, coauthor Walker found the character of the 1996 election, which he also observed, to be a disappointment. In the politically polarized atmosphere of Nicaragua at the time, the right wing insisted on a series of last-minute changes in the electoral law and in the personnel of the Supreme Electoral Council. The procedural modifications were hard to operationalize on such short notice, and the personnel changes introduced many people into the system who were inexperienced or lacking in commitment to democracy. Each step of the election was flawed by anomalies—from registration and campaigning to election-day voting and postelection vote-counting.

The worst problems occurred in the counting of the vote after the polls had closed. There were so many irregularities that the Supreme Electoral Council did not announce official results for more than a month after the election. Such confusion reigned in some places that the entire tallies of hundreds of voting stations were ultimately thrown out. Perhaps significantly, the bulk of them occurred in Managua, Jinotega, and Matagalpa—the three departments whose electoral councils were under newly appointed Liberal presidents.

Against this background, the Liberal Alliance was triumphant. Its presidential candidate, Arnoldo Alemán, beat perennial FSLN candidate Daniel Ortega by winning 51 percent of the vote; only 37.7 percent of the vote went to Ortega. In the National Assembly, the Liberals took forty-two seats, the FSLN took thirty-six, and fifteen seats were divided among nine minor parties. Both Ortega and the presidential candidate who placed third denounced the Liberal victory as illegitimate.[5]

THE ALEMÁN ADMINISTRATION

The fifty-year-old lawyer/farmer who was inaugurated as president in January 1997 had been a Liberal since the days of the Somozas. Though he had developed a burning hatred for the Sandinistas, he was widely rumored to have made a financial killing during the revolution by purchasing heavily subsidized veterinary medicines in Nicaragua and smuggling them into neighboring countries for sale at much higher market prices.[6] Elected to the Managua City Council in 1990, he then engaged in complicated deal making—some of it quite deceitful—to get himself appointed mayor by his peers. In that position he governed as a sort of "neopopulist." Using USAID funds to carry out highly visible public works for which he took full credit, he employed the politically faithful, mixed with and proclaimed his concern for the poor, and identified the Sandinistas as the cause of most of the country's problems. With financial and moral support from the Cuban and Nicaraguan exile communities in Miami, he and other Liberal mayors worked to create the Liberal Alliance out of various Liberal microparties that had survived the fall of Somoza.

Ironically, the Liberal victory of 1996 was also facilitated by the behavior of some leaders of the FSLN in the 1990s. These people had weakened the party's image by engaging in a legal but unseemly property grab (dubbed *la piñata*) during their lame-duck months early in 1990 and by clinging to the party leadership when challenged in 1994. The break-off of the Renovating Sandinista Movement (MRS) into a separate party in 1995 took most of the professional and intellectual leaders out of the FSLN just as the united and well-financed Liberals were gearing up for the 1996 election.

The Alemán administration was a disappointment for anyone concerned with democratic consolidation in Nicaragua. It was marked by extreme polarization, confrontation, administrative incompetence, and unprecedented corruption. The disastrous impact of Hurricane Mitch in October 1998 only highlighted and accentuated these failings.

In many ways, Arnoldo Alemán was a quintessential neopopulist—a category of leader that had emerged in various parts of Latin America by the end of the twentieth century.[7] Like the populists of earlier decades (Getulio Vargas in Brazil, Juan Perón in Argentina, José María Velasco Ibarra in Ecuador), the neopopulists used personal charisma and dramatic rhetoric to appeal—almost as secular messiahs—to large blocks of socially and economically marginalized and stressed citizens. Characteristically, they championed the weak and vulnerable—the "people"—as against the evil and "repugnant other"—often, though not always, the privileged classes.[8] However, unlike the old populists who promoted labor unions and other organs of civil society, neopopulists (such as Carlos Menem in Argentina, Alberto Fujimori in Peru, and Abdalá Bucaram in Ecuador) appealed directly to the politically unorganized sectors of society. Indeed, such leaders actually feared and disliked organized civil society, be it in the form of grassroots civic organizations (of peasants, workers, women, etc.) or nongovernmental organizations (NGOs)—national and international—that provided assistance to such organizations. And finally, unlike the old populists with their schemes for government intervention in the economy, the neopopulists—though usually elected on platforms criticizing neoliberal economics—often eventually adopted neoliberalism (government downsizing, emphasis on agro-export, and a retreat from state involvement in the economy) and, indeed, found that in the short run, at least, implementing structural reforms was popular with their marginalized supporters.[9]

By the 1990s, Nicaragua was ripe for the emergence of neopopulism. The U.S.-orchestrated Contra War and its related programs of economic strangulation had ruined the economy and created an ever-growing segment of impoverished people—unemployed workers, demobilized combatants, and informal-sector vendors. Most of these people were not members of organized civil society. In addition, massive U.S.-generated anti-Sandinista propaganda promoted in the 1980s through the local and international media, by the Catholic Church hierarchy, and by opposition parties—together with the inability of the Sandinistas to bring peace and solve the country's economic problems—had demonized the Sandinistas in the eyes of many. Thus, neopopulism in Nicaragua had both an accessible base of stressed and angry but unorganized people to which to appeal and a ready-made "repugnant other"

President Arnoldo Alemán. (Photo by and with permission of Jorge Lopez, *La Tribuna*)

(the Sandinistas) to serve as a target in mobilizing that anger. Furthermore, as noted earlier, the neopopulists were bolstered by USAID programs in the early 1990s (from which pro-Sandinista municipalities were excluded) and by popular reaction to Sandinista excesses, starting with the *piñata* in 1990 and continuing throughout the decade as a tiny group of old revolutionaries clung stubbornly to the reins of party power.

Thus, Alemán rose to power—and initially attempted to rule—as a neopopulist. Harboring an intense hatred of the Sandinistas and not having played a central role in the bargaining and consensus building that went into the National Assembly's rewriting of the "rules of the game" in the mid-1990s, Alemán and his Liberal plurality in the legislature immediately called into question the legitimacy of the 1994 Military Code, the 1995 amendments to the 1987 constitution, and the 1996 Property Stability Law 209. In addition, seeing the Sandinistas as irredeemably evil, they maneuvered to deprive them of the full number of seats on the executive body of the National Assembly to which they appeared entitled.

These moves resulted in months of chaos. There were general strikes and demonstrations led by the National Union of Farmers and Ranchers and joined by urban workers to protect the properties that had changed hands in the 1980s. In addition, there were raucous and hate-filled invective, renewed armed insurgency, FSLN boycotts of the National Assembly, constitutional challenges, sporadic attempts at public dialogue, and behind-the-scenes bargaining between the leaders of the two major political forces. On the positive side, grassroots organizations representing peasants and urban workers were again active in defending their interests—especially as they related to the property issue.

Eventually, pressure—both international and domestic—for a compromise solution became irresistible, and Alemán was forced to adopt a new strategy that would add behind-the-scenes deals with his Sandinista enemies to his neopopulist public posture. In the fall of 1997, private negotiations between legal teams representing the FSLN and the government culminated in an agreement on the thorniest issue of the 1990s, that of property. In November, after only four hours of debate, seventy-three of the ninety-three members of the National Assembly voted to approve the Law of Urban and Rural Reformed Property.[10]

For a while it appeared that with the settlement of the property issue a "new normalcy" was beginning to emerge in Nicaragua. Soon, however, the leaders of the two major parties each suffered personal scandals. Alemán was engulfed in escalating charges of corruption. First came the "Narcojet" scandal, in which traces of cocaine were found in a rented (previously stolen) jet that had been serving as the presidential plane since December 1997. Then, in February 1999, Comptroller General Agustín Jarquín announced the results of an investigation of the president's personal assets, which showed that Alemán's personal fortune had grown by 900 percent from 1990 to 1996. Though Alemán eventually resorted to jailing Jarquín for a number of months, the scandal would not go away. Ortega, too, was besieged by scandal. In 1998, he suddenly found himself accused by his thirty-year-old stepdaughter of having sexually abused her over a period of nearly twenty years.

Although both Ortega and Alemán would survive the scandals and retain control of their respective political movements, their behavior hurt their parties and dramatically eroded their popularity. In April 1999, nearly half of those questioned in an *Envío* survey saw the Alemán administration as "the most corrupt government in Nicaragua's history,"[11] and a CID-Gallup poll of public opinion found that fully 77 percent of Nicaraguans had doubts about their president's honesty.[12] In the latter poll, public support for the two major parties—FSLN and Liberal—had dropped to 20 percent each.[13]

On top of this, support for Alemán and the Liberals was also diminished by their poor handling of the disaster visited on Nicaragua by Hurricane Mitch in October 1998. More than 2,400 people were killed, and nearly one-fifth of Nicaragua's population was left homeless. Economic damage totaled more than $1.5 billion.[14] Working with a civil service stripped to the bone by a decade of neoliberal downsizing and further debilitated by corruption, cronyism, and incompetence, the Alemán administration was painfully slow in helping those hurt by the disaster. Furthermore, as a neopopulist, Alemán channeled Nicaraguan public relief aid through local governments where Liberals were in power or through Liberal party organizations where they were not. He even attempted at first to deflect the flow of international assistance away from nongovernmental organizations (seen by him as Sandinista), which he could not control.[15]

The increasingly weak positions of both Alemán and Ortega would lead in turn to a strange series of pacts between the two archenemies.[16] Whereas the agreement on the 1997 property law could be seen as serving a national good, it would be hard to defend subsequent deals between the two *caudillos* in such terms. While publicly attacking each other in the most visceral terms, Alemán and Ortega now made deals that simply served their own or their parties' narrow interests. Late in 1999, the two crafted a pact that the FSLN/PLC majority in the Assembly quickly converted into law the following year. Among other things, it "packed" the Supreme Court, the Office of the Comptroller General, and the Supreme Electoral Council (CSE) with FSLN and PLC partisans. As a result, Alemán was relieved of scrutiny by the comptroller general, and both *caudillos* were free—for the time being, at least—of the threat of successful prosecution under the judicial system. Furthermore, the electoral laws were revised to effectively exclude any meaningful challenges from third parties.

By the turn of the century, Nicaragua appeared to be at a critical political juncture. Once dramatically dissimilar, the Liberals and what was left of the FSLN had become much more alike. Since the days of Somoza, the Liberal movement had long been essentially a vehicle for personal aggrandizement and ambition. Now in the late 1990s, a tiny remnant of the original FSLN controlled a party that had seen the defection of most of its middle- and upper-level cadre and a near-complete dissolution of its once-strong relationship with the various organs of civil society created in the 1970s and 1980s.

THE 2001 ELECTIONS

It was against this background that national elections were held in 2001. As had been the case in 1996, what transpired was not entirely uplifting. In 2000, the now-partisan Supreme Electoral Council, working under new electoral laws, arbitrarily rejected attempts by all third parties—except the relatively weak Conservative party—to qualify for the elections. The latter reportedly had been saved under pressure from the U.S. Embassy, which initially was apparently worried that the PLC was too discredited to defeat the FSLN.

The most notable characteristic of the 2001 campaign period was the degree to which it was subjected to manipulation by the U.S. government. For instance, as the official campaign heated up that spring with perennial FSLN presidential candidate Daniel Ortega showing a seven-point lead in the polls, the United States reportedly reversed course and pressured the Conservative presidential candidate to withdraw so as not to split the anti-Sandinista vote.[17] Then, as the gap narrowed between Ortega and his Liberal opponent, seventy-three-year-old businessman Enrique Bolaños Geyer, U.S. officials, from Secretary of State Colin Powell on down, made a series of anti-Sandinista statements. After the attacks of September 11, 2001, Washington even tried to connect Ortega with world "terrorism," and one U.S. official publicly predicted a "vicious" response should an Ortega government be found to have links to terrorism.[18] As in 1996, the Catholic Church hierarchy also aligned itself against the FSLN.

Ortega attempted to present himself as a "new man," able to coexist with practically anyone. His campaign organization at one point even tried unsuccessfully to win the endorsement of former archenemy Anastasio Somoza Portocarrero, the son of the deposed dictator.[19] But the opposition of the United States, vocally joined by the Catholic hierarchy, was overwhelming. On November 4, the Nicaraguan electorate—well aware of the pain the United States could inflict on independent countries within

its sphere of influence—gave Bolaños a fourteen-point victory over Ortega. The Conservative party, which had hastily fielded a new presidential
slate, won only 1.4 percent of the ballots—far short of what was needed to
qualify to run in the next election

Former U.S. president Jimmy Carter, in Managua as the head of his
center's electoral observer team, was remarkably frank in his condemna-
tion of the heavy-handed U.S. role: "I personally disapprove of statements
or actions by any country that might tend to influence the vote of people
in another sovereign nation."[20]

THE BOLAÑOS ADMINISTRATION

The country over which Bolaños was to preside was awash in problems.
The economy was nearly prostrate, and the human condition of most Nicaraguans desperate. Furthermore, the "structural adjustments" and neoliberal economic policies begun in the late 1980s and accelerated under
IMF and U.S. pressure in the 1990s had so shrunk the state that it was now
utterly incapable of dealing with the dire human condition of the impoverished majority. Finally, though international nongovernmental organizations and some elements of grassroots civil society were still trying to
address the country's social problems, neither of the two political parties
left standing in 2002 had the integrity to articulate and organize an effective response to the national crisis. Alemán's Liberal party was as morally
bankrupt as when it served the Somozas. And the FSLN, once a vehicle for
change, was now a discredited instrument of personal ambition.

The new president, a businessman with strong anti-Sandinista creden-
tials, had served quietly as vice president to Arnoldo Alemán. Though the
PLC's presidential candidate, Bolaños, apparently had not even been con-
sulted when Alemán selected the PLC candidates for the Assembly. Now
the PLC would have a working majority in the National Assembly—a bloc
strong enough to modify the constitution. Alemán—a member of the Assembly for life by virtue of his status as ex-president—had set himself up
to dominate his country's politics as the central figure in that body. The
Somoza-like *caudillo* clearly envisioned Bolaños as a figurehead who would
formally occupy the office of the presidency until he, Alemán, could return
to it after the next election.

However, there was more to Bolaños than Alemán had envisioned. Having a reputation for honesty and having campaigned on an anticorruption

platform, the conservative entrepreneur seemed determined not simply to be a stand-in for Alemán. If he were to be a real president, he would have to confront and defeat Alemán. Thus, after first attacking lower-level corruption during the Alemán administration, he eventually went after Alemán himself. In August 2002, he and acting Attorney General Francisco Fiallos accused Alemán, his family members, and close allies of misdirecting $100 million in public funds to bank accounts they controlled in Panama. "Arnoldo," the new president said, "I never dreamed you would betray your people like this. You took the pensions from the retirees, medicine from the sick, salaries from the teachers. You stole the people's trust."[21]

Those statements were a dramatic effort to convince the National Assembly to strip Alemán of his legislative immunity, which it did in 2002, thanks to a fleeting alliance between the FSLN and a handful of Bolaños's loyal legislators. However, although Alemán was sentenced to a twenty-year jail term in 2004, it was soon apparent that the ongoing Ortega/Alemán pact process would give Alemán a large measure of freedom. Indeed, he served most of his time under house arrest and his conviction was completely overturned in January 2009 by the politicized Supreme Court.

Meanwhile, Bolaños's anticorruption campaign, particularly his crusade against Alemán, served largely to isolate him within the PLC and the larger political arena. In 2004, Bolaños left the PLC and created the Alliance for the Republic (Alianza para la República, APRE). This split within the right helped the FSLN in the 2004 municipal elections, in which it won eighty-four municipalities, including Managua, the majority of them in coalition with other parties.

Through the pact, the FSLN and the PLC worked to oust Bolaños. In October 2004, the by-then thoroughly politicized Comptroller's Office, citing the president's failure to disclose the source of campaign funds in the 2001 election, called for his impeachment. While Ortega did announce the following month that the FSLN would not support impeachment, the legislature passed constitutional reforms clearly designed to limit presidential authority. These included requiring legislative approval (60 percent) in appointing government ministers and diplomats, giving the legislature the power to dismiss cabinet members and to override a presidential veto, and creating several new administrative bodies.[22] Bolaños attempted to use state institutions to stop the reforms, but to no avail: All were controlled by the FSLN and PLC. In turn, the two parties even refused to pass laws Bolaños introduced that were required for the disbursement of IMF loans. At one point, Ortega even proposed holding early presidential elections to remove Bolaños from office.[23] This resulted in a prolonged constitutional crisis that became a matter of international interest, ultimately mediated by the Organization of American States (OAS).[24] In October 2005, Bolaños and Ortega agreed that the new laws—the Framework Law—would not be implemented until after the 2006 elections and that the FSLN would stop blocking laws required for the country's IMF agreement and the ratification of the Central American Free Trade Agreement.

THE 2006 ELECTIONS

By 2006, the Supreme Electoral Council had been thoroughly politicized by the country's two *caudillos*. And, since Alemán's conviction on corruption charges had given Ortega the upper hand in ongoing iterations of the pact, Ortega's interests would be reflected in the nature and behavior of that key entity. First, Roberto Rivas—widely seen as a favorite of Cardinal Miguel Obando y Bravo or, as *La Prensa* put it, "his protected one" (*su protegido*)[25]—was made president of the CSE. This and an Ortega decision to support the outlawing of therapeutic abortion, even when necessary to save the mother's life, was apparently sufficient to cause former anti-Sandinista Obando to support Ortega in the elections. Second, and even more important, the electoral laws were changed to allow a presidential candidate to win with less than a majority if he or she were to obtain 40 percent of the vote or 35 percent with a five-point margin over the nearest rival. This adjustment in the rules favored Ortega, whose vote total had hovered around 40 percent in the previous three elections.

Ortega was also favored by a split in his conservative opposition. Alemán's old Constitutional Liberal Party ran José Rizo, a coffee grower and former vice president under Bolaños. However, the corruption of the PLC had caused a large segment of that party to break off and form a new party, the Nicaraguan Liberal Alliance (ALN), under the leadership of banker Eduardo Montealegre. The ALN and the Conservative party united in 2006 to back Montealegre's presidential candidacy. Two groups that had split from the FSLN also fielded candidates—Edmundo Jarquín for the MRS and Edén Pastora for a new microparty, the Alternative for Change—but they were not a serious challenge to Ortega.[26]

The election itself was relatively clean. It was observed by international teams from the Organization of American States and the Carter Center as

Jubilant Ortega supporters celebrate following ET's announcement of the results of their "quick count" only hours after the polls closed in the 2006 national elections. (Photo by David Evans)

well as two major domestic groups.[27] This level of observation meant that all involved knew from the start that patterns of fraud would not go undetected and would be denounced if they took place. In addition, the major domestic observer group, Ética y Transparencia (Ethics and Transparency, or ET), fielded such a large team that ET workers were in almost every voting place in the country to observe and report the vote count after the polls closed. Within hours of the closing, ET had an extremely accurate "quick count" of the results—thus ensuring that any later manipulation of the tallies would be detected.

All observers agreed that Daniel Ortega had won the presidency with 38 percent of the vote, followed by Montealegre (28.3), Rizo (27.1), Jarquín (6.3), and Pastora (0.3). Fraud—favoring the FSLN—was detected by ET in only four municipalities of one coastal department, the RAAN.[28] And, though the Carter Center made a series of suggestions for improving the system, its overall assessment of the 2006 election was positive.[29]

Probably the least clean aspect of the 2006 election was the role the U.S. government played in its effort to manipulate the outcome. As in the previous three presidential contests, U.S. personnel spoke out and worked behind the scenes in an effort to orchestrate the victory of one candidate—in this case the ALN's Eduardo Montealegre.[30] Ironically, however, their efforts actually helped split the anti-Sandinista forces, thus helping to ensure the Ortega victory, which could not have taken place without that split.

THE ORTEGA ADMINISTRATION

While a change from the prior conservative administrations, the Ortega administration was also a departure from the democratic values of the Sandinistas of the 1980s. Though he introduced important social policies (see Chapter 6), Ortega's administration also intensified the corruption of the rule of law begun during the pact making of the previous decade. Ortega now had tight control of what was left of the FSLN and, within the pact, he held a clear advantage over Alemán, whose corruption in the 1990s had been so extensive that additional charges could always be raised by the Ortega-controlled judiciary if they were ever necessary. In addition, Ortega and Alemán were in a position to control their mutual opponent, the ALN's Eduardo Montealegre, whose legislative immunity to prosecution under corruption charges dating from the Bolaños administration could easily be lifted whenever the two *caudillos* saw fit.[31]

The Ortega administration also exhibited little tolerance for dissent. Journalists, former FSLN members, and civil society organizations complained of intimidation and violence by Ortega's sympathizers. Among the most prominent targets of government harassment were former FSLN members Carlos Fernando Chamorro and Ernesto Cardenal, both of whom were the subject of legal investigations and public smear campaigns, and a handful of women leaders who continually spoke out against the criminalizing of therapeutic abortion.[32] *Turbas,* pro-Ortega youth gangs, were increasingly used as a tool to intimidate the opposition. Moreover, the administration sought to extend control over civil society through the establishment of Citizens Power Councils (CPCs) (discussed in Chapters 6 and 7) and heavy-handed intervention in municipal governments (discussed in Chapter 7).

2008 Municipal Elections

The municipal elections of 2008—held in 146 of 152 municipalities—appear to have been yet another example of the corrupting nature of the pact.[33]

Though it had immediately certified Ortega's victory in the 2006 elections, the huge and prestigious domestic observer group ET was barred by the politicized CSE from observing in 2008 on the grounds that it had assumed "political positions."[34] In addition, all credible international observation was also barred. Prior to the elections, the CSE limited the electoral field by ruling that the MRS and Conservative party were not eligible to participate because they could not present a full slate of candidates. Critics viewed this as an effort to protect the FSLN and PLC from electoral competition, particularly in light of the fact that two tiny parties that surely did not meet all the requisites were allowed to run.[35] The PLC and ALN united two enemies, Alemán and Montealegre, against the FSLN. The move was forced, in part, by the CSE's hasty decision to reduce the time frame for parties, alliances, and their candidates to register. The alliance fielded Montealegre, who continued to be dogged by accusations of fraud in the Central Bank's Negotiable Investment Certificate (CENI) scandal, as its candidate in the Managua mayoral race.[36]

According to official results, the FSLN won 105 municipalities, including Managua, followed by the PLC with 37 and the ALN with 6. Allegations of fraud quickly surfaced. But verifying where the truth lay—especially in the absence of credible on-site observation—was another matter. FSLN representatives and supporters maintained that the party's success was a result of Ortega's popular programs and good governance at the municipal level. They contended that preelection polls had given the FSLN—most notably the FSLN's Managua mayoral candidate, triple crown boxing champion Alexis Argüello—an advantage. In truth, there was no dispute that the FSLN won sixty municipalities and that results in ninety-five municipalities were uncontested.[37] The majority of the forty contested municipalities were those that Montealegre's faction would have received, per the alliance with the PLC. Finally, they pointed out that no claims of fraud had been brought to the CSE.[38] Much of this was true and yet ET investigated extensively, finding nine major areas of irregularities ranging from the expulsion of party monitors (*fiscales*) from voting places, fraudulent annulment of votes, and early closing of some voting places to failure to properly guard and secure electoral materials and open intimidation at voting stations.[39] Another report offered evidence of vote tampering, as some tallies from the voting tables were different than those the CSE presented. Additionally, it appeared that total votes in some districts (such as Nindiri) exceeded the number of registered voters.[40] As of July 2009, the Supreme Electoral Council still had not reported the results of some 30 percent of the tables, many of them in

Managua.[41] The allegations of fraud resulted in the loss of aid from the United States and the European Union.[42]

In the aftermath of the 2008 elections, Nicaragua's two *caudillos* prepared for their next electoral showdown. In January 2009, the Supreme Court overturned Alemán's sentence, and the latter quickly announced his intention to run for president in 2011. Some alleged that the court's move was the price Ortega had to pay for some of the municipalities the FSLN "won" in 2008. Next, in October 2009, the FSLN justices in the Supreme Court Constitutionality Commission met alone at night and ruled that the constitutional prohibition against the presidential reelection did not apply in Ortega's case.[43] Although highly disputed by independent jurists long afterward, the Liberal justices lacked a majority to overturn it in plenary. This cleared the way for Ortega to run again. Given the advantage he held over Alemán in the pact, it seemed almost certain that Ortega would be president of Nicaragua for some time. Had Nicaragua become an "incipient institutional dictatorship" as the MRS put it?[44]

NOTES

1. For a comprehensive examination of this period, see Thomas W. Walker, ed., *Nicaragua Without Illusions: Regime Transition and Structural Adjustment in the 1990s* (Wilmington, Del.: Scholarly Resources, 1997).

2. In this context, *reactionary* is a better word than *conservative*, since in social and economic matters, the new administration was trying not to conserve what it had inherited from the Sandinistas but rather to "turn the clock back" to a real or imagined past.

3. *Recompa* comes from the word *compa*, which is short for *compañero* (comrade in arms), a term often used for Sandinista soldiers. *Revueltos* is used in other contexts for scrambled eggs.

4. See, for instance, "Nicaragua: Atlantic Coast Groups Rearm," *Central America Report*, vol. 25, no. 22 (June 11, 1998), p. 3.

5. For information concerning the election, see Thomas W. Walker "Epilogue: The 1996 National Elections," in Walker, ed., *Nicaragua Without Illusions,* pp. 305–311.

6. From a Walker interview with Ricardo Chavarría, former vice minister of social welfare (INSSBI), July 18, 1998.

7. For good discussions of this interesting phenomenon, see Carlos de la Torre, "Populism and Democracy: Political Discourses and Cultures in Contemporary

Ecuador," *Latin American Perspectives*, vol. 24, no. 3 (May 1997), pp. 12–24; and Kurt Weyland, "Neopopulism and Neoliberalism in Latin America: Unexpected Affinities," *Studies in Comparative International Development*, vol. 31, no. 3 (Fall 1996), pp. 3–31.

8. De la Torre, "Populism and Democracy," pp. 19–20.

9. See Weyland, "Neopopulism and Neoliberalism in Latin America."

10. Nitlapán-*Envío* Team, "An Accord Besieged by Discord," *Envío*, vol. 16, no. 196 (November 1997), pp. 3–4.

11. "After Stockholm and Before the Pact," *Envío*, vol. 18, no. 215 (June 1999), p. 4.

12. "Nicaragua: Government and FSLN Weakened by Protests," *Central America Report*, May 14, 1999, p. 2.

13. "Nicaragua: FSLN Hardliners Maintain Control," *Central America Report*, June 18, 1999, p. 7.

14. "Nicaragua: Mitch Redefines Political and Social Scenario," *Central America Report*, May 28, 1999, p. 6.

15. Ricardo Chavarría, executive director of the Instituto de Promoción Humana (Nicaragua's oldest nongovernmental organization), in a lengthy e-mail communication with coauthor Walker on January 14, 1999.

16. Strange as this turn of events may seem, it actually was predicted as a strong possibility by Nicaraguan political observer Oscar René Vargas in an interview with the Hemisphere Initiatives/Washington Office on Latin America election observer team (of which co-author Walker was a member) in October 1996.

17. *Envío* Team, "The Road to the Elections Was Paved with Fraud," *Envío*, vol. 20, nos. 244–245 (November–December 2001), p. 37.

18. John F. Keane, director of the Office of Central American Affairs, U.S. Department of State, in response to a question at a conference on "Nicaragua's Presidential Election," University of Pittsburgh, October 4, 2001. With Cristiana Chamorro, a prominent member of Nicaragua's elite and a writer for that country's leading daily, *La Prensa,* present on the panel, Keane paused to think before he chose the term "vicious."

19. Nitlapán-*Envío* Team, "Between Two Evils and Many Dreams," *Envío,* vol. 20, no. 242 (September 2001), p. 2.

20. Jimmy Carter, November 4, 2001, as quoted in NicaNet, "Election Update," *Nicaragua Network Hotline* (Supplement), November 8, 2001.

21. Quoted in Gioconda Belli, "Nicaragua: A Crusader Looks to the U.S.," *Los Angeles Times,* September 8, 2002.

22. David Kolker, "An Unjust Attack on Nicaraguan President Enrique Bolaños," Council on Hemispheric Affairs, November 18, 2004, www.coha.org/an-unjust

-attack-on-nicaraguan-president-enrique-bolanos; Latin American Database, "Nicaragua's Legislature Looks to Limit Presidential Powers; Aleman Could Rescue Bolanos," NotiCen, January 13, 2005.

23. Shelley McConnell, "Can the Inter-American Democratic Charter Work? The 2004–05 Constitutional Crisis in Nicaragua," presented at the International Studies Association meeting, February 28–March 3, 2007, p. 15.

24. For a more complete discussion of the crisis and the negotiations, see McConnell, "Can the Inter-American Democratic Charter Work?" and Council on Hemispheric Affairs, "Nicaragua: A Three-Way Political Ground," COHA memorandum to the press, July 20, 2005.

25. "Inicia proceso Roberto Rivas en Costa Rica," *La Prensa*, March 13, 2010.

26. The original MRS candidate, former Managua mayor Herty Lewites, died in July 2006 and was succeeded in the race by Jarquín. Lewites had been a member of the FSLN and served as the minister of tourism in the revolutionary government. He left the FSLN to join the MRS in 2005.

27. Coauthor Walker was part of the Carter Center team.

28. "Observacíon Electoral Nicaragua 2006," Carter Center, Atlanta, May 2007, pp. 39, 40.

29. Ibid., pp. 42, 43.

30. Nicaragua Network Delegation to Investigate U.S. Intervention in the Nicaraguan Election of November 2006, *The 2006 Nicaraguan Elections and the U.S. Government Role*, June 2006.

31. Montealegre, who served as treasury minister under Bolaños, was implicated in a scandal involving Negotiable Investment Certificates (CENIs), which resulted in the collapse of several banks.

32. El Centro Nicaraguense de Derechos Humanos (CENIDH), Derechos Humanos en Nicaragua Informe 2008 (Managua: CENIDH, 2009); Tina Rosenberg, "The Many Stories of Carlos Fernando Chamorro," *New York Times*, March 22, 2009.

33. Municipal elections in the North Atlantic Autonomous Region (RAAN) were delayed upon request by the regional Yatama government due to the lingering effects of Hurricane Felix, which devastated the region in September 2007.

34. "La Entrada de Roberto Rivas," *El Nuevo Diario*, February 28, 2010.

35. Asier Andres Fernández, "Court Dashes Third Party Hopes in Municipal Elections," *Central America Report*, June 27, 2008; Asier Andres Fernández, "A Murky Pact Between Liberals and Sandinistas," *Central America Report*, July 18, 2008.

36. Nitlápan-*Envío* Team, "Lots of Clashes, Little Light, and Still No Way Forward," *Envío*, vol. 27, no. 320 (March 2008).

37. Instituto para el Desarollo y Democracia, "Elecciones Municipales 2008/2009: Informe Final," IPADE, May 2009, pp. 110.

38. Coauthor Wade interview with Paul Oquist, minister of national policy and private secretary to President Ortega, Managua, July 2009.

39. Grupo Cívico Ética y Transparencia, "Valorizacíon Preliminar de Problemas Encontrados Elecciones Municipales 2008," Managua, November 12, 2008, and Grupo Cívico Ética y Transparencia, "Informe Final Elecciones Municipales 2008," Managua, 2009.

40. See Instituto para el Desarollo y Democracia, "Elecciones Municipales 2008/2009.

41. Coauthor Wade interviews with Carlos Fernando Chamorro and Judy Butler, July 2009.

42. Matthew Lee, "US Cuts Aid to Nicaragua," *Washington Post*, June 11, 2009.

43. Brendan Riley, "This Ongoing Institutional Crisis Brought to You by Nicaragua's Daniel Ortega," Council on Hemispheric Affairs' *Washington Report on the Hemisphere*, June 16, 2010.

44. Nitlápan-*Envío* Team, "Abuse as Usual Means Many Accounts to Settle," *Envío*, no. 330 (January 2009); Nitlápan-*Envío* Team, "Mirages," *Envío*, no. 345 (April 2010).

5
🖋 *The Economic Dimension*

When the revolutionary government that replaced the Somoza regime in 1979 drew up its first comprehensive economic plan—*The 1980 Program for Economic Reactivation in Benefit of the People*—it was well aware that it faced a stark reality. "We are confronting," the government observed, "the effects of a hundred years of dependent capitalism which expresses itself in the appropriation of the national wealth by an extremely small group, leaving the vast majority of the population in misery and ignorance."[1] The term *dependent capitalism* as used in this statement is not a rhetorical or demagogic expression. It refers to an objective reality—a socioeconomic pattern predominant throughout Latin America that seemed—and still seems—to persist whether the political form of the moment be liberal "democracy" (for example, Colombia from the late 1950s on), one-man dictatorship (the Dominican Republic under Rafael Trujillo or Venezuela under Marcos Pérez Jiménez), progressive military rule (Peru, 1968–1975), or rightist military dictatorship (Brazil, 1964–1985, or Chile, 1973–1989).

There is a profound difference between what is loosely called free enterprise or capitalism in the United States and its counterpart in Latin America. Capitalism in the United States coexists with relatively high levels of social justice precisely because it is dependent on the bulk of the American people as consumers. Most of what U.S. industry produces is consumed in the United States. The economic system, therefore, would collapse if the majority of citizens were exploited to the extent that they could no longer consume at relatively high levels. Quite the opposite is true in Latin America, where the so-called capitalist economies are overwhelmingly externally oriented, placing great emphasis on the production of products for export. Under these dependent capitalist systems, the common citizen is important as a cheap and easily exploitable source of labor rather than as a consumer. Therefore, there is little or no economic incentive for the privileged classes that dominate most Latin American governments to make the sacrifices necessary to improve the conditions of the majority of the people.

While prerevolutionary Nicaragua was not at all unusual as an example of a society distorted by dependent capitalism, it was nevertheless an exceptionally and strikingly tragic case. Unlike certain other countries— such as Bolivia, where at the time natural resources were thought to be in relatively short supply—Nicaragua is, and always has been, a land of impressive economic potential. The population/land ratio is very favorable. Not only is Nicaragua the largest of the Central American countries, it is the least densely populated, with approximately 43 persons per square kilometer as opposed to 79 for the region as a whole and approximately 292 for El Salvador. The land itself is rich and varied, with different soil, climatological, and altitude characteristics suitable for the production of a wide variety of crops and livestock. The country's many rivers and volcanoes offer easily exploitable sources of both hydroelectric and geothermal energy, and internal waterways facilitate inexpensive domestic transportation and present the possibility of exploitation as part of some future transoceanic waterway. Nicaragua has both Caribbean and Pacific coastlines, providing direct access not only to the food and mineral resources of the seas but also to the major markets of the world. The country has significant timber resources—from pine forests in the highlands to hardwood stands in the lowland tropics. Among the known mineral assets are silver and, particularly, gold. Finally, the Nicaraguan people, with their relatively homogeneous culture and language and their indomitable spirit and joie de vivre, are themselves a very important national asset.

The tragedy—indeed the gross injustice—of prerevolutionary Nicaragua was that in spite of all this potential and some apparent signs of "development," such as frequent spurts in gross national product (GNP), the vast majority of the Nicaraguan people, even in the late 1970s, led a stark existence while a small, privileged minority monopolized and misused the national resources to their own nearly exclusive benefit. This fact is illustrated by income distribution figures for the late 1970s that show that 20 percent of the population (i.e., the upper and middle class) received 60 percent of the national income while 80 percent (the lower classes) were expected to make do with the other 40 percent. The poorest 50 percent had access to only 15 percent of the national income, for an average of a little more than a couple hundred dollars per person per year.[2]

EVOLUTION OF THE ECONOMIC SYSTEM

The best way to understand the inequities of the Nicaraguan economic system is to examine its historical roots. Nicaraguan economic history prior to the Sandinista Revolution is divisible into four distinct time spans: (1) the colonial period, from the 1520s to the 1820s; (2) the first half century of independence, from the 1820s through the 1870s; (3) the period of primitive dependent capitalism, from the late 1870s through the 1940s; and (4) the rise of modern dependent capitalism, from the 1950s through the 1970s.

The Colonial Economy

When the Spaniards arrived in western Nicaragua in the early sixteenth century, they found a relatively advanced agrarian society. The approximately 1 million native inhabitants of the region—descendants of colonizers and refugees from the Mayan and Aztec civilizations to the north—lived in villages and cities ranging in population from a few hundred to tens of thousands. This was a feudal society, with chiefs, subchiefs, and commoners, in which tribute flowed from the lowly to the lofty. However, land was held collectively and each inhabitant of the villages and cities had access to a designated plot nearby. The rich soils of the region yielded agricultural products in abundance ranging from corn, cassava, and chili to beans, tobacco, and a variety of vegetables. Each population center had one or more local markets at which agricultural products were sold. Though periodic crop failure and intertribal warfare undoubtedly inflicted occasional acute hardship, the economy in general was relatively self-sufficient and self-contained. The market system, intraregional trade, and general access to rich agricultural lands provided the material wherewithal to satisfy basic human needs.

The Spanish conquest, as we noted earlier, had an immediate and devastating impact on this economic system. Superimposing themselves on the existing feudal structure, the *conquistadores* demanded tribute in gold and, when that was depleted, Indian slaves. Within a few decades the near total destruction of the native population through death by contact with European diseases and the export of slaves created a severe manpower shortage that all but destroyed the labor-intensive agricultural base of the region's economy. To be sure, some lands remained under intensive cultivation throughout the colonial period, providing some export products such as corn and cacao, as well as food to meet the region's much reduced internal demand. But for the most part, the rich lands of Nicaragua reverted to jungle or were exploited for the raising of cattle to produce hides, tallow, and salted meat for sale to other colonies.

In a few decades, therefore, the economy essentially had become externally oriented. In addition to the sale of corn, cacao, and cattle products, the tiny Spanish elite accrued wealth through the exploitation of forest products, shipbuilding, and intermittent gold mining—all to meet external rather than internal demands. The underpopulation of the colony and the concentration of wealth in the hands of the privileged classes of León and Granada made Nicaragua a prime target for attacks by pirates from England and elsewhere in Europe, further contributing to the region's status as a colonial backwater. The process of underdevelopment had begun.

The First Half Century of Independence

The partial interruption of foreign dominance resulting from the disintegration and eventual collapse of Spanish colonial rule in the early nineteenth century was reflected in important changes in the Nicaraguan economic system. It is true that British traders were quick to provide the landed elite with an outlet for their traditional export products, but the relative political anarchy and international isolation of the first half century of independence also encouraged the growth of a number of other types of economic activity. There was a rapid growth in the number of self-sufficient peasant farms or *huertas*. A fragile, indigenous marketing system was reestablished. And in the villages and cities, various types of cottage industries began to develop.

For most of the Nicaraguan people this economic system, though certainly not highly developed, was fairly benign. Although he may have been exaggerating slightly, one observer writing in the early 1870s noted that "peonage such as is seen in Mexico and various parts of Spanish America does not exist in Nicaragua. . . . Any citizen whatever can set himself up on a piece of open land . . . to cultivate plantain and corn."[3]

Primitive Dependent Capitalism

The relative isolation of Nicaragua and the gradual development of an internally oriented economy were abruptly interrupted by the coffee boom that hit Central America in the late 1800s. Coffee was probably introduced into Nicaragua as an exotic curiosity in the first quarter of the nineteenth century. By 1848 it was being produced commercially on a small scale. In the early 1850s it was a favorite beverage of the 20,000 or so foreign passengers each month who utilized Cornelius Vanderbilt's Accessory Transit Company route across Nicaragua on their way to California.[4] But it was not until the 1870s that coffee really came into its own. By then the international demand was so strong that the country's ruling elite were motivated to monopolize and redirect much of Nicaragua's productive capacity toward the cultivation of that one export product.

Two factors of crucial importance to coffee production are fertile land in the right climatological setting and a large, essentially unskilled workforce that can be called upon to offer its services for a few months during the harvest season. In Nicaragua in the early 1870s both were in short supply. The coffee culture had already moved into most of the exploitable lands around Managua, and other promising lands in the northern highlands were occupied by independent peasants and members of Indian communes engaged in traditional subsistence farming. And as the rural masses had access to their own land, there was no pool of vulnerable and easily exploitable peons.

The traditional elite solved both of these problems with ingenuity and speed. In the late 1870s and 1880s they took the land they coveted and created the workforce they needed through a combination of chicanery, violence, and self-serving legislation. Individual squatter farmers and Indians working the land through communal arrangements were extremely vulnerable to legal manipulation because, in most cases, these people held rights to the land by tradition rather than by legal title. For several decades the agrarian elite had attempted, through legislation, to abolish communal and squatter landholdings. In 1877, under the presidency of Conservative Pedro Joaquín Chamorro, an agrarian law was passed that outlawed communal holdings and gave individuals the right to buy "unoccupied" national lands. The resulting massive dislocation of Indian communal farmers and individual peasants led inevitably to the War of the Comuneros of 1881 in the Pacific and north-central regions of Nicaragua.

After a series of cruel battles in which as many as 5,000 Indians may have been killed,[5] the new order was imposed on the region. Coffee was free to expand into new land.

The laws that forced the small farmer off the land also helped create a vulnerable rural proletariat. To reinforce this phenomenon, the elite-controlled governments also passed laws against "vagrancy" and the cultivation of plantain—the banana-like staple food of the peasants.[6] Obliged to buy staples at high prices in the commissaries of the plantations where many now worked, former peasants were forced to rely on credit from these company stores. Before long they were trapped into a very effective system of debt peonage. In less than a decade, the self-sufficient peasantry of a large section of the country had been converted into a dependent and oppressed rural proletariat. Most rural Nicaraguans began to lead a life of insecurity, fluctuating between the good times of the coffee harvest, from November through February, and the hardship and unemployment of the *tiempo muerto* (dead period) between harvests.

The growth of the coffee culture also marked the birth of dependent capitalism in Nicaragua. Before this period the economy was based on traditional cattle ranching and subsistence peasant and communal farming. Neither involved a significant use of capital. Coffee, however, was different. First, years before the first harvest, the planter had to make a significant investment in preparing the land and planting and nurturing the seedlings. When the trees began to bear fruit, it was necessary to spend considerable sums of money on manpower and machinery. A large workforce was needed for the handpicking of the coffee berries, and more people and machinery were employed in weighing, pulping, drying, sorting, sacking, and transporting the product.

It is not surprising, then, that although some small farmers converted to coffee bean production, most of those who went into this new enterprise were large landholders, prosperous commercial speculators, and, in some cases, foreigners. The Conservative oligarchy used its control of the legislative process to pass the Subsidy Laws of 1879 and 1889, which gave planters of all nationalities cultivating more than 5,000 trees a subsidy of 5 cents per tree.[7] Among other things, these laws encouraged foreign colonists to seek their fortunes on the fertile slopes of the central highlands. With them came an infusion of new capital.

Once established as the cornerstone of the Nicaraguan economy, coffee held that position until the 1950s. This is not to say that other forms of agriculture were completely wiped out. Some farsighted peasants chose to flee the new coffee zones entirely, moving on to subsistence farming on land in other regions that were not yet coveted by the landed elite. In addition, the traditional precapitalist cattle *hacienda* (ranch) of the lowlands, though now less important, was by no means completely eclipsed. But overall, coffee was clearly the mainstay of the country's economy.

With the growth of the coffee industry, Nicaragua developed what is often loosely referred to as a "banana republic" economy—one based heavily on a single primary export product. Typically, the benefits of the system flowed heavily to a small domestic elite and its foreign trading partners. Taxes on coffee profits, which might have helped redistribute income to the impoverished majority, were virtually nonexistent. The common citizen was an abused instrument of production rather than a beneficiary of the system. The Nicaraguan economy also became subject to periodic "booms" and "busts" produced by the fluctuating world price of its single product. In good times the economy grew and coffee planters imported luxury goods and machinery, invested money abroad, and educated their children in the United States and Europe. The first of the Somoza dictators received his U.S. education as a result of such a boom. In bad times, such as those following the onset of the 1929 Depression, coffee prices plummeted and the economy stagnated. Planters hunkered down, lived off savings and investments, and imported fewer luxury items and less machinery.

Typical also of the banana republic syndrome was the fact that throughout most of the period, little effort was made by the governments of Nicaragua to see that the economy served the purpose of genuine national development. The notable exception to this rule was the regime of Liberal strongman José Santos Zelaya from 1893 to 1909. Zelaya had no real quarrel with laissez-faire economics or with coffee. Indeed, he helped the coffee industry by opening up "new" lands and improving Nicaragua's transportation network. Nevertheless, he also emphasized education, brought fiscal responsibility to the government, created the rudiments of a modern administrative structure, and insisted on national economic self-determination. His refusal to concede to the United States canal rights that would have diminished the economic and political sovereignty of his country and his subsequent negotiation with other powers for a more equitable canal treaty contributed to the U.S. decision to encourage, and then reinforce militarily, the Conservative rebellion of 1909. After Zelaya, the Conservatives, and later the much-chastened Liberals, provided governments whose economic policies fit the banana republic model closely. Within a few years of their ascent to power, the Conservatives gave their U.S. protectors essentially the same canal treaty Zelaya had rejected. The United States had no intention of building a Nicaraguan canal. It simply wanted to buy up the rights to preclude the possibility that any other country would do so. From then until the 1950s virtually no effort was made to alter Nicaragua's established role as a provider of a single primary product.

Modern Dependent Capitalism

The quarter century preceding the War of Liberation was a time of economic modernization and dependent "development." New products were added to Nicaragua's portfolio of exports, technology and technocrats became faddish, the government bureaucracy grew rapidly by expanding— at least on paper—into various social service areas, and the gross national product grew in respectable spurts. But the benefits of the changes and growth did not "trickle down" to most Nicaraguans. Their perilous standard of living remained essentially constant as the gap between them and the tiny middle and upper classes widened relentlessly.

One of the most obvious changes to occur during this period was the diversification of Nicaragua's exports. In addition to coffee and beef products, Nicaragua now exported significant quantities of cotton, sugar, bananas, wood, and seafood. The most important new product was cotton. The sharp increase in the world price of this raw material in the early 1950s, flowing out of heightened demand during the Korean War, motivated Nicaraguan planters and speculators to invest in cotton production in the Pacific lowlands. Nicaragua, which had exported only 379 metric tons of cotton in 1949, increased that figure to 43,971 metric tons in 1955. Eventually as much as 80 percent of the cultivated land on the Pacific coast was converted to cotton.[8] Some cattle ranches became cotton plantations, but, as in the case of the coffee boom seven decades earlier, much of the land that went into the production of this new export product was appropriated in one way or another from peasant producers of grains and domestic staples. Once again independent farmers were transformed into a rootless rural proletariat in the name of "progress" and "development" for the privileged few.

Cotton, like coffee, was subject to cycles of boom and bust. The first period of bust began in 1956, three years after the end of the Korean War. Cotton was an even more capital-intensive enterprise than coffee. It required great investments in machinery, fertilizer, insecticides, and labor. In Nicaragua's case, cotton came to account for almost all of the tractors and harvesters, most of the irrigation systems, and more than three-fourths of the commercial fertilizer used in the country.[9] Small-scale production of cotton was simply out of the question.

Another factor that affected the Nicaraguan economy in this period was the birth of the Alliance for Progress in the early 1960s. A U.S.-sponsored response to the revolutionary success of Fidel Castro in Cuba, the alliance was designed to bring about social and economic development in Latin America through politically moderate means. Enlightened reform from above would, it was hoped, defuse the "threat" of popular revolution from below. The Somozas and the traditional elite of Nicaragua found the idea of the alliance very appealing. Not that they were particularly concerned with its lofty objectives of social and economic justice. Rather, they saw it in more practical terms as a legitimizing device and a source of a variety of economic opportunities. In return for rather painless paper reforms and the creation of a modern social-service bureaucracy, they would receive increased foreign aid and technological assistance and have access to numerous new business opportunities.

Nicaragua in the 1960s was typified by a peculiar type of neopositivism reminiscent of Mexico in the days of Porfirio Diaz. Technology, foreign investment, and "development"—as defined in terms of growth in gross national product—were the new articles of faith. A group of highly trained developmentalists known as the technocrats or, less respectfully, the "miniskirts," were elevated to positions of great responsibility. The heart of their operations was the Banco Central in downtown Managua. There the dictator-president, the head of the "miniskirts" (Francisco "Ché" Láinez, the bank's director), and the cream of Nicaragua's technocratic community met late into the night planning the country's economy as if they were the board of directors of a large corporation. Feasibility studies were ordered, foreign investment was wooed, and joint ventures were embarked upon. Once a year the Banco Central issued an annual report brimming with tables and analyses concerning the national economy. To help train even more business technocrats, Harvard University's School of Business Administration cooperated in the creation of the Central American Institute of Business Administration (INCAE), located in the outskirts of Managua.

A parallel stimulus for capitalist development in Nicaragua, which coincided with the Alliance for Progress, was the birth of the Central American

Common Market in 1960. This attempt at regional economic integration provided increased incentive for both incipient industrialization and the diversification of export products. As such it was, for a while, an additional boon to the privileged domestic and international groups who controlled these activities. However, the Soccer War of 1969, between El Salvador and Honduras, brought about the demise of this integrative effort.

The developmentalist optimism of the 1960s proved to be a hollow illusion. Compared with the rest of Latin America, Nicaragua received relatively little foreign investment—perhaps because doing business in that country normally entailed paying off the Somozas in one way or another. Though economic growth did take place, its benefits were concentrated in relatively few hands. The Somozas and their allies simply used their control of the expanded governmental apparatus and the country's new technocratic expertise to increase their own fortunes. Eventually, in the late 1960s and early 1970s, the technocrats themselves were pushed aside as the corrupt and intemperate Anastasio Somoza Debayle replaced skilled administrative personnel with National Guard officers and other cronies to whom he owed rewards for personal loyalty.

The problem of corruption had existed throughout the Somoza period. Anastasio Somoza García had encouraged corruption in his subordinates as a way of isolating them psychologically from the people and thus making them dependent on him. Although the corporate image of the Somoza system improved during the developmentalist years of Luís and the puppets, official corruption continued unabated. In a conversation with coauthor Walker in 1977, Luís Somoza's close adviser and confidant, Francisco Láinez, the chief of the "miniskirts" during that earlier period, related an interesting story. One day Luís Somoza, in a pensive mood, asked Láinez to tell him in all frankness what one thing he, Láinez, would do, if he were in Luís's shoes, to bring development to Nicaragua. Láinez thought for a moment and then responded that he would take each of the major categories in the national budget—health, education, etc.—and see to it that *at least half* of that money actually went for the purposes for which it was ostensibly destined. According to Láinez, Luís simply smiled sadly and responded, "You're being unrealistic."[10] This is not to say that, at the highest levels, money was being stolen openly. That would not have been acceptable to Washington—which was footing much of the bill—nor was it necessary, since the Somozas' absolute control of the government gave them the ability to apply a legalistic patina to the flow of public funds. Even after the patent and massive misuse of international relief funds following the 1972 earthquake, the U.S. government, intent on not embarrassing a good ally, was able for several years to produce audits that appeared to refute claims that these funds had been misappropriated.

A final important economic phenomenon of this last prerevolutionary period was the emergence of three preponderantly powerful economic groups each composed of an assortment of influential firms, individuals, and families with financial operations rooted in distinct major banking systems. The function of these groups seems to have been to pool influence, expertise, and financial power in such a way as to give group members an economic advantage over nonmembers. The negative impact on society was that by reducing competition, they tended to contribute to "a greater inequality of both power and wealth."[11]

The oldest of the groups had its roots in the first half of the twentieth century. Clustered around the Banco de América, this so-called Banamérica Group probably originally was an economic response by Conservative Granada-based families and firms to the vagaries of doing business in a country dominated by a dictator from the other party. Whatever its early roots, the Banamérica Group burgeoned into a powerful association of interests and firms including sugar, rum, cattle, coffee, export-import businesses, department stores, and supermarkets. Banamérica's international banking ties were with the Wells Fargo Bank and the First National Bank of Boston.

A second group, clustered around the Banco Nicaragüense, emerged in the 1950s and 1960s as an apparent response to the Banamérica Group. With a clearer identification with León and the Liberal tradition, the BANIC Group included coffee and cotton interests, a major beer industry, merchants and commercial enterprises, land development and construction, and lumber, fish, and vegetable oil processing. BANIC's major banking ties were with the Chase Manhattan Bank.

The third important group was that of the Somozas. It consisted of the family's wide holdings in practically every segment of the economy. For several decades its banking needs had been covered by the national banks—first the Banco Nacional and then the Banco Central. These banks frequently extended loans to the Somozas that would not have been available to private citizens and that often were never repaid. Though it probably was not necessary, the Somoza group eventually set up its own bank, the Banco Centroamericano.

Interestingly, the Somoza financial empire in prerevolutionary Nicaragua—though vast and impressive—was less clearly recognized as a "group" than were the BANIC and Banamérica networks.[12] This was probably due to the fact that Somoza interests defended themselves not through their group association per se, but rather through the family's direct control of the government and all of its institutions. The founder of the dynasty, Anastasio Somoza García, acquired many of his agrarian properties at the outset of the Second World War by simply taking over the numerous coffee plantations and cattle ranches that the government confiscated from German landholders. In addition, he used his unchallengeable coercive power to acquire other prime properties by simply making Mafia-style "offers that couldn't be refused" to the hapless owners. He and his sons also used their control of the government to pass legislation favorable to their agrarian and business interests, to avoid taxes, to award themselves lucrative contracts, and to create obstacles for economic competitors and political adversaries.

Though the Somoza financial empire had the reputation of being poorly and inefficiently run, this was more than compensated for by the tremendous advantage it enjoyed through direct control of government. By the time the dynasty was overthrown, the family had accrued a portfolio worth well in excess of $500 million—perhaps as much as $1 billion or $1.5 billion. The Somozas owned about one-fifth of the nation's arable land and produced export products such as cotton, sugar, coffee, cattle, and bananas. They were involved in the processing of agricultural products. They held vital export-import franchises and had extensive investments in urban real estate. They owned or had controlling interests in two seaports, a maritime line, the national airline, the concrete industry, a paving-block company, construction firms, a metal extruding plant, and various other businesses including Plasmaféresis de Nicaragua, which exported plasma extracted from whole blood purchased from impoverished Nicaraguans. Finally, the Somozas had huge investments outside Nicaragua ranging from real estate and other interests in the United States to agricultural enterprises throughout Central America to textiles in Colombia. Shortly before their overthrow, they even bought controlling interests in *Visión*, the Latin American equivalent of *Newsweek* or *Time* magazine.

The events of the 1970s accentuated the abuses and defects of the Nicaraguan economic system. In the last years of the Somoza dynasty, it had reached a state that, from the point of view of most citizens, was intolerable. For over a century, the country's rich natural resources had been plundered, appropriated, and abused for the benefit of a tiny minority. Millions of Nicaraguans had become economic instruments rather than fulfilled and participating human beings. Public revenues and foreign aid officially destined "to meet basic human needs"[13] had been routinely laundered to end up in the pockets of the ruling family and its allies. The nation's public and private banks had been used first as instruments for the concentration of wealth and finally as conduits for the export of capital as the erstwhile ruling class began to flee into exile. The War of Liberation of 1978–1979 was as much a product of systemic socioeconomic factors as it was an expression of intense political opposition to a particularly venal dictator.

SANDINISTA ECONOMIC POLICY

The economic policy and programs of the revolutionary government that took power in July 1979 constituted a radical departure from those of previous regimes. Nicaragua's new political leaders, though varied in their ideological and social backgrounds, were remarkably united in their sense of historic responsibility and their determination to carry out a social revolution rooted in a New Sandinista Economy that, they said, would "make possible *a just, free, and fraternal human life in our fatherland.*"[14] Intensely aware of the tremendous human costs of the old patterns of dependent capitalism, they were determined to fashion an economic system that would not only eradicate past abuses but also transfer the "center of attention" from the privileged minority to the exploited "masses." Significantly, however, the economic tactics they adopted during their nearly eleven years in power were pragmatic and in no way rigidly tied to any preconceived ideology. The Sandinistas made no attempt to impose a Socialist economic system, much less a Communist one.

One of the first signs of the pragmatic, nonorthodox nature of Sandinista economic policy was the decision, taken by the Sandinistas at the time of the Triumph, to honor Somoza's onerous $1.6 billion foreign debt. Although they had absolutely no moral obligation to pay for the dictator's scandalous misuse of international funding, the new government realized that servicing Nicaragua's financial obligations was necessary for the country to remain creditworthy in international financial circles. Therefore, unable to pay according to the schedule worked out with Somoza, they immediately entered into a long process of negotiation with a group of private banks to which Somoza owed $580 million and ultimately won a more real-istic repayment plan. Then, "between 1980 and 1982, Nicaragua made every interest payment . . . , a record almost unparalleled anywhere in Latin Amer-ica in those crisis-ridden years."[15] Only in 1983, when it simply became im-possible to continue all payments as scheduled, did Nicaragua begin to prioritize the servicing of some debts while renegotiating others.

A further indication of pragmatism in international economic policy was the Sandinistas' decision to adopt a policy of "walking on four legs" in the development of aid and trade relations with the rest of the world. The objective was to actively pursue economic relations with four groups of countries: the Socialist Bloc, the United States, other developed countries, and the Third World. Accordingly, one finds that from 1978 to 1982, Nica-raguan exports to and imports from the Socialist Bloc rose from 0 and 1 percent, respectively, to 7 and 11 percent of the Nicaraguan relationship with the world. By mid-1985, the overall value of trade with the Socialist Bloc stood at 20 percent. For the United States, equivalent figures were 23 and 31 percent (1978), 24 and 19 percent (1982), and an overall 17.5 per-cent just before the 1985 trade embargo. For the rest of the developed world the tally was 38 and 25 percent (1978), 43 and 22 percent (1982), and an overall 36 percent in mid-1985.[16] Finally, for the Third World, equiva-lent statistics were 39 and 43 percent (1978), 26 and 47 percent (1982), and an overall 26.5 percent in mid-1985. In other words, throughout the nearly six years prior to the 1985 U.S. embargo, Nicaragua maintained a diversi-fied trade policy. Even at the end of this period, only about one-fifth of its world trade was with the Socialist Bloc. It was only after the embargo that relationships with the Socialist Bloc began to expand significantly.

Diversity was also the rule in the areas of aid and credit. Throughout its years in power, the Sandinista government sought and received assistance from a wide variety of countries. The major disappointment, of course, was the United States, which, immediately after Ronald Reagan's inauguration in 1981, cut off all economic assistance to Managua. However, very few other countries followed the U.S. lead. Throughout the ensuing years, Nica-ragua received assistance from such politically disparate states as Argen-tina, Austria, Brazil, Canada, Denmark, Libya, Mexico, Peru, Sweden, and various countries in the Socialist Bloc (to name just a few). Indeed, when the Reagan administration declared its full trade embargo in 1985, a variety of countries immediately expressed their disapproval by offering additional assistance or credit. Significantly, such assistance was about evenly balanced between the Socialist Bloc and Yugoslavia ($202 million) and Western Europe ($198 million).

The Sandinistas also demonstrated pragmatism in the domestic sphere with their decision not to socialize the Nicaraguan economy completely. Such a move would have been counterproductive, as the public sector already faced a severe shortage of trained manpower due to the inevitable flight into exile of many members of the middle class and the already greatly expanded role of the state. Furthermore, the Cuban experience of oversocialization served as a useful negative example. It is true that all of the properties of the Somozas and their accomplices were immediately confiscated, making the people the collective owners of 20 percent of the arable land, numerous industrial and commercial enterprises, and thousands of private homes and mansions. In addition, the government nationalized the banking and insurance systems—the latter because it was unable to cope with the needs of a war-ravished country, and the former so as to block the continued flight of capital abroad and instead to direct loans to those segments of the economy in which they could have the greatest impact. Moreover, in the ensuing years some other properties were nationalized for reasons of overriding national interest or because the owners underutilized, decapitalized, or otherwise abused their rights. However, during the entire period of Sandinista rule, the private sector accounted for between 50 and 60 percent of the gross domestic product (GDP). In fact, echoing an argument that coauthor Walker heard other Sandinistas make, Daniel Ortega claimed that "the Sandinista revolution . . . invented perestroika." In a March 1990 interview with *Paris Match*, he recalled

a conversation with Gorbachev at the end of April 1985. At that time, he [Gorbachev] wasn't yet talking about perestroika. For three hours I explained to him the specific policies we were following in Nicaragua. . . . How, for example, we had distributed individual plots of land to peasants so that they would become landowners. He responded by telling me that he thought that that was the right path to follow and that we, the Sandinistas, should absolutely avoid committing the errors that they, in the USSR as well as in the eastern bloc countries, had committed.[17]

The government demonstrated its determination to preserve the private sector by taking several important measures. Especially in the first few years, it made considerable sums of money available in the form of loans to capitalists willing to reactivate their enterprises. It also provided key private producers access to foreign currency at low rates of exchange. It quickly established the *Ley de Amparo* (Law of Protection), which provided Nicaraguan citizens the right to seek redress for and question the legality of the everyday activities of the government (including the confiscation of property). And beginning in 1983, it issued "guarantees of inexpropriability" for rural properties being efficiently utilized.

It is true that figures showing production by the private sector of a relatively constant 50–60 percent of GDP mask certain important changes that were taking place *within* that sector. A few urban enterprises—such as the luxurious Club Terraza in Managua, which the government confiscated and put under worker ownership and management, and certain large, private rural properties that were seized and subsequently turned into peasant cooperatives or parceled out to individual small farmers— were still part of the private sector, even though the nature of ownership had changed significantly. Yet, overall, traditional private property was normally respected as long as the owner obeyed the law and remained productive.

Behind such flexibility and pragmatism, however, was the Sandinistas' determination to control Nicaragua's mixed economy in such a way as to serve the interests of all Nicaraguans. Pursuing what they described as "the logic of the majority," the Sandinistas immediately set up a state monopoly over the sale of export products in order to channel a substantial part of the earnings from exports into badly needed social and economic infrastructure. They also tightly controlled imports to conserve scarce foreign exchange for high-priority social and economic inputs. In addition, they issued and enforced laws for the protection of urban and rural workers and peasants renting parcels from large landholders. Finally, they used the state's influence and financial leverage to promote the production of greater quantities of basic food products.

The economic problems facing the Sandinista government during the first half decade were awesome. The Somozas and their accomplices had left Nicaragua with a $1.6 billion foreign debt (in per capita terms, the highest in Latin America) and another $500 million in war damage. Adding insult to injury, they had also pilfered the banking system of all but about $3 million. The world market value of almost all of Nicaragua's export products declined sharply from 1980 onward. In 1982, the country suffered its most costly natural disaster in its recorded history—extensive flooding followed by drought. And finally, starting in the early days of the Reagan administration, the new government faced an elaborate U.S.-orchestrated program of economic destabilization, which featured the severance of economic aid; the curtailment and, in 1985, the complete embargo of all U.S.-Nicaraguan trade; attempts to create an international economic boycott; the blocking of loans from international lending organizations such as the World Bank and the Inter-American Development Bank; the use of *contras* to inflict infrastructural and crop damage and to necessitate the divergence of scarce funds into defense; and the direct use of the CIA to destroy oil-storage facilities at Corinto (1983) and to mine Nicaragua's harbors (early 1984).[18]

It should not be surprising, therefore, that the Nicaraguan economy was in markedly worse shape in the mid-1980s than it had been at its prerevolutionary high-water mark in 1977 or that it declined precipitously in the second half of the 1980s. But when the Kissinger Commission argued in January 1984 (1) that Sandinista economic performance had been "poor" and (2) that this alleged bad performance had been due in part to "mismanagement invariably associated with regimes espousing Marxist-Leninist ideology,"[19] it was engaging in clever sophistry. The Sandinistas had clearly not used Marxist-Leninist ideology as a major model in their economic planning. What is more, Kissinger's use of 1977 as a base year was deliberately deceptive. Although Nicaragua's per capita GDP *had* declined around 38 percent from 1977 through 1983, it had actually *risen* by 7 percent overall in the years 1980, 1981, 1982, and 1983. Kissinger had been able to show a decline *only* by including two years of economically devastating civil conflict during which the Sandinistas were not even in power! Furthermore, even though a 7 percent per capita GDP growth over a period of four years would not ordinarily be impressive, it was not bad when compared with the negative 14.7 percent registered for Central America as a whole during the same years.[20] Indeed, Nicaragua had not merely the best growth rate in Central America but one of the best in all of Latin America—and this in spite of the formidable array of economic problems mentioned earlier.

The relatively strong economic performance of the first several years appears to have been the product of various factors. In the first place, with its low population density, rich lands, and industrious people, Nicaragua had always been a country of considerable economic potential. Previously bottled up by the corrupt, inefficient, and elitist Somoza system, this potential could now be more fully realized. It is not surprising that total production of most agricultural products—both domestic and export—rose to or

Ruined grain storage facility. Built by the new government as part of its effort to ensure more universal access to food, this depository in Ocotal—destroyed in June 1984—was but a small fraction of the hundreds of millions of dollars' worth of social and economic infrastructure destroyed by the contras as of mid-1985. (Photo by the coauthor Walker)

exceeded prewar levels within a few years after the ouster of the dictator. The new government was even successful in stimulating the production of nontraditional export products such as castor seed, garlic, ginger, onions, mangoes, melons, peanuts, and sesame seed, which by 1983 accounted for 10 percent of the total value of exports.[21]

The second possible reason for such growth may be the practical, non-ideological behavior of the Sandinistas themselves. Instead of engaging in "guerrilla economics," they had preserved a mixed economy and had carefully weighed alternatives in making economic decisions. These measures not only bore fruit in the domestic economy but also gave the Sandinistas a moderate image abroad, thus enabling them to build trade and aid relationships with a wide variety of countries.

Whatever the successes of the first four years, they were not to last; the heavy impact of the U.S. destabilization campaign fell painfully on the country during the rest of the Sandinista period. Gross domestic product per capita fell continuously from 1984 onward (see figure below). Hemmed in by decreasing revenues on the one hand and sky-rocketing military expenses (by 1985 over half of the national budget was going to defense) and war-related social costs (caring for refugees, wounded, maimed, orphaned, etc.) on the other, the revolutionary government chose to fill the gap by printing ever-increasing volumes of paper money. This, in turn, triggered high rates of inflation, which, as we noted in Chapter 3, crested in 1988 at over 33,000 percent.

It is difficult for anyone who has not experienced this type of inflation to understand what it is like. Perhaps it would help to note that foreigners and those few Nicaraguans who could still afford to eat in a restaurant frequently paid the bill with bound bundles of the highest denomination paper *cordobas*. Often, as long as the paper binding was still in place, the waiter would simply count the bundles rather than bother to look at the

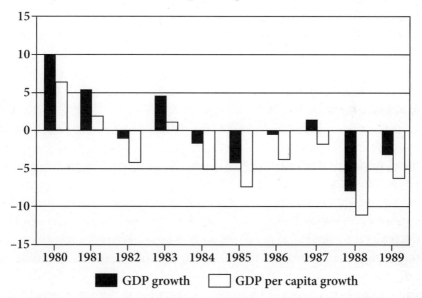

Nicaraguan Economic Growth, 1980–1989
(in percentages)

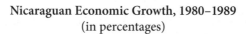

Source: Michael E. Conroy, "The Political Economy of the 1990 Nicaraguan Elections," paper presented at the Coloquio sobre las Crisis Economicas del Siglo XX, Universidad Complutense de Madrid, April 17–19, 1990; statistics generated by the UN Economic Commission on Latin America.

individual notes. People on fixed salaries, including upper-level government officials, often found what they earned on the job inadequate for the simple maintenance of their families. One high-ranking Sandinista coauthor Walker knew supplemented his salary by renting his car to foreign news teams and making and selling pizzas at night. The wife of a vice minister friend of coauthor Walker sold dresses from their garage and rented their eldest son's room to visiting American scholars.

For ordinary Nicaraguans, of course, the impact was strikingly more dramatic: "Urban wages in 1988 had fallen, according to some statistics, to only 10 percent of 1980 levels."[22] Although urban salaries were often augmented by work in the "informal sector" and work and resources secured in the rural areas, ordinary Nicaraguans suffered terribly. It was not uncommon in those years for schoolteachers, for example, to quit their jobs upon realizing that more money could be made even by preparing and selling *tamales* on the street than by continuing to teach. Major intersections in Managua swarmed with desperate men, women, and children selling anything they thought passing motorists might buy. Begging, prostitution, and petty crime, which had declined during the first several years of the revolution, increased markedly from the mid-1980s onward.

Only by imposing an extremely harsh austerity program, with massive layoffs and sharp cutbacks in social programs, was the government able to significantly reduce inflation in 1989. In doing so, however, it simply added to its political woes by appearing to be callously betraying the social objectives of the revolution.

It is undeniable that the Sandinistas made some significant economic mistakes during their nearly eleven years in office. In the first place, pursuing their policy of maintaining a mixed economy, they made largely futile efforts throughout the period to convince large private landowners and businessmen to remain productive. Considerable government resources were expended in the form of loans, favorable foreign exchange rates, and so forth to try to win the cooperation of this sector. Even in 1988–1989, the government was still begging the monied private sector to join it in *concertación*, a cooperative, dialogue-driven approach to solving the woes of the economy. When all was said and done, most of the monied private sector, with a few notable exceptions such as that of the big rice growers, remained uncooperative, unproductive, and even downright subversive. Critics on the left argued that the resources spent in wooing the rich would have been better used to improve workers' salaries and to give more support and better prices to peasant producers.

And there were other errors. The use of price controls to ensure more equitable distribution of basic staples distorted the market, hurt production, and helped augment shortages. Attempts to build large state agro-industrial projects as a device to generate foreign exchange consumed funds that might have had a more positive impact if spent on small-scale public and private productive activities.

On top of all this the Sandinistas were buffeted by structural problems and "acts of God." Programs aimed at improving the lives of the rural poor in the early 1980s had the negative effect of accentuating the historical problem of labor shortages during the harvest season. As their lives became less precarious due to greater access to land and government social and extension programs, the rural poor became less inclined to accept the low wages and hard work involved in following the agro-export harvests. Though the revolutionaries were able to convince tens of thousands of committed urban folk to volunteer to take in the crops, some of what had been grown often went to waste for lack of pickers.[23] Finally, in September 1988, Nicaragua's efforts to bring hyperinflation under control were literally blown asunder by Hurricane Joan, which cut an east–west swath across the country, obliterating Atlantic coast cities, destroying valuable timber resources, chewing up infrastructure even in the west, and necessitating a massive burst of emergency government spending. As a result, 1988 "price increases [that] had reached an historical monthly peak of 98% in June, [but] had fallen to 20% in August, . . . began an inexorable climb in September that climaxed with 126% in December."[24]

Overall, however, the collapse of the Nicaraguan economy in the late 1980s was mainly the product of deliberate U.S. policy. Though the Sandinistas had made their share of economic mistakes, they were not the wild-eyed "Communist" ideologues that they were often portrayed to be in the United States. Indeed, as we noted, one of their major errors was a costly and essentially wasted effort to win the cooperation of the monied private sector. Furthermore, until the impact of the Contra War and other U.S. destabilization techniques really began to hit in the mid-1980s, Nicaragua was one of the few countries of Latin America that actually registered growth in GDP per capita. Some of this is attributable to inevitable "bounce back" from the destruction of the war years. But that there was still growth in 1983, a full four years after the end of the War of Liberation, says something about Sandinista economic policy.

POST-SANDINISTA ECONOMIC POLICY

If economic planning based on "the logic of the majority" had been set aside by the Sandinistas under the austerity programs of the late 1980s, it was discarded and buried under the conservative Chamorro and Alemán governments that followed. The new emphasis was on economic recovery and growth through private commercial agro-export. The Reaganesque logic was that everyone would benefit if private business could just be left alone to go about the task of reactivating the economy and exporting lots and lots of traditional agro-export products. In June 1990, a triumphant U.S. Embassy official expressed this philosophy when he announced confidently to a group of visiting U.S. scholars that Nicaragua's recovery lay in one word: "cotton."[25] He neglected to point out that cotton had been a major product under the banana republic economy of the Somozas, one whose production entailed tremendous negative social consequences such as land concentration, exploitation of workers, and exposure to pesticides. He also failed to mention that cotton normally requires the importation of costly inputs such as machinery, fertilizers, and pesticides, which—though they benefit the economy of the supplier country (traditionally the United States)—tend to cancel out most of the foreign exchange–earning benefits of the product.

The Chamorro and Alemán administrations enthusiastically implemented the neoliberal model of economics that was de rigueur at that time throughout most of Latin America. The term *neoliberal*, as used by social scientists, plays off the word *liberal*, which is used to describe the economic philosophy that dominated the region at the end of the nineteenth and well into the twentieth century. Liberal economics had featured an emphasis on the free market, international trade, a very limited role for government, and, in practice, the increasing concentration of rural property into the hands of the agro-exporting elite. Though it often resulted in economic growth, it usually featured maldistribution of income and increased social unrest. Nicaragua, as we pointed out earlier, was simply an extreme example of this general phenomenon.

Throughout Latin America, neoliberalism featured (1) the downsizing of government; (2) privatization of state-owned enterprises; (3) deregulation of private enterprise; and (4) a sharp reduction in or an elimination of tariff barriers to foreign trade. All of these, it was believed, would eliminate inflation, strengthen local currency, increase productivity, stimulate international trade, and result in rapid economic growth. Although many people would be dislocated and suffer in the short run, long-term economic growth would eventually benefit all.

In the case of Nicaragua, the implementation of neoliberalism meant that government programs in health and education were cut back and public servants were encouraged to resign. In the wake of this austerity, inflation was reduced to practically nothing, and a new currency, the "gold *cordoba*," which replaced the currency of the Sandinista era, remained relatively stable vis-à-vis the dollar from then on. In addition, state-owned enterprises—from the national airlines, energy, and telecommunications companies to smaller "people's property" urban enterprises and large state farms—were privatized. Furthermore, many Sandinista-era rules regulating private enterprise were abolished. Finally, tariffs were reduced, and Managua and secondary cities experienced "market glitter" as imported goods—which only a privileged minority could afford—crowded merchants' showcases.

An additional twist to Nicaraguan neoliberalism was what appears to have been a deliberate attempt to dismantle the agrarian peasant cooperatives set up during the Sandinista era. Whereas in those years the land was inalienable from the cooperative—members could use it but not sell it—now the peasants were given the "right" to sell their individual shares. Faced with emergencies, many did. (The modification of the Mexican constitution to give Mexican *ejidatarios*—cooperative members—the same "right" was one factor that triggered the Zapatista revolt in Chiapas in 1994.) On top of this, the state then cut back on loans to the cooperatives—giving preference instead to agrobusiness—and banks demanded repayment of debts.

As in most of Latin America, the neoliberal "reforms" enacted in Nicaragua from 1990 onward were actively promoted by the United States and enforced by the multinational lending agencies—the International Monetary Fund, the World Bank, and the Inter-American Development Bank—in which Washington exercised de facto veto power. Though the Sandinistas had sought World Bank and IDB support (until the United States vetoed their proposals in the early 1980s), they had never even approached the IMF; the regressive social implications of IMF loans were simply incompatible with their visions of a more just society. The Chamorro and Alemán administrations, however, had no such qualms. True, organized resistance by the poor sectors hurt by neoliberal reform often slowed their compliance with international dictates, but comply they did. In return for formal agreements (called "enhanced structural adjustment facilities") with the lending agencies and the international donor community, Nicaragua received foreign aid and loans to address its fiscal problems and help in various projects. And in 2001, in spite of deep concern over high levels of corruption in the Alemán administration, the international donor community formally admitted Nicaragua to the Highly Indebted Poor Countries Initiative, thus canceling much of its foreign debt.

Added to Nicaragua's economic troubles and lack of policy "wiggle room" was the fact that from 1990 onward, Washington insisted that if U.S. (and by implication international) aid were to flow to Nicaragua, then the new government would have to reinstate or compensate claims by U.S. citizens whose properties had been confiscated by the Sandinistas. The clear implication was that the confiscation of largely ill-gained properties of the Somozas and their cronies—some of them U.S. citizens—had been without justification. Further, though few U.S. citizens had actually suffered confiscation, Washington now insisted that a far larger number of subsequently naturalized U.S. citizens—Somocistas who had fled to the United States from 1979 onward—be treated as fully equal to U.S. citizens at the time of the Sandinista victory. "There are no second-class U.S. citizens," U.S. ambassador John Maisto intoned solemnly to a group coauthor Walker was with in 1994 when he questioned Maisto about the apparent absurdity of including the Somoza-era noncitizens in the U.S. claim.[26]

The degree to which Nicaragua in the 1990s was obliged to yield its economic sovereignty to the international lending and donor community was brought home to coauthor Walker during an off-the-record interview conducted the day after the 1996 general election by an observer group, of which he was a member, with an individual heading one of those institutions in Nicaragua.[27] When asked what he thought of the results of that election, he responded that either outcome would have been the same to him, since neither Alemán nor Ortega would have had many options concerning how to run the economy. After elaborating on that point, he then confided that his institution had an economic plan for Nicaragua and that he had arranged for President-elect Alemán to come to his—the international bureaucrat's—office to see it.

The results of the "reforms" imposed on Nicaragua were predictable. Inflation was brought under control. The currency became relatively stable. By the mid-1990s, the economy actually began to grow. This pattern continued under the Bolaños administration. In fact, the economy grew approximately 3.4 percent during Bolaños's term.[28] Such growth, however, was very poorly distributed. Indeed, as we discuss in the next chapter, the social impact of this type of growth was extremely regressive and did little to alleviate poverty. Much of the growth was the result of the importation of luxury goods and the creation of luxury services—hotels and restaurants—to cater to the privileged minority. There was also some agro-export, although it contributed little to growth. To that end, Bolaños secured access to the U.S. market through the Central American Free Trade Agreement (CAFTA), which was approved by the National Assembly in October 2005. Although it was too early at the time of this writing to gauge the medium- or long-term effects of the agreement, early indications were that imports from the United States and the trade deficit increased during the first few years and small and medium-size farmers were being forced out of business. Those working in *maquilas*—foreign-owned sweatshops located in special areas where Nicaraguan labor laws do not apply—earned $60 a month, half of the regional monthly salary.[29]

ORTEGA'S ECONOMIC POLICY

The new Ortega administration's economic policy was a bit puzzling. First, it did not mark a dramatic departure from that of the other post-1990 governments in spite of the fact that Nicaragua would now receive many hundreds of millions of dollars annually from the Bolivarian Alliance for the Peoples of Our America (ALBA)—the Venezuelan alternative to the U.S.-promoted Central American Free Trade Area and Free Trade Area of the Americas. Curiously, the Ortega administration retained its membership in CAFTA and chose to take relatively small loans from the International Monetary Fund, which obliged it to submit to the neoliberal, socially regressive dictates of that U.S.-dominated entity.[30] True, the IMF was now insisting on some "poverty alleviation" policies, but being involved with the IMF was still a continuation of post-1990 conservative policy and a dramatic reversal of the FSLN stance during the revolution.

Another puzzlement involved social spending itself. Starting in 2007, Nicaragua would receive over $600 million annually in support from Venezuela/ALBA. Half would be outright grants. The other half came in the form of virtual grants: the "purchase" of half of the $600 million in oil imported annually on twenty-five-year, 2 percent interest terms—essentially free to the generation in power.[31] Critics complained of a lack of transparency regarding ALBA funds particularly with regard to the state-owned oil distributor, PETRONIC, and ALBANISA, a jointly owned private company with ties to Ortega that had been created to manage oil profits.[32] Both ALBA and ALBANISA holdings were without public oversight. [33] While some of Nicaragua's neighbors were enjoying lower prices at the gas pump as a result of similar Venezuelan aid, fuel prices in Nicaragua remained as high as ever. So where were the oil money and other ALBA funds going? When coauthor Walker told one of Nicaragua's leading independent economists, Adolfo Acevedo, that he was looking for "hard data" on social spending, the latter simply threw up his hands and exclaimed, "If you find some, let me know."[34]

While most people with whom the authors talked in 2009—including harsh critics such as former Sandinista Vice President Sergio Ramírez and the former editor of the Sandinista daily *Barricada*, Carlos Fernando Chamorro—admitted that the Ortega administration was definitely doing more for the poor—in terms of the poverty reduction programs noted in Chapter 6—than its post-1990 predecessors,[35] many felt that what was being done was not nearly what was possible with the money available. Acevedo argued that an opportunity to really improve public education and, hence, invest in Nicaragua's future was being squandered in spite of ample resources.[36] And it was clear the government's failure to let Venezuelan petroleum largess be reflected in reduced fuel prices hurt Nicaraguans not just at the fuel pump but also in terms of the knock-on effect high fuel costs have on the cost of everything.

Overall economic performance under the Ortega administration was mixed. Average annual growth during the first two years was 3.2 percent but fell to negative 1.5 percent in 2009.[37] Any economic growth, however, was undermined by rising fuel costs, inflation, and growing unemployment. The cost of the *canasta basica*—the price of a standard market basket of household consumer products—more than doubled in 2007, leaving it beyond the reach of almost 55 percent of Nicaraguans.[38] Moreover, real wages declined to 1996 levels despite an 18 percent minimum wage increase in 2007 and a second minimum wage increase in January 2008 of 15 percent.[39] The energy crisis also had a significant impact on productivity, as extensive rolling blackouts plagued the country during 2007.

Seemingly, then, the "logic of the majority"—the guiding principal of Sandinista economic policy in the 1980s—was, at best, muted under this later Ortega government.

NOTES

1. Ministerio de Planificación, *Programa de Reactivación Económica en Beneficio del Pueblo* (Managua: Secretaría Nacional de Propoganda y Educatión Política del FSLN, 1980), p. 98.

2. Ibid., p. 99.

3. Paul Levy as quoted in Jaime Wheelock Román, *Imperialismo y Dictadura: Crísis de una Formación Social* (Mexico City: Sigo Veintiuno Editores, 1975), p. 29.

4. David Richard Radell, *An Historical Geography of Western Nicaragua: The Spheres of Influence of León, Granada, and Managua, 1519–1965* (Ph.D. dissertation, University of California–Berkeley, 1969), p. 77.

5. Wheelock Román, *Imperialismo y Dictadura*, p. 77.

6. Ibid., p. 71.

7. Radell, *An Historical Geography*, p. 202.

8. Wheelock Román, *Imperialísmo y Dictadura*, pp. 125, 126.

9. Ibid.

10. From a lengthy conversation with Francisco Láinez in his home in Managua during the second week of December 1977.

11. Harry Wallace Strachan, *The Role of the Business Groups in Economic Development: The Case of Nicaragua* (D.B.A. dissertation, Harvard University, 1972), p. 7.

12. Ibid., pp. 16, 17.

13. A favorite expression of U.S. officials during the Carter administration.

14. Ministerio de Planificación, *Programa de Reactivación Económica*, p. 11. The emphasis is in the original.

15. Sylvia Maxfield and Richard Stahler-Sholk, "External Constraints," in *Nicaragua: The First Five Years*, ed. Thomas W. Walker (New York: Praeger, 1985), p. 258.

16. The 1978 and 1982 statistics are from "Lunes Socio-Económico," *Barricada*, May 23, 1983; those for 1985 are from "Reagan Wields a Double-Edged Trade Sword," *Central America Report*, vol. 12, no. 17 (May 10, 1985), p. 129.

17. Daniel Ortega as quoted in Pierre Hurel, "Ortega ne rend pas les armes," *Paris Match*, March 22, 1990, pp. 78–81.

18. For more details about the U.S. destabilization effort, see Maxfield and Stahler-Sholk, "External Constraints"; and Thomas W. Walker, "Nicaraguan-U.S. Friction: The First Four Years, 1979–1983," in *The Central American Crisis: Sources of Conflict and the Failure of U.S. Policy*, ed. Kenneth M. Coleman and George C. Herring (Wilmington, Del.: Scholarly Resources, 1985), pp. 157–189.

19. Kissinger Commission, *Report of the National Bipartisan Commission on Central America* (Washington, D.C.: U.S. Government Printing Office, 1984), p. 30.

20. For the sources behind these statistics as well as an excellent discussion of the economic model followed by the Sandinistas and the overall results, see Michael E. Conroy, "Economic Legacy and Policies: Performance and Critique," in Walker, ed., *Nicaragua: The First Five Years*, pp. 219–244.

21. Maxfield and Stahler-Sholk, "External Constraints," p. 252.

22. Latin American Studies Association Commission to Observe the Nicaraguan 1990 Election, *Electoral Democracy Under International Pressure* (Pittsburgh: LASA, March 15, 1990), p. 19.

23. For an excellent discussion of this problem, see Laura J. Enriquez, *Harvesting Change: Labor and Agrarian Reform in Nicaragua, 1979–1990* (Chapel Hill: University of North Carolina Press, 1991).

24. Michael E. Conroy, "The Political Economy of the Nicaraguan Elections," a paper prepared for presentation at the Coloquio sobre las Crísis Económicas del Siglo XX, Universidad Complutense de Madrid, April 15, 1990, p. 25.

25. From a briefing by John Leonard, U.S. Embassy deputy chief of mission, Managua, for the 1990 Latin American Studies Association Research Seminar in Nicaragua, June 19, 1990.

26. Interview by the Latin American Studies Association Seminar on Nicaragua with U.S. ambassador John Maisto, U.S. Embassy, Managua, June 27, 1994.

27. The individual in question was interviewed by the election observation team of the Washington office on Latin America/Hemisphere Initiatives in February 1996.

28. ECLAC, *Statistical Yearbook 2009*.

29. CENIDH, *Derechos Humanos en Nicaragua: 2006*, January 2007, p. 66.

30. Arturo Grigsby, "The Economy Will Be Austere and Uncertain in 2010 and 2011," *Envío*, vol. 29, no. 344 (March 2010).

31. Coauthor Walker interview with Nicaraguan economist, Adolfo Acevedo, December 18, 2009.

32. "Congress Divided over Venezuelan Oil Deal," *Central America Report*, no. 3422, June 8, 2007; "Opposition Accuses FSLN of 'Privatizing' Venezuelan Aid," *Cen-*

tral America Report, February 1, 2008; Tim Rogers, "Nicaragua's Newest Tycoon? 'Socialist' President Daniel Ortega," *Christian Science Monitor*, October 14, 2009.

33. Rogers, "Nicaragua's Newest Tycoon?"

34. Walker interview with Acevedo.

35. Wade interview with Chamorro, July 27, 2009, and Walker interviews with Chamorro, December 14 and 17, 2009, and Ramirez, December 17, 2009.

36. Walker interview with Acevedo.

37. ECLAC, *Statistical Yearbook 2009*.

38. CENIDH, *Derechos Humanos en Nicaragua 2007*, January 2008.

39. "Inflationary Spiral Rocks Population," *Central America Report*, January 18, 2008.

6
Culture and Society

When the outsider travels for the first time in Central America he or she may expect—as we did on our first trips there—to find relatively similar little countries. After all, could a handful of contiguous ministates with little geographic extension, tiny populations of a few million each, and a long history of colonial and early postcolonial union be much different from one another? Yes, they could be, and they are. Undoubtedly the unique character of original native populations, varying climatological influences, and dissimilar patterns of colonization and economic exploitation all had something to do with Central America's variety. Whatever the causes, the individuality of each country is striking indeed. Nicaragua, for instance, is practically as different from the neighbors with which it shares borders (Costa Rica and Honduras) as it is from those with which it does not (Guatemala and El Salvador). The uniqueness lies more in the areas of cultural traits and national character than in social patterns and structures.

CULTURE

Nicaraguan culture is rich and fascinating. In an obvious sense it is part of the wider Hispanic American culture. Like other Latin Americans, most Nicaraguans speak Spanish, are at least nominally Roman Catholic, and place great importance on the family and the defense of personal *dignidad* (dignity). Yet, embedded in this matrix of Hispanic universality are various traits that Nicaragua shares with only a few other countries or exhibits in complete isolation.

Language is an area in which Nicaraguans have their own special quali-
ties. Unlike most other Latin Americans, they rarely, if ever, use the standard
tú form of informal address. Instead, like the Argentines, a few Colombians,
and some peoples on their borders, they address each other with the ar-
chaic, nonstandard, informal pronoun *vos* and modify the person of their
verbs to fit. Soon after the Sandinista victory, customs officials were busily
stamping each incoming passport with an exuberant colloquial greeting
that translates: "Nicaragua awaits thee (*vos*) with the smile of lakes and volcanoes and the brilliant and dignifying sun of liberty."

Nicaraguan language is also spicy. One regional song that is practically
the functional equivalent of a national anthem ends with the phrase "Long
live León, *jodido!*" *Jodido* and forms drawn from the same root (to screw),
unacceptable for use in mixed company elsewhere in Latin America, are an
almost essential condiment in Nicaraguan speech. People of all classes and
both sexes revel in the appropriate use of pungent vocabulary, double en-
tendre, and off-color jokes. Little is off-limits to the irreverent tongue of the
fun-loving Nicaraguan. In the old days, the Somozas themselves were the
brunt of hundreds of jokes. Priests and Americans have always been favorite targets. Under the revolutionary government, the Sandinistas were
mercilessly roasted. Subsequently, Violeta Chamorro, Arnoldo Alemán,
and Enrique Bolaños suffered the same indignities.

Nicaraguan vocabulary also includes a number of words of non-Spanish
origin. Place names and forms used for common rustic items such as green
peppers, corn, and turkey reflect the lingering influence of Nicaragua's ancient Indian heritage. On the other hand, the many years of U.S. occupation
have left their linguistic impression in the form of numerous adopted English words. To use just one example, when coauthor Walker hitchhiked
from the Honduran border to Managua in July 1979, he was, as the Nicaraguans put it, going by "ride."

On a more serious plane of verbal expression, Nicaragua has evolved a
rich literary tradition. At the turn of the twentieth century, a young native
poet, Rubén Darío, won international acclaim as the founder of Latin America's first clearly original literary movement, "modernism." To this day, his
birthplace is preserved as a national shrine, and poets and writers in Nicaragua are held in particularly high esteem. Darío was followed in the first half
of the twentieth century by a number of writers: Santiago Argüello (prose,
poetry, and drama); Gustavo Alemán-Bolaños (novels, poetry, and political
tracts); and Salomón de la Selva (poetry). More recently, the poet Pablo An-

tonio Cuadra, who examines the essence of things *nica* in his famous book *El Nicaragüense* (*The Nicaraguan*), distinguished himself as a contributor to the columns of *La Prensa* and as the editor of the prestigious literary journal *El Pez y la Serpiente* (*The Fish and the Snake*). Pedro Joaquín Chamorro, the martyred editor of *La Prensa*, also turned his talents to creative literature. Shortly before his assassination in 1978, Chamorro produced a volume of short stories and two novels, *Richter 7* (which depicts the decadence of the Somoza system and the tragic erosion of Nicaraguan culture in the period of "reconstruction" following the earthquake of 1972) and *Jesús Marchena* (dealing with, and written in the colloquial language of, the dispossessed rural poor).[1] Another contemporary writer-philosopher, José Coronel Urtecho, emerged from a conservative background to become a highly respected intellectual catalyst for the War of Liberation and an important revolutionary poet thereafter. Also on the left was the famous priest Ernesto Cardenal, who won international acclaim as a revolutionary poet before joining the FSLN forces as a pastor in the field and subsequently serving as minister of culture in the revolutionary government. Numerous other leaders of the revolutionary government—among them Interior Minister Tomás Borge and Vice President Sergio Ramírez—also turned their hand to prose or poetry.

Similarly, Nicaraguans have made notable contributions in the fields of art and music. There is a rich indigenous artistic heritage dating back to precolonial times that currently manifests itself in the pottery, leather work, woodcarving, embroidered clothing, and other handicrafts available in local public markets. On a more sophisticated plane, the National School of Fine Arts, founded in Managua in the early 1940s, produced a number of well-known figures including the abstract painter Armando Morales. In the area of music, Nicaragua also has its formal and folk components. The outpouring of popular revolutionary music generated by the War of Liberation was particularly interesting. Pressured by the Carter administration to improve his human rights image by allowing limited freedom of expression, Somoza relaxed his censorship of radio broadcasts slightly in the year before his fall. As a result, some radio stations devoted considerable airtime to thinly veiled or openly revolutionary music. In a very real sense, the haunting and inspiring tunes and lyrics of such revolutionary singers and composers as Carlos Mejía Godoy became the background accompaniment of the young people who fought at the barricades.

Nicaraguans also exhibit their cultural uniqueness in their religious ceremonies. Like Catholics throughout Latin America, the inhabitants of each

Nicaraguan city and village hold annual festivities honoring patron saints. But unlike the people of any other Latin American country, Nicaraguans have a weeklong celebration for the Immaculate Conception of Mary. The festivities of *La Purísima*, which culminate on December 8, far outshine other holidays, including Christmas. During *La Purísima*, altars to the Virgin are erected or decorated in homes or workplaces throughout the country and the people of each neighborhood or village, especially the children, go from altar to altar singing songs and reciting prayers. For their piety, they are rewarded with small gifts—usually edible—that normally include a piece of sugarcane. Even in the wake of the War of Liberation—a time of great economic hardship—Nicaraguans of all classes and political persuasions celebrated *La Purísima* with tremendous enthusiasm. Indeed, one of the most moving sights coauthor Walker saw in that period was that of two teenage war heroes, dressed in FSLN battle fatigues, standing enraptured in front of a tiny home altar—their Belgian automatic rifles temporarily abandoned on the floor like children's playthings.

Another delightful aspect of Nicaraguan culture is the cuisine. Again, there are elements of both the universal and the particular. Like Mexicans and other Central Americans, Nicaraguans eat corn in the form of *tortillas*. *Tortillas* vary in size, color, and thickness from country to country. In Nicaragua they are large, thin, and made of finely milled white corn. They are often used as an edible utensil in which to wrap barbecued meat, beans, or whatever one happens to be eating. Another absolutely essential item in Nicaraguan cookery is beans. As elsewhere in Latin America—since most people cannot afford the regular consumption of animal protein—beans serve as the main source of protein. The small red bean to which Nicaraguans are particularly addicted is refried with rice to produce a delicious dish called *gallo pinto* (spotted rooster)—a favorite breakfast food of people of all classes. Like many other Latin Americans, *nicas* also enjoy *tamales*. Their *nacatamal*, however, has its own particular character. Wrapped in a pungent leaf from a banana-like plant rather than a corn husk, it consists of corn *masa* (dough), rice, tomatoes, potatoes, chili, cassava root, and often a small piece of meat. Another very typical Nicaraguan dish is *vaho*, which is prepared by slowly steaming salted meat and various vegetables in layers over the same banana-like leaves in a large covered container. In general, Nicaraguan cuisine is well worth trying. Though usually tastefully seasoned, it is seldom hot. For lovers of "hot stuff," however, a bottle or bowl of fine, lip-mummifying *salsa de chile* (chili sauce) is seldom very far away.

No discussion of food would be complete without some mention of drink. The favorite nonalcoholic beverage in Nicaragua is coffee—the best (very good, indeed) coming from the high country around Matagalpa. Like other Latin Americans, Nicaraguans who can afford it drink their coffee 50-50, with hot milk, at breakfast and black with sugar during the rest of the day. Other typical sweet drinks are made from toasted cacao and green or toasted corn. In the field of alcoholic beverages, Nicaragua excels. The typical lightly alcoholic drinks are beer and the more traditional and indigenous *chicha*, made from fermented corn mash. The favorite hard liquor is rum, of which Nicaragua has one of Latin America's very best, Flor de Caña (Flower of the Cane).

In all, Nicaraguan culture is rich, varied, and unique. Ironically, however, one of the many sins of the Somozas and their accomplices was to ape and promote foreign culture—especially North American—at the expense of what was authentically *nica*. Not surprisingly, the preservation and strengthening of Nicaraguan culture was a high priority of the FSLN when it seized power. Their determination in this respect was signaled immediately by the creation of the Ministry of Culture, housed, ironically, in one of the deposed dictator's former residences, El Retiro. Before long, there was also a Sandinista Association of Cultural Workers (ASTC), which, in addition to advancing the interests of people in the visual and performing arts, worked in promoting Nicaraguan culture. The ministry, the ASTC, and other groups and individuals did much in the next decade to stimulate a burgeoning of cultural expression. Small museums were created, performing groups (such as the national circus) were encouraged, an award-winning movie industry came into being, mural art flourished, a huge annual exhibition and sale of hand-crafted children's toys, *la Piñata*, became a Managua Christmas tradition, and new cultural journals (such as *Nicaráuac*, published by the Ministry of Culture) were printed. Even on Sandinista television, inexpensive foreign programming gradually gave way to relatively expensive but more appropriate locally produced material. Under Somoza, 95 percent of the programming had been foreign—mainly of U.S. origin. However, in 1985, just prior to the total U.S. embargo, 20 percent was Nicaraguan. U.S. programming had dropped to 59 percent, and the Socialist countries and the rest of the world were contributing 3 percent and 18 percent, respectively.[2]

Inevitably, the economic collapse of the late 1980s and the conservative restoration in the 1990s had a negative impact on the expression of Nicaraguan culture. The Sandinista austerity program of the late 1980s led to the abrupt closing of the Ministry of Culture in 1988 and the replacement of it and the ASTC with a new Institute of Culture in 1989. Many observers, including high-ranking Sandinistas, complained bitterly that these austerity moves represented a serious reversal of the process of "democratization" of culture that had flowered in the early to mid-1980s.[3] Austerity also diminished Nicaraguan cultural content on national television during the last several years of the Sandinista period. After the Sandinista defeat in 1990, the situation deteriorated even further. Murals were destroyed, museums were closed, literary works in some public libraries were burned, and state-run TV, now controlled by the new government, used more and more foreign programming.

SOCIETY

In social conditions and structures, Nicaragua has much more in common with the rest of Latin America than it does in many aspects of culture. This is not particularly surprising, since most social phenomena are at least partly the product of fairly universal economic and political factors. Nicaragua shares with the other Latin American countries the twin legacies of Iberian colonialism and dependent capitalist "development." Throughout Latin America, the human exploitation and rigid social stratification institutionalized during the colonial era were intensified by the income-concentrating tendencies of modern dependent capitalism.

Demographic Conditions

Like most other Latin American countries, Nicaragua experienced tremendous demographic change in the twentieth century. Population growth rates soared, the median age dropped to around fifteen, and there was a population shift away from the country toward the urban areas.

The population explosion is a fairly recent phenomenon. True, Nicaragua traditionally has had a very high birthrate. High birthrates seem to be a predictable by-product of poverty—especially in rural societies. Yet until the mid-twentieth century, the country's fertility was very nearly counterbalanced by the high death rate, resulting in only gradual net gains. In the late twentieth century, however, major advances in medical science made it fairly easy throughout the world to significantly reduce death by contagious disease, especially among infants and children. Prodded and assisted by international organizations such as the United Nations, even the most socially insensitive regimes such as the Somoza dictatorship were able to introduce new technologies that significantly reduced the death rate. In the 1950s and 1960s this meant that the Nicaraguan population grew at an annual rate approaching 3 percent. To compound the problem, the population was becoming younger and, as a result, even more fertile. This in turn pushed the growth rate in the early 1970s to 3.4 percent annually,[4] which meant that if nothing changed, the population would double every twenty-one years. Fortunately, by 2008, the country's population growth rate had dropped to about 1.3 percent.[5]

The Somoza regime's response to the population trend was to encourage the people to use birth control devices. A family planning program was created in 1967, which after about a decade was operating out of approximately seventy clinics. Even so, it is estimated that only about 5 percent of all women of fertile age used birth control devices.[6]

Sandinista policy toward birth control was not as revolutionary as some might have expected. Though they did bring sex education to public schools and to television, the revolutionaries, anxious to avoid unnecessary conflict with the powerful Catholic Church, systematically skirted the issue of abortion. Although no one was prosecuted for having or performing one, abortion was never legalized during the Sandinista period. In addition, as happens almost anywhere there is war, there was a prolonged baby boom in war-torn Nicaragua. This, coupled with significantly reduced infant mortality, meant that from 1979 to 1989 the population grew by a phenomenal 52 percent, from 2.5 million to 3.8 million.

In the wake of the Sandinista electoral defeat of 1990, there were reasons for both optimism and pessimism in the area of population control. On the one hand, the end of the Contra War brought hope that the baby boom might abate. On the other, the Chamorro government's official opposition to abortion and its termination of sex education on TV and the curtailment of it in the public schools meant that family planning would be more difficult. In addition, because there is normally a high correlation between poverty and high birthrates, the continuing deterioration of living conditions was not a good sign. In all, the country's population continued to rise in the post-Sandinista period, reaching about 6 million by 2010, more than twice the 1979 total of 2.5 million.

Urbanization in Nicaragua, as elsewhere in Latin America, was also a twentieth-century phenomenon. In 1900, fewer than one in every three

Nicaraguans lived in towns and cities of 1,000 inhabitants or more. By 1980, however, approximately half were urban dwellers. Since birthrates in the cities are lower than those in the country, the urbanization of Nicaragua appears to have been essentially the product of rural to urban migration. People were leaving the countryside. They were motivated on the one hand by "push" factors, such as land concentration, seasonal unemployment, and inhumane rural working conditions. Although the new government began to alleviate these problems by the early 1980s, the activities of the *contras* soon provided another powerful incentive for rural folk to flee to more protected urban areas. On the other hand, the cities exercised a certain "pull" by offering somewhat better health care and educational opportunities and the illusion of a better standard of living.

Urbanization has had some important effects on Nicaragua. In a very real sense, it made possible the Sandinista Revolution. Decades of government corruption and insensitivity in the face of the miserable condition of many poor urban dwellers throughout the country provided a powerful incentive for the urban insurrection. Without mass urban participation, the small FSLN army in the field would surely have had a much more difficult time in defeating the murderous National Guard. Another effect of urbanization—one with which both the revolutionary and subsequent governments had to come to grips—is the maldistribution of the workforce. Throughout its period in power, the Sandinista government was faced paradoxically with manpower shortages in some rural areas and massive unemployment in the cities. This problem is bound to plague the post-Sandinista governments, too, for the foreseeable future.

Social Cleavage

By comparison with many other Latin American societies, Nicaragua is relatively integrated. However, measured against an ideal standard, it still had a long way to go when the Sandinistas took power in 1979. The most obvious dimensions of cleavage in Nicaraguan society relate to region, ethnic origin, sex, and class. The first three present less serious problems than the last.

Over the past century, the problem of regionalism has become steadily less important. The relocation of the national capital to Managua in 1852 and several generations of elite intermarriage have reduced the old rivalry between the colonial cities of León and Granada to a triviality. In addition, the construction of highways and railroads in the twentieth century tended to integrate other formerly remote areas. Perhaps the greatest single problem of regional integration relates to the much neglected Caribbean region, where large segments of the population still look upon the central government with distrust.

That large but sparsely populated territory is also Nicaragua's major ethnic problem. It has five culturally and racially distinct peoples of African or indigenous origin, plus an ever-growing population of Spanish-mixed origin that has emigrated from the Pacific, and a history of separateness that dates to pre-Columbian times. Unlike the original inhabitants of western Nicaragua, who were largely of Meso-American origin, the pre-Columbian peoples of the eastern coast were believed to have been descendants of immigrants from South America. Later, during the colonial period, when the region fell under the control of the British, English-speaking black slaves were introduced into the region. As a result of these factors, most of the people there speak English and/or indigenous languages rather than Spanish, are Protestant rather than Catholic, and have a variety of cultural traditions distinct from those of the country's Hispanic majority.

Not surprisingly, the region in which the Sandinista government found the greatest difficulty in implementing its revolutionary programs was the Atlantic coast. This was not for lack of good intentions. Immediately after the liberation, the government affirmed its interest in the region's welfare. Attractive billboards in Managua enthusiastically proclaimed, "The Atlantic Coast: An Awakening Giant." The Sandinista television network featured Miskito dance groups. Misurasata, an organization of Indians living in that region, was given a seat on the Council of State. The literacy campaign and virtually every government social program had a component designed for the Atlantic coast. Indeed, the new government spent more per capita on social and economic projects for the people of the Atlantic region than for any other part of the country. Nevertheless, although people at the higher levels of government seemed to appreciate the need to treat the country's indigenous minorities with respect and care, soldiers and middle- and lower-level bureaucrats were sometimes quite insensitive and abusive. The ugly incidents that resulted tended to increase the distrust that many *costeños* (coastal people) already felt for the people of western Nicaragua.

The problem had deep historical roots. When the British crown and pirates dominated the coast, local natives allied themselves with those groups against the "Spaniards"—as western Nicaraguans are still known locally. The Somozas used them in disproportionate numbers in the National Guard because of their willingness to fight westerners. Neither Sandino in the 1930s nor the FSLN in the 1970s had much following on the coast. Indeed, many *costeños* in the 1980s remembered and resented the fact that some of Sandino's guerrilla operations in Zelaya disrupted foreign-owned extractive industries in which they had once been employed.

This historical legacy, coupled with mistakes made early in the period of Sandinista rule, meant that the Atlantic coast was a highly visible Achilles' heel by the time Ronald Reagan came to office in the United States. It appears to have become almost immediately the focal point of CIA-sponsored activity against the Sandinistas. Powerful radio stations beamed scare propaganda into the region. Miskito young people were recruited or pressed into *contra* forces operating out of bases in Honduras. By late 1981, the Nicaraguan government had uncovered "Operation Red Christmas," a CIA plot to separate the Atlantic region from the rest of Nicaragua and thus provide a possible seat for an alternative government.[7] For both humanitarian and security reasons, the Sandinista government soon responded to increased *contra* raids along the Río Coco in northern Zelaya by moving almost 10,000 Indians to safer locations farther south. Though conducted in a humane fashion,[8] these moves *were* involuntary, thus further exacerbating Miskito-Sandinista tensions. Over the next year or so the situation worsened. During the ensuing security operations, several hundred indigenous leaders suspected of subversive activities were detained without adequate due process, and as many as 150 individuals either disappeared permanently after being arrested or (as in the case of the massacre at Leimos) were executed outright.[9] Although the persons committing these acts had clearly disobeyed orders (many were later tried and punished), relations with the Atlantic peoples remained very poor until the government late in 1983 began a series of attempts at reconciliation. Starting at that time with an amnesty for Miskito prisoners, the government then began a process of dialogue and negotiation, which eventually resulted in laws that gave the peoples of the Atlantic region a high degree of self-rule based legally in both the 1987 constitution and the Autonomy Statute passed by the National Assembly that September. Yatama, the unified Miskito military organization that became a regional indigenous party after its return in 1989, has been consistently competitive with the FSLN and PLC in municipal and regional elections.

Post-Sandinista governments apparently had learned little or nothing from Sandinista experience in dealing with the peoples of the Atlantic coast. Openly hostile to the concept of autonomy, Chamorro ignored the Autonomy Statute and instead moved quickly to appoint a government overseer for the region. In doing so, she generated widespread animosity among *costeños*, the majority of whom had voted for UNO that February. The Alemán and Bolaños administrations, elected with significant support on the coast, were no less paternalistic toward *costeños* than their predecessors. Still, some significant progress was made in land demarcation and titling, one of the most heated areas of contention between the communities and the central government. In a 2001 ruling by the Inter-American Court in the case *Mayagna (Sumo) Awas Tingni Community v. Nicaragua*, the government was ordered to title the Awas Tingni's land. In December 2002, the Demarcation Law Regarding the Properties of the Indigenous Peoples and Ethnic Communities of the Atlantic Coast, Bocay, Coco, and Indio Maiz Rivers formally recognized indigenous ownership of the land. The surveying and demarcation process took much longer than the fifteen months mandated by the court. After returning to power in 2007, the Ortega administration accelerated the process of titling communal lands along the Atlantic coast, although not without some conflict. In December 2008, the Awas Tingni community finally received the title to its territory. The government expected to complete the titling process by the end of 2010, ultimately distributing more than 22,000 square miles.

Frustration with the long-simmering land issue spilled over into other areas. Outrage with the central government's response to the aftermath of Hurricane Felix, a category 5 hurricane that battered the Atlantic coast in September 2007, the postponement of the 2008 elections in the RAAN, and economic disputes led to a resurgence of Miskito nationalism. In 2009, the Miskito Council of Elders declared independence from Nicaragua— although the claim was not embraced by everyone in the community and was not recognized by any outside entity.[10]

Though the problem of integrating the Atlantic coast affects less than 8 percent of the country's population, the issue of sexism affects more than 50 percent. As elsewhere in Latin America, values and ideas connected with the concept of machismo (manliness) have traditionally affected sex roles in Nicaragua. Though things were changing, Nicaragua was still very much a man's world in the 1970s. A woman's place was in her home, and a strict double standard of sexual behavior applied. On the whole, women received less education and, when employed, earned less money than men. The plight of poor women was especially aggravated by the nature of the Somoza dictatorship and its National Guard. Officers of the Guard controlled a flourishing prostitution industry, and soldiers were rarely punished for rape.

Though it would be naive to think that, even in a revolution, sexism could be abolished overnight, it is clear that the national liberation struggle and the revolution greatly advanced the cause of women's liberation in Nicaragua. The vital part played by women in the War of Liberation caused a healthy reevaluation of sex stereotypes. The Association of Women Confronting the National Problem (AMPRONAC) set up neighborhood committees that helped organize the urban resistance, and many young women fought and died alongside their male counterparts in the FSLN guerrilla army. According to male soldiers with whom coauthor Walker spoke, women—who made up more than 25 percent of the FSLN army—were not camp followers but fully integrated soldiers who shared all of the responsibility of the campaign. They were admired and respected by their male counterparts. The women veterans spoke of warm bonds of respect and love that marked their guerrilla experience.

In postliberation Nicaragua, women continued to play an active role. They were prominent not only in the new government but also in the Sandinista Popular Army, the Sandinista National Police (which was eventually headed by a woman), and the Sandinista Popular Militias. In addition, AMPRONAC metamorphosed into a Sandinista organization, the Luisa Amanda Espinosa Association of Nicaraguan Women (AMNLAE), which was represented on the Council of State. There, and in the National Assembly inaugurated in 1985, AMNLAE members pushed for and frequently won legislation promoting women's interests. However, the Sandinista Revolution by no means brought complete equality to women. Though more rigorously prosecuted, domestic violence continued. Abortion remained technically illegal. And AMNLAE, which was supposed to fight vigorously for women's rights, tended more often in the late 1980s to do the bidding of the state and the FSLN.[11]

Post-Sandinista governments marked a clear step back for women's rights. Therapeutic abortions, which had been legal since 1890, were halted in Managua's women's hospital. The use of artificial contraception was condemned by education officials. A total abortion ban was passed in 2006 with the votes of the FSLN, which supported the measure in exchange for the Church's support in the 2006 presidential elections. While contraceptives remained widely available, most poor women did not have access to health centers or sex education. As a result, Nicaragua had one of the region's highest teen pregnancy rates and the lowest average age of mothers.[12] Further, the deteriorating economic situation impacted most heavily on women. The "last hired and first fired," they tended disproportionately to lose their jobs as overall unemployment grew. As a result, women increasingly looked for work elsewhere. This "feminization" of migration was particularly common among young, slightly more educated women, many of whom were single mothers. While most went to Costa Rica, those with resources also went to the United States and Spain. Evidence indicated that they sent home more money than their male counterparts.[13] All of this, however, tended to reactivate and give purpose to the previously declining AMNLAE. In addition, a number of other women's rights groups soon took to the field. Having experienced some advances and a degree of liberation during the Sandinista period, many women were now unwilling to lapse back into their highly exploited prerevolutionary role.

By far the most serious dimension of social cleavage in Nicaragua is that of class. Before the revolution, there was a very wide gap in the standard of living between the privileged 20 percent of the population and the impoverished 80 percent. As elsewhere in Latin America, the usual European and North American class categories were inadequate to describe the Nicaraguan class structure. The problem lay in the fact that although the bulk of the privileged class could be described as belonging to a "middle group" or "middle sector" by virtue of occupation and standard of living, they were definitely not a distinct "middle class." Rather than having their own set of values and distinct group identification, members of the middle sector tended to ape and identify with the tiny upper class. The real distinguishing factor in Nicaragua was whether one worked with one's hands. Quite simply, 80 percent did and 20 percent did not. Since any physical work was viewed as degrading, the privileged minority was accustomed to hiring lower-class individuals at very low pay to cook their meals, care for their children, clean their homes, tend their yards, shine their shoes, and tote their luggage. This was the "natural" order of things. And whereas *la sociedad*, the people of the upper class or high society, often looked down on members of the middle sector, there was much less distance between the two privileged groups than between them and the impoverished majority.

The distance between the masses and the privileged classes was also maintained symbolically. Titles denoting university degrees—doctor, licentiate, engineer, architect, and so on—were taken very seriously in pre-revolutionary Nicaragua. Lower-class individuals were expected to use them with the family name or the respectful *don* or *doña* with the given name in addressing their "superiors." And whereas the privileged minority were accustomed to employing the familiar *vos* form with their inferiors, the latter were expected to respond with the respectful formal *usted*. This verbal underscoring of class distance even applied in communication between privileged children and their nursemaids. The child was *usted* and the servant, *vos*.

Privileged status was also demonstrated in a number of other ways. Membership in a country club or prestigious social organization, the consumption of imported luxury goods, travel abroad, and the affectation of foreign mannerisms all helped distinguish *gente decente* (decent people) from the masses.

Although the overthrow of the Somozas was a product of the combined efforts of all classes, it was inevitable that if it were to be a real revolution with meaningful change, there would be class tension and conflict after the liberation. By definition, social revolution involves a reordering of the relationship between classes. Former privileged groups are asked—or obliged—to make sacrifices so that the nation's limited resources can be redirected into the human development of the majority.

In the case of Nicaragua, the revolution affected the former privileged classes negatively in a number of ways. The use of *don* or *doña*, or of university titles, became less common—at least for a while. *Compañero* or its more common variants, *compa* or *compita*, became the usual form of address, at least among revolutionaries. Country clubs were confiscated and put to other uses including recreation for the public. The importation of luxury goods was curtailed. Many rural and urban properties were seized, and stiff taxes were levied on property, income, and domestic luxury items such as cigarettes and rum.

Many Nicaraguans understood and were able to accommodate themselves to this new reality. The relatively privileged parents of the tens of thousands of high school and college students who participated in the Literacy Crusade of 1980, for instance, demonstrated their willingness to cooperate with the revolution by giving their children the required permission to join the crusade. Some businessmen and landholders responded to government pleas to reactivate the economy by returning their properties to normal production.

But many members of the former privileged classes were a good bit less generous and understanding. Some simply liquidated their assets and fled the country, joining more than 10,000 Somoza followers already exiled in northern Central America and the United States. Others stayed on, grumbling and resisting. Within days of the liberation, for instance, co-author Walker was asked by a lawyer friend to help get his teenage children into an English-language program in the United States so they, in his words, would not "waste" the months that school would be out during the literacy campaign. Bitter jokes about the revolution and its leaders became standard fare at some gatherings. Rumors of all sorts spread like wildfire in privileged circles (one even claimed that the immediate postwar shortage of beans and medicine was due to the fact that these precious materials were being diverted to Cuba).

More seriously, fearing that Nicaragua was becoming "another Cuba," many landholders and businessmen refused to cooperate in the reconstruction. They began decapitalizing their properties instead of reinvesting in spite of repeated assurances that a responsible private sector would be preserved and provided with very generous government loans, tax incentives, and concessionary rates of currency exchange.

As we noted earlier, bourgeois resistance began almost immediately after the Triumph. Several recently founded or reorganized microparties began issuing shrill statements reflecting the fears of the privileged classes. In May 1980, *La Prensa* took a sharp political jag to the right. At the same time, several tiny counterrevolutionary "armies"—such as the so-called Democratic Armed Forces (FAD), which had been organized by disgruntled cattlemen—began harassing the government. Though posing no real threat to the regime, these "armies" and former National Guardsmen operating out of safe sanctuary in Honduras did manage to inflict property damage and take innocent lives, including those of seven young literacy campaigners.

The position of the privileged classes hardened even more after the election of Ronald Reagan in the United States in November 1980. At that point, paramilitary activities increased and the Catholic Church hierarchy, *La Prensa*, the opposition microparties, and the Superior Council of Private Enterprise (COSEP) closed ranks in a more concerted effort to reverse history. Although their activities were couched in terms of the defense of "freedom of the press" and of the preservation of "religious liberty" and a "mixed economy," those were not the issues. Neither of the latter two had been threatened at all, and press freedom was severely limited only in 1982, almost three years after the Triumph, when the country was clearly under internationally organized paramilitary attack. In reality, the heart of the matter was power. The Catholic Church hierarchy feared an erosion of religious control and authority in the face of the immense popularity of the revolution and the new process of democratization within the Church that had begun at Medellín. The privileged classes in general sensed, quite accurately, that they had lost political power. The Sandinistas had been quite willing to allow these groups political participation at least equivalent to the percentage they represented within the population. But that was not enough. As long as the expectation remained that the *contras* or the U.S. Marines might someday deliver power back into their hands, there would be no incentive to adjust to the new system.

SANDINISTA SOCIAL PROGRAMS

The most important long-term concern of the Sandinista Revolution was to improve the human condition of the downtrodden majority of the Nicaraguan people. From its founding in 1961 to its final triumph in 1979, the FSLN repeatedly advocated a variety of sweeping social reforms. Immediately after their victorious entry into Managua, therefore, the revolutionaries began to put promises into effect. Ironically, their efforts were made very difficult by the terrible domestic economic situation and the huge international debt inherited from the departing dictator and his cronies. The government had very little in public revenues with which to finance social programs and was forced to ask the working classes to show restraint in making admittedly justifiable wage demands—especially in the public sector.

In spite of these problems, the revolutionaries made impressive progress in the social area, especially in the early 1980s. Almost immediately after their victory, in order to combat unemployment in urban areas, they embarked on a variety of labor-intensive public works projects financed out of a special Fund to Combat Unemployment. The revenues for this fund were raised through a tax on the "thirteenth month" salary that all employers were obliged to pay their employees at Christmas. The privileged minority of wage earners entitled to more than $150 in their extra month's salary were required to forgo that part of their bonus in order that thousands of their less fortunate countrymen be employed. The middle sector complained bitterly, but this fund and other monies—some from international sources—allowed the government not only to provide jobs but also to engage in public works projects designed to improve the lives of the people. These included a fifty-square-block children's park in the heart of old Managua, public dance and assembly facilities, several clean and well-constructed public marketplaces, simple and hygienic concession stands, covered picnic areas, sidewalks, paved roads in poor neighborhoods, and the reconstruction of war-damaged roads in urban areas.

The new government was also concerned with improving the lives of the rural poor. Immediately after the liberation, the government confiscated the agrarian properties of Somoza and his cohorts—about one-fifth of the nation's cultivable land. During the following years additional confiscations took place for other reasons, so that by 1984, large private landholdings, which had represented 52 percent of total farmland in 1978, had been reduced to 26 percent. Although some of the land confiscated had been distributed to individual peasants, the major beneficiaries of this change at first were peasant cooperatives and state farms; they had not even existed in 1978, but now they controlled 36 percent and 19 percent of the land, respectively.[14] On the state farms and cooperatives, efforts were made to improve the lives of the rural poor by upgrading working conditions; providing small health units, schools, housing projects, and day-care centers; and opening rural stores in which the prices for basic necessities were kept artificially low. From the mid-1980s onward there was a movement away from state farms, which resulted in the redistribution of those lands to private cooperatives and individual peasants. In fact, by 1989, almost a third of former state farm acreage had been reassigned in this fashion.[15] Not only had the state farms shown relatively low productivity, but equally important, the war had created a political imperative to address the land hunger of the rural populations.

In the segment of private agriculture that had not been organized into cooperatives, the government worked on behalf of the poor in a number of additional ways. To help the agricultural proletariat working on large private farms, it began strict enforcement of laws governing minimum wages and working conditions and encouraged workers, through their unions, to insist on their rights. In addition, for the first time in history, small producers were given access to substantial amounts of public credit. In the first

A cartoon commentary on the attitude of the privileged classes (as represented by the figure in the derby hat). (Courtesy of *Cartoons from Nicaragua: The Revolutionary Humor of Roger* [Managua: Committee of U.S. Citizens Living in Nicaragua, 1984])

year over 50 percent of all public loans to the agrarian private sector went to credit and service cooperatives formed by peasants. Later a program was begun that gave titles of ownership to large numbers of peasants who had previously occupied and used land without legal guarantees. Small farmers were also helped by strict controls governing water usage and maximum rents for agricultural lands.[16]

In spite of severe economic constraints, the government also implemented sweeping changes in public policy toward health, social security, food, housing, and education.[17] Efforts in the area of health were impressive. Even during the insurrection, the FSLN, through its neighborhood Civil Defense Committees (CDCs), had organized health volunteers to deal with the most pressing medical needs of people in the insurgent neighborhoods. Immediately after the liberation, the poorly coordinated, chaotic, clientelistic health care system inherited from Somoza was thoroughly reorganized into one administratively centralized ministry. The overriding philosophy of the new system was to make health care available to everyone in rural and urban areas alike.

A major dilemma for the Sandinistas in these years was to decide whether, on the one hand, to emphasize expensive curative health care (hospitals, doctors, etc.) or, on the other, to opt for more effective but also less politically glamorous preventative programs. In the long run, the government ended up doing both. Government expenditures in the area of health increased over 200 percent from 1978 to 1983. The most costly aspect of the program related to the rebuilding, expansion, and staffing of curative facilities such as hospitals and clinics. At the same time heavy emphasis was also placed on primary or preventative health care, and in 1981 the United Nations Children's Fund (UNICEF) chose Nicaragua as a demonstration site for this type of approach to health. Here, voluntary labor was crucial. Within months of the Sandinista victory, inoculation campaigns had been carried out, at low cost, by mass organizations. By 1982, over 78,000 volunteer health *brigadistas* had been mobilized to work in a variety of preventative projects on designated Popular Health Days (Jornadas Populares de Salud). As a result of these efforts, not a single confirmed case of polio occurred in 1982, and by 1983 infant diarrhea, mountain leprosy, and malaria were down 75, 60, and 50 percent, respectively. Infant mortality in general was down from 121 per 1,000 in 1978 and 1979 to 90.1 per 1,000 in 1983. Life expectancy had crept up from 52.2 to 57.6 years.

Early on, the social security and social welfare functions of the government were reorganized, separated from those having to do with health, and consolidated into one institution—the Nicaraguan Social Security and Welfare Institute (INSSBI). The latter not only extended social security coverage to a wider segment of society but also took on the responsibility of dealing with problems related to social welfare, such as the rehabilitation of prostitutes and delinquent minors, the care of orphans, the creation of day-care centers, the building and administration of workers' recreation facilities, and so on. Eventually it was also put in charge of handling the emergency needs of displaced persons—first the victims of the 1982 flood and later the hundreds of thousands of persons made homeless by the CIA-coordinated Contra War and by the ravages of Hurricane Joan in 1988.

The revolution also brought an abrupt change in government policy regarding food. Under the Somozas, the majority of Nicaraguans had suffered from malnutrition. Much of the country's best lands had been used to produce agro-export products for the benefit of the few. Domestic food production was inadequate. Much food was imported. Prices were high. The Sandinistas, however, immediately placed a high priority on making basic staples available to all at reasonable prices. The tactics employed were complex. Farmers were given incentives to increase the production of staples while, at the same time, the state played a prominent role in the storage, distribution, and pricing of basic foods through its new state-owned food marketing enterprise (ENABAS). Because demand shot up and imports went down before production in all areas reached a sufficient level, the government also found it necessary to institute a system of rationing of certain basic staples so that all people could have relatively equal access to those items regardless of class. But there were problems: Middle- and upper-class people grumbled about scarcity in supermarkets (most Nicaraguans shop in people's stores and public markets), ration cards, standing in line, and so forth. Market people were upset that they had fewer imported products to sell and that consumer prices in people's stores were artificially low. But by 1983, the program was showing results. Although the per capita intake of corn had remained stagnant over 1977 levels and that for beans had increased only slightly, the consumption of rice was up 66 percent. In addition, although the consumption of beef and milk were down 10 and 4 percent, respectively, the intake of eggs, cooking oil, and poultry were up 21, 30, and 80 percent, respectively.[18]

The new government was also concerned with helping the people secure what the Sandinistas viewed as the basic human right to shelter. As in the area of other social services, the devastation caused by the war accentuated an already bleak situation in housing. The basic philosophy of the new Ministry of Housing and Human Settlements (MINVAH) was both humanitarian and practical. In the practical sense, aware of the inadequacy, waste, and high cost of public housing programs in capitalist and socialist countries alike, the revolutionaries decided not to embark on a massive government program of housing construction. Some government housing was constructed—especially in connection with agricultural production centers. But the major thrust of new Sandinista policy was to provide legal protection to the renter and homeowner and to supply infrastructural, technical, and organizational support for the construction of new housing. Accordingly, drastic rent reduction and controls were immediately implemented. Illegal subdivisions, in which wealthy landowners had been selling small building plots on the installment plan without supplying basic services, were nationalized. The government also moved to outlaw urban land speculation and passed legislation that allowed it to confiscate unused lands needed for housing projects. In 1981, it began implementing a "sites and services" approach to housing. In projects called "progressive urbanizations," which markedly increased in number following the population dislocations caused by the 1982 floods, the homeless were given title to plots and provided with basic utilities and services, but were left on their own to improve their dwellings and create their own organizations to solve community problems.

Clearly the greatest strides in social reform in these years were made in the area of education. The first and most dramatic event in this respect was the National Literacy Crusade of 1980. From March to August of that year all schools were closed as over 60,000 young volunteers dispersed throughout the country while another 25,000 worked in the cities in an attempt to bring literacy to the majority of the population over ten years old who could neither read nor write. According to official results, the illiteracy rate for persons age ten and older was reduced in those five months from over 50 percent to less than 13 percent. Though many people hostile to the revolution claimed that the Sandinistas had greatly exaggerated their achievement, a fair examination of methods, tactics, and resources reveals that gains in the general neighborhood of those claimed by the government were at least plausible.

A literacy campaign of the type carried out by Nicaragua in 1980 would have been impossible in most of the prerevolutionary societies of Latin America. Prohibitively expensive in an unmobilized society, such a campaign would also have amounted to an administrative and logistical nightmare of the first magnitude. For the highly mobilized society of postliberation Nicaragua, however, this crusade was neither inordinately expensive nor exceptionally difficult to coordinate and implement. The key to its success was the voluntary participation not only of the young teachers and their previously illiterate students but also of various Sandinista popular organizations (described in this chapter), which provided free and vitally important logistical support. Their efforts were also backed by a substantial segment of the Catholic Church, the private sector, and various other organizations. Under such circumstances, the government's major function was simply to plan the campaign, train the literacy volunteers, and provide some material assistance. Given a target illiterate population (ten years or over) of under 800,000, the student-teacher ratio was very favorable and the time involved was sufficient to teach basic reading and writing skills.[19]

The idea of a literacy crusade had been gestating for some time. The FSLN—and in particular one of its martyred founders, Carlos Fonseca Amador—had often stressed the need for such a campaign. Planning sessions had taken place before the final FSLN victory. After the liberation, Nicaragua's new leaders forged ahead with this ambitious project in spite of dire warnings by learned international authorities that their effort was premature and destined to fail.

The Nicaraguans were blessed in that they could draw selectively upon the experience of several mass literacy campaigns attempted previously in other parts of the world. In the 1920s, the Mexican Revolution made a primitive attempt at a literacy campaign. In mid-century, Paulo Freire developed a methodology that he first attempted to apply in his native Brazil and then, after the military coup of 1964, took with greater success to other Third World countries, including Guinea-Bissau in the mid-1970s. In 1961, Cuba carried out its revolutionary literacy campaign. Not surprisingly, therefore, the Nicaraguan crusade received the enthusiastic assistance of many international experts. Paulo Freire himself was an adviser to the crusade's national coordinating body, Cuba sent advisers, the United Nations Economic and Social Council (ECOSOC) supplied verbal support and technical advice, and many individuals, including some U.S. citizens, volunteered.

The crusade was planned in stages. Soon after the liberation, the popular organizations (CDS, AMNLAE, etc.) conducted a surprisingly thorough and sophisticated nationwide census to determine the characteristics and problems of the Nicaraguan people, especially in the area of literacy. At the same time a team of literacy experts worked to prepare a twenty-three-lesson literacy primer. The crusade took place in concentric waves. First eighty selected educators took a fifteen-day seminar in literacy training. After testing what they had learned in the field, each member taught another group; then they and the members of the second group taught hundreds of additional educators, bringing the total of literacy trainers to several thousand. At that point all of the trainers were dispersed to various regions of the country to teach the volunteers. Finally, from March to August 1980, the volunteers themselves fanned out across the land to teach the illiterates who had been identified by the census.

In 1980, the Year of Literacy, the crusade became the focus of national attention. The imagery employed flowed out of the previous year's War of Liberation. This second war of liberation was designed not only to free the masses from ignorance and intellectual subjugation, but, equally important, to liberate the largely middle-class volunteers themselves from their prejudices and stereotypes about Nicaragua's impoverished majority. The country was broken into "fronts" corresponding to the six zones of combat during the liberation struggle. Within each front, there were literacy "columns," "squadrons," and individual *brigadistas* (brigadiers). In many cases the *brigadistas* lived and worked during the day with the peasants and workers whom they taught at night.

From the start, the teaching of "political literacy" was also very much a part of the campaign. Paulo Freire's concept of *concientização* (consciousness-raising) was essential. Key words, phrases, and sentences in each of the lessons were designed to stimulate discussion and a new patriotism, pride in the revolution and its martyrs, and, especially, a sense of the dignity and importance of the individual. The first lesson, for instance, focused on *la revolución*, words of central political importance that, at the same time, contained all of the basic vowels. Predictably, many members of the privileged classes, as well as a number of foreign observers, saw the campaign as little more than a systematic program of Marxist or Communist indoctrinations. However, there was nothing in the primer or the teachers manual, or in any of the other teaching aids used, that would justify that charge.

The 1980 Literacy Crusade. In March, 60,000 volunteer teachers departed for rural areas (top) while 25,000 stayed in the cities, teaching at night in such unlikely locations as the onion stall of a public market (bottom). Though the initial and most ambitious phase of the crusade was completed and commemorated with a

celebration in August (top), other aspects of this program, such as follow-up education for the newly literate and literacy education in English and Miskito (bottom), demonstrated the new government's ongoing concern for basic popular education. (Photos courtesy of Ramón Zamoras Olivas of the central office of the National Literary Crusade)

There *was* a political message. But it was nationalist and revolutionary, somewhat analogous to the message young people in the United States receive when they learn about the American Revolution in grade school. Interestingly, the director of the crusade was a Jesuit priest, Father Fernando Cardenal.

In the end, the key to the success of the crusade lay in massive voluntary participation. No one was forced to participate. Indeed, minors were not allowed to join without the permission of their parents. Yet for five months the streets of Managua and other major cities were strangely quiet as a significant segment of the country's urban teenagers and young adults waged Nicaragua's second war of liberation in the countryside. In all, this participation, the logistical support of the Catholic Church and the Sandinista popular organizations, and money and materials from all over the world ultimately made it possible for the government to coordinate a massive project at a small cost to itself.

The literacy crusade, which won for Nicaragua the 1980 award of the United Nations Educational, Scientific, and Cultural Organization (UNESCO) for the best program of its kind, was not intended as a one-shot affair. It was followed later in that year by literacy crusades in Miskito and English for the peoples of the Atlantic region and by a massive adult education program aimed at eventually lifting all Nicaraguans to the equivalency of a minimum of four years of schooling. By 1982, total enrollment at all levels of education was approximately twice what it had been in 1978. And in 1983, Nicaragua was claiming an illiteracy rate of only 10 percent—one of the lowest in Latin America.

The Sandinista Revolution in the early 1980s had embarked on an ambitious and multifaceted program of social change. By 1983, these programs were registering impressive results. Even the Kissinger Commission Report, published in January of the following year, admitted grudgingly that "Nicaragua's government has made significant gains against illiteracy and disease."[20] But as that report was being issued, the administration for which Kissinger was working was already two years into a program of low-intensity conflict against Nicaragua that, among other things, was deliberately designed to incapacitate the Nicaraguan Revolution, destroy its ability to uplift the lives of the common people, and thus not only to delegitimize it in the eyes of Nicaraguans but also to invalidate it internationally as a model for social change. In the second half of the 1980s this objective would be largely achieved.

The U.S.-sponsored surrogate war and associated forms of economic aggression impacted on social conditions in Nicaragua in a variety of ways. First, throughout the war, the *contras* targeted social service infrastructure and personnel. Numerous rural schools, clinics, food storage facilities, day-care centers, and basic development projects were destroyed.[21] One hundred and thirty teachers, 40 doctors and nurses, 152 technicians, and 41 other professionals were killed.[22] The dead also included eleven foreign social and developmental volunteers. Among them was Benjamin Linder, a U.S. citizen executed by the *contras* in June 1987 after a *contra* attack on a small hydroelectric project he was helping to develop in northern Nicaragua. This destruction and murder not only deprived rural people of the facilities and personnel who were directly affected but also discouraged other individuals from working in remote rural areas.

In the second half of the decade the war-related expenditures also consumed over half of the national budget, thus inevitably depriving social programs of badly needed resources. Government-sponsored school construction came to a complete halt in the late 1980s. War-driven inflation turned public sector salaries into a cruel joke. As a result, many teachers, health workers, and others quit their government jobs when they found they could no longer support their families with what they were earning.

Specific social programs were affected in specific ways. In the area of agrarian reform, although popular demand motivated the government to accelerate the distribution of land, the war severely limited its ability to supply credit, basic inputs, and extension services. Health services were strained to the breaking point by the large number of wounded needing immediate, often costly, curative attention. Urban housing programs were overwhelmed and incapacitated by hundreds of thousands of destitute war refugees who poured into the cities to seek safety and a better life. Similarly the Nicaraguan Social Security and Welfare Institute (INSSBI) found itself having to cope not only with its normal client load but with the large numbers of displaced persons, war orphans, war disabled, and other victims of the conflict. As part of the austerity program brought on by war-driven inflation, basic food distribution programs were ended in the late 1980s.

Thus, as the decade drew to a close, the social programs of the revolution had been drastically damaged or, in some cases, completely eliminated. In Managua hospitals, women were giving birth two to a bed with only a small piece of sheet under the birthing area of each. Children with limbs blown off by mines were screaming inconsolably for lack of sedatives. Illiteracy, disease, infant mortality, homelessness, and so forth were on the rise.

POST-SANDINISTA SOCIAL POLICY

The three conservative administrations that followed the Sandinistas oversaw a considerable reversal of Sandinista social policy and programs. In part, these programs had already been partially reversed by the impact of the Contra War on social service infrastructure and by the emergency austerity program implemented by the Sandinistas themselves to combat inflation. But the reversal was also the inevitable by-product of the Chamorro, Alemán, and Bolaños administrations' almost religious devotion to neoliberal economic principles as advocated by the United States and enforced by the International Monetary Fund, World Bank, and Inter-American Development Bank.

However, it is also fair to say that the reversal of Sandinista social gains also reflected a true insensitivity on the part of the newly reempowered traditional elites to the suffering of the impoverished majority. The elite attitude was starkly exemplified in an anecdote told in June 1990 by Reinaldo Antonio Téfel, the former minister of the Nicaraguan Social Security and Welfare Institute and a lifelong champion of the poor. According to Téfel, shortly after the 1990 election he had invited the president-elect to send a transition team to INSSBI to be briefed on its history, administration, and functions. While explaining the social welfare functions of his institute (programs for the disabled, orphans, street children, and so on), Téfel noticed that one obviously aristocratic member of the Chamorro team was becoming increasingly bored and frustrated. Unable to contain herself any longer, she eventually broke in and observed with indignation, "It is a duplication of effort that the government would have these programs when, for such things, [organizations like] the Rotary Club and the Lions Club [already] exist!"[23]

Attacks on the social programs began almost immediately after the Sandinistas left office in April 1990. Not long after Chamorro's inauguration, the many church and other international nongovernmental organizations that had been promoting social development in Nicaragua throughout the 1980s found that the new government was placing a high import tax on much of the material that they were bringing into the country to use in their programs. Under Nicaraguan law, nonprofit organizations are exempt from this type of tax. Accordingly, those affected viewed the new taxes as an illegal and blatantly political effort to stop international support for health, education, and other social projects associated in some minds with "Sandinismo."[24]

Chamorro government behavior in the area of agrarian reform was also alarming to many. Although it had repeatedly promised to respect the changes accomplished under the Sandinista agrarian reform, the new government appeared in practice to be intent on doing just the opposite. State farms were deliberately undercapitalized, and efforts were made to return these consequently "underutilized" properties to their former owners. The UNO government looked the other way as UNO/*contra* thugs attacked and seized peasant cooperatives. Even peasant recipients of individual plots of land under the Sandinistas found themselves threatened. The revolutionary government had given tens of thousands of peasants land-use titles, which were written in such a way as to guard against the reconcentration of rural property by stipulating that although the plots could be used by the peasants and passed on to their heirs, they could not be sold. The new government, however, favored "real" titles, which, by allowing sale, would once again leave the rural poor vulnerable to pressure by big holders. Finally, new policies allowing bank foreclosures in the event of default on farm loans were particularly threatening to both cooperatives and individual peasants.

Chamorro administration behavior in the field of education also gave little comfort to progressives. The new minister and vice minister of education were Sofonías Cisneros and Humberto Belli, ultraconservatives whose appointments had been arranged by the openly counterrevolutionary Cardinal Miguel Obando y Bravo. Cisneros had been a member of the Catholic hierarchy's Education Committee. With the alleged financial backing of the CIA,[25] Belli had created the U.S.-based Puebla Institute during the early 1980s and had published a series of slanted and alarmist books, articles, and op-ed pieces portraying the Sandinistas as demonic persecutors of religion. Claiming to be advocates of a "scientific" perspective and "Christian values," Cisneros and Belli moved quickly to "desandinize" education in Nicaragua. In August 1990, four months after the Sandinistas left office, the second- and third-grade elementary text *Carlitos*, with its emphasis on pride in Nicaraguan history and patriots, was replaced by a generic "Blue and White" reader that had been purchased and imported with USAID funds and featured "drawings of blue-eyed children, references to Santa Claus, and sentences about 'riding a bicycle to market.'"[26] Furthermore, all new teachers hired were members of the pro-UNO Nicaraguan Teachers' Union Federation (FSMN). By October 1990, 370 teachers and principals had been fired or transferred for what appeared to be political reasons.[27]

The Chamorro government frequently bragged that it was spending a higher percentage of the national budget on health and education than had the Sandinistas. This was true since, unlike the besieged Sandinistas, it was no longer having to spend much on defense. But what this boast hid was that as the overall budget was cut to conform to international demands, real amounts being allocated to those areas soon shrank to well below the real expenditures of the Sandinista era.

In its social policy, the administration of Arnoldo Alemán was simply more of the same. Driven by the United States and the international lending agencies to conform to IMF-prescribed structural reforms, this administration continued cutting public expenditures—especially in the social area. At the same time, Alemán squandered some resources otherwise available for real expenditures on social programs by dramatically increasing the salaries of political cronies whom he placed in top administrative positions. Finally, the unprecedented corruption of the Alemán administration depleted funds that might otherwise have been used to help the impoverished majority.[28]

The degree to which Nicaragua's social service infrastructure had been allowed to decay in the 1990s was dramatically illustrated in the wake of Hurricane Mitch, which struck Central America late in 1998, leaving 2,400 Nicaraguans dead and another 700,000 displaced. In stark contrast to the effectiveness and efficiency with which the Sandinista government had dealt with a similar disaster, Hurricane Joan, a decade earlier, Alemán's decrepit social service infrastructure was simply overwhelmed in 1998. As it turns out, most of the relief effort was furnished by international and domestic nongovernmental organizations. Even then, the Alemán government tried to channel that assistance through departmental governments where Alemán's Liberal party was in control or through Liberal party headquarters where it was not. That, and Alemán's idea of taxing such relief, met with such strong international disapproval that the government eventually had to back down.

By the end of his administration, the Alemán government had acquired such an unsavory reputation for its handling of public funds and international aid that many donor governments had resorted to the unusual practice of channeling humanitarian assistance through nongovernmental organizations rather than the government itself. By 2001, even the United States—which normally has a rather strong stomach when it comes to the peccadilloes of ideologically friendly regimes—was beginning to follow this practice with its food aid program.[29]

By the first decade of the twenty-first century, it was clear that the human cost of the abandonment or reversal of Sandinista social policy had been tremendous. This fact was clearly demonstrated by changes in Nicaragua's relative status in the world as measured by the United Nations Development Program's Human Development Index (HDI). The HDI is a composite index drawn from indicators of social (life expectancy and adult literacy) as well as economic (gross domestic product per capita) development. When the Sandinistas left power in 1990—in spite of the Contra War and an externally orchestrated effort at economic strangulation—Nicaragua had ranked 60th among the nations of the world. By 1997, when Violeta Chamorro left power, the country's ranking had dropped to 127th. By 2000, in spite of reasonably good growth in GDP, it was only up to 116th.[30] While it improved slightly during Bolaños's term to 112th in 2003 and 110th in 2005, it dropped to 124th in 2007—further evidence that economic growth had been ineffective at promoting sustainable development or reducing poverty.[31] In 2006, more than 70 percent of the rural population had no access to potable water and seven in ten working Nicaraguans could not afford the entire contents of the *canasta basica*.[32]

Increasingly, however, Nicaragua's poor turned to other means to support themselves. The UNDP estimated that more than 800,000 Nicaraguans left the country between 1990 and 2005—and projections by some nongovernmental organizations were higher.[33] Nicaraguan migration to Costa Rica and the United States increased significantly in the 1990s in response to structural adjustment policies. Remittances—money sent home from citizens abroad—totaled $250 million in 1996 and $600 million in 2000 (almost one-quarter of GDP).[34] Like those of other countries in the region, Nicaragua's people were becoming its most lucrative export.

THE RETURN OF DANIEL ORTEGA

Daniel Ortega's return to office brought with it a renewed emphasis on social programs. A new literacy campaign, initiated by FSLN municipal governments in previous years, reduced illiteracy from almost 21 percent in

2007 to less than 5 percent in 2009. The campaign, "From Martí to Fidel," was modeled on the Cuban "Yo sí Puedo" (Yes, I Can) program and was recognized by UNESCO. A later Program Amor, sponsored by the Ministry of the Family, focused on the disintegration of the family, child labor, and getting street children into school. Additionally, the Ortega administration immediately eliminated all school fees and lifted the requirement on school uniforms, which had prevented many poor children from attending school. School enrollments increased dramatically in 2007 (more than 15 percent) but fell in 2008 and 2009. However, increasing enrollments were met with insufficient expenditures (the lowest in Central America) and students experienced overcrowded classrooms without desks or enough teachers.

The Zero Usury program—modeled on similar microcredit programs throughout the developing world—provided small, low-interest loans to help women start small businesses. By July 2009, more than 82,000 women had received "solidarity loans" totaling 458 million *cordobas*.[35] However, since program participants were selected by Citizens Power Councils (CPCs), there were allegations that the program was politicized and clientelistic. The Zero Hunger program targeted hunger and food scarcity among the rural poor by providing a package of one pregnant cow, a sow, hens, seeds, and construction materials to those with at least a *manzana*—1.68 acres—of land. The land requirement meant that a significant portion of the rural population, who are landless, were excluded from the program. Program participants had to agree not to sell the animals. As with the Zero Usury program, the transfers were made to the women of the household. By July 2009, more than 32,000 families of the target 75,000 were participating.[36] The program had its critics—who pointed to the difficulties and expense for poor families of maintaining a cow, the lack of linkages to a larger, coherent development strategy, and in a number of cases alleged political favoritism in the choice of recipients[37]—but, though the long-term impact on poverty remained unclear, the programs did appear to be having a positive impact on the poorest sectors living in rural areas.[38]

The lack of a comprehensive development strategy had come to characterize post-Sandinista Nicaragua. Neither the market-based strategies of the three conservative administrations nor the rather modest state-supported initiatives of the Ortega administration offered a long-term solution to structural injustices. Meaningful fiscal reform, which might have included much needed tax and land reform, would have been incompatible with the neoliberal model and elite self-interest, and was not attempted by the new

Ortega government. Instead, the country became increasingly reliant on remittances—$740 million in 2007—to offset the costs of adjustment. According to one poll, as many as 60 percent of Nicaraguans were considering migrating abroad to solve their economic problems.[39] The fact that the young and educated constituted a growing segment of Nicaragua's migrants—more than two-thirds were under age twenty-nine, 41 percent had secondary education, and nearly 20 percent had some higher education[40]—could not help but have significant ramifications for the country's future. Twenty years of neoliberal policies had failed to build a country that could provide for the basic needs of its people.

NOTES

1. For a review of Chamorro's works and complete bibliographical citations, see Grafton Conliffe and Thomas W. Walker, "The Crucified Nicaragua of Pedro Joaquín Chamorro," *Latin American Research Review*, vol. 13, no. 3 (Fall 1978), pp. 183–188; and Grafton Conliffe and Thomas W. Walker, "The Literary Works of Pedro Joaquín Chamorro," *Caribbean Review*, vol. 7, no. 4 (October–December 1978), pp. 46–50.

2. Walker interview with Oscar Miranda, Sandinista Television System (SSTV), June 20, 1985.

3. For information about culture in the Nicaraguan Revolution, see David Craven, "The State of Cultural Democracy in Cuba and Nicaragua During the 1980s," *Latin American Perspectives*, vol. 17, no. 3 (Summer 1990), pp. 100–119.

4. United Nations, *1978 Statistical Yearbook* (New York: United Nations Publishing, 1979), p. 70.

5. World Bank, World Development Indicators, http://data.worldbank.org/indicator/SP.POP.GROW.

6. An anonymous informed source.

7. "Nicaragua: Sandinista Accusations of Reagan Destabilization," *Central America Report*, March 6, 1982, p. 70.

8. Amnesty International, for instance, stated outright that "reports of shootings of civilians and other deliberate brutality during the transfer were later shown to be false, and government medical and other civilian personnel assisted residents during the transfer." See Amnesty International, "Nicaragua Background Briefing: Persistence of Public Order Law Detentions and Trials" (London, 1982), p. 8. Ironically, the Reagan administration had painted quite a different picture, accusing the Sandinistas of wholesale human rights violations equivalent to those perpetrated by the

Nazis during the Second World War. For a discussion of how the Reagan administration misinformed the public on this issue, see Thomas W. Walker, "Nicaraguan-U.S. Friction: The First Four Years, 1979–1983," in *The Central American Crisis: Sources of Conflict and the Failure of U.S. Policy*, ed. Kenneth M. Coleman and George G. Herring (Wilmington, Del.: Scholarly Resources, 1985), pp. 183–184.

9. For a lengthy examination of this matter, see Inter-American Commission on Human Rights, Organization of American States, *Report on the Situation of Human Rights of a Segment of the Nicaraguan Population of Miskito Origin* (Washington, D.C.: OAS, 1984).

10. Salvador Garcia Babini and Juan Carlos Ocampo Zamora, "The Caribbean Coast: Independence or Desperation?" *Envío*, no. 340 (November 2009).

11. For excellent detail and analysis of the situation of women in the Nicaraguan Revolution, see Patricia Chuchryck, "Women in the Revolution," in *Revolution and Counterrevolution in Nicaragua*, ed. Thomas W. Walker (Boulder, Colo.: Westview Press, 1991).

12. Coauthor Wade interview with Marta María Blandón, director of Ipas Central America, July 2009.

13. CENIDH, *Derechos Humanos en Nicaragua 2007*, January 2008.

14. Jaime Wheelock Román, *Entre la crisis y la agresión: la Reforma Agraria Sandinista* (Managua: Editorial Nueva Nicaragua, 1985), p. 119.

15. Kent Norsworthy with Tom Barry, *Nicaragua: A Country Guide* (Albuquerque, N.M.: Inter-Hemispheric Education Resource Center, 1990), p. 80.

16. For more details about agrarian reform in Nicaragua, see Joseph R. Thome and David Kaimowitz, "Agrarian Reform," in *Nicaragua: The First Five Years*, ed. Thomas W. Walker (New York: Praeger, 1985), pp. 299–316.

17. For more information about these major social programs, see (1) Deborah Barndt, "Popular Education," (2) Thomas John Bossert, "Health Policy: The Dilemma of Success," (3) Reinaldo Antonio Téfel et al., "Social Welfare," (4) Harvey Williams, "Housing Policy," and (5) James E. Austin and Jonathon Fox, "Food Policy," in Walker, ed., *Nicaragua: The First Five Years*, pp. 347–422.

18. These statistics are from Austin and Fox, "Food Policy," p. 409. For an excellent book on food in Nicaragua, see Joseph Collins and Francis Moore Lappé, *What Difference Could a Revolution Make? Food and Farming in the New Nicaragua*, 2nd ed. (San Francisco: Institute for Food and Development Policy, 1985).

19. Previously illiterate individuals were ultimately reclassified as literate if they were able to pass a basic reading and writing test upon completing all twenty-three lessons in the literacy primer.

20. Kissinger Commission, *Report of the National Bipartisan Commission on Central America* (Washington, D.C.: U.S. Government Printing Office, 1984), p. 30.

21. Coauthor Walker personally viewed destroyed infrastructure of this type on various visits to the war zone throughout the late 1980s.

22. From the final statistics on the human cost of the war given to coauthor Walker by the Nicaraguan Ministry of the Presidency in January 1990.

23. From a Walker conversation with Reinaldo Antonio Téfel in Managua on June 27, 1990.

24. Walker interview with Francisco Ortíz of the Evangelical Committee for Developmental Aid (CEPAD) in León, Nicaragua, June 17, 1990.

25. Betsy Cohn and Patricia Hynds, "The Manipulation of the Religion Issue," in *Reagan Versus the Sandinistas: The Undeclared War on Nicaragua*, ed. Thomas W. Walker (Boulder, Colo.: Westview Press, 1987), p. 106.

26. "Education: UNO Goes to School," *Envío*, vol. 9, no. 111 (October 1990), pp. 12–15.

27. Ibid.

28. For details on this corruption, see articles in *Envío*, the monthly publication of the Jesuit University, and in the Managua daily, *La Prensa*, for 1999–2001.

29. Nitlapán-*Envío* Team, "A Predictable Disaster Competes with a Predicted Electoral Process," *Envío*, vol. 20, no. 241 (August 2001), p. 3.

30. "El Desarrollo humano en Nicaragua, 2000," www.undp.org.ni/idhnicaragua/pdf.htm, Capitulo 1, p. 18.

31. According to Grigsby and Perez, in terms of absolute numbers there were more families living in poverty and extreme poverty. See Arturo Grigsby and Francisco Pérez, "RuralStruc Program. Structural Implications of Economic Liberalization on Agriculture and Rural Development in Nicaragua," MAG/FOR/World Bank/NITLAPÁN, January 2007.

32. CENIDH, *Derechos Humanos en Nicaragua 2006*, January 2007, pp. 58 and 63.

33. UNDP, *Human Development Report 2009*.

34. Manuel Orozco, "Family Remittances to Nicaragua: Opportunities to Increase the Economic Contributions of Nicaraguans Living Abroad," a report commission by the U.S. Agency for International Development, February 7, 2003, www.thedialogue.org/PublicationFiles/remittances%20to%20nicaragua.pdf.

35. Coauthor Wade interview with Minister of National Politics Paul Oquist, July 2009.

36. Ibid.

37. See, for example, Paul Kester, "Zero Hunger: Development or Just Rain-drops?" *Envío*, no. 342 (January 2010).

38. For a thoughtful argument and rebuttal regarding the antipoverty programs, see Kathy Hoyt, "Report from a Fact-finding Trip to Nicaragua: Anti-Poverty Programs Make a Difference," *NACLA*, December 12, 2009, and Alejandro Gutiérrez, "The Disconcerting 'Success' of Nicaragua's Anti-Poverty Programs," *NACLA*, February 17, 2010.

39. José Adán Silva, "Young People Exiled by Poverty," Inter Press Service, October 19, 2009.

40. Ibid.

7

Government and Politics

A political system is not simply a matter of electoral procedures, constitutions, and governmental structures. Politics also involves the relationship between groups and classes and all other factors that impinge on the character of governmental output. For this reason, a narrow examination of the formal constitutional and structural characteristics of a government—especially in the Third World context—is frequently not only misleading but also essentially an empty intellectual exercise. This is certainly true for Nicaragua, particularly in the period before the FSLN victory in 1979.

THE PREREVOLUTIONARY SYSTEM

If one had been foolish enough to take seriously the constitutional formalities and stated objectives of the Nicaraguan government during the Somoza years, one would surely have come to the mistaken conclusion that Nicaragua was blessed with a modern democratic form of government that was pursuing praiseworthy developmental goals. According to the constitution, there were free elections, separation of powers, and a full gamut of explicitly guaranteed human rights. To ensure minority participation, the major opposition party was automatically awarded 40 percent of all seats in the legislature and minority representation on boards of government agencies along with judgeships. What is more, there were a variety of public agencies and institutions such as the Central Bank, the National Development Institute, the Nicaraguan Agrarian Institute, the Institute of Internal-External Commerce, and the Social Security Institute, which were ostensibly designed to cope with the problems faced by a modernizing society. The stated policies of the government were also impressive. The major expressed goal was to develop the country through the modernization and diversification of the economy. Accordingly, highly trained technocrats were given important roles in the development process and lofty five-year plans were issued and subsequently endorsed by lists of international agencies.

All of this, of course, was simply a facade. Government and politics under the Somozas were "of, by, and for" the privileged few. Democracy was nonexistent, corruption was elaborately institutionalized, and public policy consistently ignored the well-being of the majority of the population.

Nicaragua was a democracy in name only. Although there were constitutional provisions for the separation of power—with a bicameral legislature, an executive, and a judiciary—in reality, all power was concentrated in the hands of the president. The National Guard was the president's private army. His command over the Liberal party—which in turn dominated both houses of the legislature and all government agencies—meant that the president was, in fact, the only decision maker. Mandated minority participation served only to legitimize the system and to co-opt Conservative politicians. There was never any possibility that the opposition would come to power legally since elections were thoroughly rigged. During campaign periods, there was frequent censorship of the press and intimidation of opposition candidates. On election day, there was multiple voting by the pro-Somoza faithful, tampering with the ballot boxes, and, cleverest of all, the use of a translucent "secret" ballot that, even when folded, could easily be scrutinized by government election officials as it was deposited in the ballot box.

Given the hopelessly undemocratic character of elections under the Somozas, party organization and activity were shallow and essentially without meaning. The two major parties, Liberal and Conservative, were crusty relics of the nineteenth century. The original ideological differences between them had long since faded into insignificance. Both represented the interests of a small privileged minority and, by the middle of the twentieth century, both had been co-opted and emasculated by the Somoza system.

Officially, the Somozas were Liberals and their governments were Liberal administrations. In fact, however, throughout most of the period, the Liberal party was simply a cosmetic appendage to a system that depended on brute military force. One apparent exception occurred in the late 1950s and early 1960s when Luís Somoza—who enjoyed the trappings of democracy and party politics—encouraged the Liberal party to have a life of its own. In that period, new Liberal leaders emerged and there was some hope that they might turn into real presidential prospects. In the late 1960s, after the "election" of the less politically minded Anastasio Somoza Debayle, these hopes were quickly dashed. Independent upstarts left or were drummed out of the party as the dictator began to maneuver to perpetuate himself in power, and the Liberal party lapsed into its more traditional cosmetic role.

The official Conservative opposition played an even less dignified role. If the Liberal party was the neglected wife of the Somoza system, the Conservative party was its kept woman. Since the facade of democracy was so important to the Somozas, it was imperative that there always be an opposition to run against during elections. Enticed by personal bribes and/or lucrative opportunities inherent in mandated minority participation in Congress, the judiciary, and government agencies, the leaders of the Conservative party frequently agreed to provide a legitimizing opposition during the rigged elections. Even on those infrequent occasions when the main leaders of the Conservative party mustered the dignity to refuse to participate, the dictators were usually able to convince less important Conservatives to carry that party's banner to defeat.

There were a number of microparties during the Somoza period. A few of the more notable were the Independent Liberal party (PLI), composed of Liberals who, from 1944 on, chose to dissociate themselves from the parent party over the issue of Somoza's continuing dominance; the Nicaraguan Social Christian party (PSCN), formed by young Catholic intellectuals in 1957; and the Nicaraguan Socialist party (PSN), which was founded by local Communists in 1944.

One of the more interesting of the microparties was the Social Christian party.[1] Inspired by progressive papal encyclicals, lay Catholic humanism, and Christian Democratic ideas emanating from Europe, this party attempted to take advantage of Luís Somoza's somewhat more open attitude toward competitive political activity. Stressing the importance of platform, ideology, organization, and tactics, the Social Christians not only won a significant popular following, but also penetrated the labor movement and for a while came to dominate the national students' organizations. Though many young Social Christians freely admitted their admiration for the courage and audacity of FSLN guerrillas, they felt at that time that a peaceful, democratic solution might still be possible. When it became clear in the early 1970s that they were wrong, the more progressive members of the party split from the PSCN to form the Popular Social Christian party (PPSC), which espoused an increasingly revolutionary position.

Mass interest articulation through legal channels was also a fairly hopeless activity under the Somozas. Peasants and urban labor, for instance, had almost no input into the political system. Ignorant, illiterate, and geographically scattered, the peasantry and rural proletariat were subject to constant abuse by landowners and the National Guard. An agrarian reform program legislated in the early days of the Alliance for Progress had virtually no impact on the misery of the rural poor. From 1964 on, a private Social Christian–oriented organization—the Institute for Human Promotion (INPRHU)—did struggle to organize and raise the consciousness of the peasants, but in the face of government roadblocks, its efforts were largely ineffectual. In the end, clandestine activity proved to be the only viable alternative. In the late 1970s, the FSLN began organizing rural workers and landless peasants in workers' committees. In 1978, these were fused into a national organization—the Rural Workers' Association (ATC). In the following year, as the War of Liberation neared its successful conclusion, ATC-organized peasants made their contribution by digging trenches and felling huge trees across roadways to block troop movements and by maximizing the first post-Somoza harvest through the seizure and immediate cultivation of Somocista-owned lands in the newly liberated areas.

The urban worker was only slightly better off than his country cousin. The organized labor movement encompassed a small minority of all workers and was badly fragmented. In 1977, the major union organizations included the Marxist Independent General Confederation of Labor, with 12,000 members; the government-patronized General Confederation of Labor, with 8,000 to 10,000 members; the AFL-CIO-oriented Confederation of Labor Unity, with 7,000 members; and the Social Christian Confederation of Workers of Nicaragua, with 3,000 members. The right to strike, while formally enshrined in law, was so severely restricted that most of the many strikes that took place in the 1960s and 1970s were declared illegal. Collective bargaining was made all but impossible by Article 17 of the *Regulations of Syndical Associations*, which allowed the employer to fire, without explanation, any two leaders of the striking union. In the long run, the only viable option for urban workers, too, was to organize themselves clandestinely—again under FSLN leadership. Significantly, the urban insurrections—which took place almost exclusively in working-

Whispering greed: During a Somocista gala, Somoza Debayle (right) shares a confidence with his uncle, Luis "Tio Luz" Manuel Debayle, who, during his ten years as head of the national energy agency, is alleged to have misappropriated in excess of $30 million. (Photographer unknown)

class neighborhoods—turned out to be one of the most important ingredients in the overthrow of the dictatorship.

Not surprisingly, given the nearly complete absence of institutionalized popular input into the political system, the Somoza government was virtually oblivious to the interests of the ordinary Nicaraguan citizen. Lofty-sounding social programs—ostensibly concerned with public health, agrarian reform, low-income housing, education, social security, and the like—served mainly as devices to legitimize the system, attract foreign aid, employ the politically faithful, and diversify opportunities for the pilfering of public revenues. Very little of what the government spent actually trickled down to the people. With members of Somoza's family at the head of most government agencies, a large chunk of each agency's assets went directly to satisfy the family's greed. For instance, in the ten years in which he headed the National Institute of Light and Energy, Anastasio Somoza Debayle's uncle, Luis Manuel Debayle, allegedly siphoned off more than $30 million. Under the Somozas were layer upon layer of corrupt bureaucrats who were expected and, indeed, encouraged to help themselves. Honesty, a threat to the system, was discouraged.

Often a legalistic patina was applied to these misuses of public revenues. But the end result was that when the FSLN seized power in 1979, it had to cope with acute problems in health, education, housing, and welfare. To add insult to injury, the departing dictator and his accomplices, who had left barely $3 million in the public coffers, had saddled the new government with a whopping $1.6 billion foreign debt.[2]

THE REVOLUTIONARY SYSTEM

If the old political system had been "of, by, and for" a tiny privileged elite, the revolutionary system that replaced it was clearly based in and oriented toward the interests of the impoverished majority. Whereas democracy under the Somozas meant rigged elections, the empty rhetoric of corrupt elite-oriented parties, and the suppression of popular political participation, the new political system not only featured competitive internationally supervised elections but, more important, involved and depended upon the mobilized voluntary participation of hundreds of thousands of ordinary citizens. For the first time in Nicaraguan history, the impoverished majority came to have a voice and power in many aspects of the decision making that affected their lives. Not surprisingly, this seismic change in the orientation of politics and government in favor of the "have-nots" was alarming to many of the former "haves."

The Government of National Reconstruction, 1979–1985

The governmental system of revolutionary Nicaragua came into existence gradually over a period of years. At first, its informal but central element was the nine-person FSLN National Directorate (DN) drawn equally from the three former factions of the party. Until an elected government was inaugurated in January 1985, each branch of the formal government, though by no means powerless, existed at the pleasure of the DN, which had created it in the first place. The National Directorate in turn drew its strength from the legitimacy it had acquired through its leading role in the revolutionary victory, its control of the revolutionary armed forces, and the support of hundreds of thousands of civilians who made up the grassroots organizations that had developed during the insurrection. Within the DN, as earlier noted, decision making was based on consensus or near-consensus; during the entire period of Sandinista rule, open factional disputes were completely avoided, and none of the nine *comandantes* of 1979 either resigned or were replaced.

Nevertheless, in spite of its virtually unassailable political advantage, the FSLN chose, for practical reasons, to create a formal governmental structure that would encourage the participation not just of Sandinistas but of almost all other sectors in society as well. This decision was important since the new government needed the cooperation of a variety of groups. The Sandinistas knew that if they were going to preserve a mixed economy with a major role for the private sector, they would have to institutionalize participation by the various parties and interest groups associated with former privileged classes. They had no intention of allowing these minority groups enough political power to deflect or water down their revolution, but they did sincerely want to give them involvement in the system at least equivalent to their numerical weight in the population as a whole. Accordingly, all of the institutions that were created—the plural executive, the corporatively organized legislative branch, the ministries, and the judiciary—included non-Sandinistas as well as Sandinistas.

The executive branch originally consisted of a five-person Governing Junta of National Reconstruction (JGRN) containing two Conservatives, one pro-Sandinista intellectual, and two FSLN guerrilla veterans. Eventually, through resignation and reassignment, the JGRN was reduced to one Conservative and two Sandinistas. Junta member Daniel Ortega—also a member of the Sandinista Directorate—eventually became its head. All of the ministries except interior and defense were placed under the JGRN.

The legislative body, or Council of State, which was formally inaugurated in May 1980, employed a quasi-corporative system of representation. Virtually all political parties (with the exception of the Somoza branch of the Liberal party) and major pro- and anti-Sandinista interest organizations were assigned seats. Each grouping elected or appointed its own representatives. The size and composition of the council changed over time. Originally envisioned as having thirty-three members, it actually comprised forty-seven when inaugurated in 1980. The Council was eventually expanded to fifty-one before it was superseded by the elected National (Constituent) Assembly in January 1985. These increases reflected the emergence of new interest organizations and parties and the rise or decline of old ones. The traditional parties and interest organizations complained, with accuracy, that pro-Sandinista organizations were given a majority of seats. The Sandinistas responded by indicating, with equal accuracy, that

The FSLN National Directorate. From left to right: Luis Carrión, Víctor Tirado López, Carlos Nuñez, Humberto Ortega Saavedra, Tomás Borge, Bayardo Arce, Jaime Wheelock, Henry Ruiz, and Daniel Ortega Saavedra. (Photo courtesy of *Barricada*)

the traditional parties and organizations were actually overrepresented given the small percentage of the population made up of the classes for which they stood.

Changes also occurred in the functions of the Council. Instead of being limited, as originally proposed, to the approval or disapproval of Junta decisions without modifications, the Council had the right to initiate and/or modify legislation. In the words of its first president, *Comandante* Bayardo Arce, it had acquired a "colegislative" function.[3] It is interesting to note that, whereas in 1980–1981 the Junta initiated most bills before the Council (fifty-six as opposed to thirty-nine), the Council itself initiated the majority of bills in the 1982–1983 session (forty-four as opposed to sixteen).[4]

The judicial branch, in its turn, was composed of both regular courts and special tribunals. The regular court system was similar to that of other Latin American countries with habeas corpus and various levels of appeal. The members of these courts were lawyers coming from a variety of political backgrounds. Convictions were often overturned on appeal.

The more controversial special tribunals were set up to deal with emergency overloads of the judicial system. These tribunals were created immediately after the victory to try the thousands of National Guardsmen and Somocistas taken prisoner as the old system collapsed. As in the Nuremberg trials following the Second World War, there was an element of ex post facto justice. Nevertheless, no official executions occurred, the death penalty was abolished, and the maximum sentence was thirty years. Further, those individuals sentenced on the questionable charge of "illicit association" (for instance, being a member of the National Guard) were duly released when their three-year terms were up. Later, in April 1983, another type of tribunal, the "Popular Anti-Somocista Tribunals" (TPAs), was created to try cases related to the Contra War and suspected internal counterrevolutionary activity. The TPAs were criticized for not providing sufficient due process. Among other problems, although an appeals process was included within the tribunal system, there was no right to appeal through the regular judicial system.[5] On the other hand, to view this matter in perspective, we should note that *most* governments violate due process during times of national danger. Even Great Britain, normally considered one of the world's greatest democracies, routinely imposed prolonged imprisonment without trial in the case of suspected members of the Irish Republican Army.

The Sandinistas also moved to decentralize government and administration. At the time of the Triumph, a network of local governments known as Municipal Juntas for Reconstruction (JMRs) was elected in public assemblies. These three- or five-person bodies had the responsibility of coordinating local reconstruction efforts in cooperation with local grassroots organizations and with the departmental and national governments. However, the local governments, lacking authority and resources, found themselves heavily dependent on central government bureaucrats who often had little understanding of local problems. Negative feedback ultimately led the revolutionary government to draft a plan for regionalization and decentralization that was formally inaugurated on July 19, 1982. The country was then divided into six regions and three special zones, each of which had the authority to deal with all government functions. These nine entities were created in accordance with the differing demographic and economic characteristics of different parts of the country. As a result, local officials, instead of having to deal with an overloaded central bureaucracy, could coordinate their activities directly with regional officials familiar with the needs, problems, and assets of the region.

Groups and Power in the Early 1980s

The conduct of government in this period was made easier, less expensive, and more responsive to the people by the existence of a variety of volunteer

Grassroots mobilization and mass participation. (Above) Liberation theologist Teófilo Cabastrero (at right) takes notes as lay Catholic Delegates of the Word discuss their experiences in teaching the "social gospel" in rural Nicaragua. (Below) Leaders of the UNAG (National Union of [Small] Farmers and Ranchers) from the region around Estelí conduct an end-of-the-year meeting to assess their success and failure in meeting the goals they had set for themselves at the beginning of the year. (Photos by coauthor Walker)

In July 1979 members of the rebel militias pose at a checkpoint near the northern town of Condega. The makeshift uniforms and old M-1 weapon were fairly typical of the urban militias. (Photo by coauthor Walker)

grassroots organizations (*organizaciones de masa*). Eventually involving approximately half of the adult population, these included the Sandinista Defense Committees (CDSs), the Sandinista women's organization (AMNLAE), the Sandinista Youth (JS-19), the Rural Workers' Association (ATC), the Sandinista Workers' Central (CST), and the National Union of (Small) Farmers and Ranchers (UNAG).

The grassroots organizations, especially the neighborhood CDSs, were bitterly criticized by disgruntled Nicaraguans and detractors in the United States as being little more than vigilante committees or gangs of thugs (*turbas*) acting as mindless puppets of their Sandinista masters. Although there were occasional excesses—such as a few instances of disruption of opposition political activities and one brief occupation of fundamentalist Protestant church buildings—no overall pattern of behavior emerged that would justify in any way such an Orwellian picture of Sandinista Nicaragua.

On the contrary, the grassroots organizations, whose behavior was in fact normally orderly and correct, actually served numerous functions of crucial importance to the new society. One of these *was* vigilance. After all, the country was under attack. It was only fitting that the people for whom this revolution was being carried out would have the opportunity to defend it against subversion. In addition to helping block the formation of an internal "fifth column," the mass organizations (especially the CDSs) conducted *vigilancia revolucionaria*, a sort of neighborhood crime watch that spectacularly reduced the incidence of common violence and petty crime. Second, the grassroots organizations were also facilitators. Their role in mobilizing the enthusiastic voluntary participation of hundreds of thousands of Nicaraguans was an indispensable boost to the literacy crusade, health and housing programs, the organization of sports and cultural activities, the production and distribution of food, and the reactivation of the economy. Third, these organizations were vehicles for citizen input and participation. Through them hundreds of thousands of ordinary citizens learned how to hold meetings, elect leaders, debate issues, make collective decisions, and implement projects. Fourth, they frequently channeled feedback about common concerns to the government. For instance, demonstrations and other pressure from the ATC were clearly responsible for an important shift in government policy away from a heavy emphasis on state farms toward a policy of land distribution to peasant cooperatives and individual small-holders. Finally, these organizations played a crucial role in political socialization. All societies have ways of transmitting from generation to generation a common body of knowledge and attitudes toward national history, heroes, values, and principles. Through group activity and discussion, the new grassroots organizations helped replace old Somoza-era values with ones appropriate to a more sovereign, just, and humane society.

The Sandinista Armed Forces were also an important pillar of the new system. Forged in long years of difficult struggle against the Somozas, they were explicitly Sandinista and therefore very unlikely to stage a coup against their own government—a phenomenon quite common elsewhere in Latin America. During the years of guerrilla warfare and throughout the eighteen-month War of Liberation, the FSLN army was vastly outnumbered and outgunned by Somoza's U.S.-trained and -equipped National Guard. Numbering only a few hundred during the urban uprisings of September 1978, the regular FSLN forces had grown to only a few thousand by the beginning of the Final Offensive of June 1979. It is remarkable that one unit of this tiny force was able to launch the attack on Managua with only "approximately 125 weapons of war [FALs, M-1s, M-16s, Uzis, Galils, and the like] and ten light

A seventeen-year-old veteran—hero of the FSLN army—and a friend pose for coauthor Walker in November 1979. His Belgian FAL automatic rifle was the favorite weapon in the small regular guerrilla army.

machine guns and bazookas."[6] The FSLN won the war not because of its military superiority, but because it was convinced of the rightness of its cause and enjoyed the support of most Nicaraguans. The combination of a lean but well-trained and dedicated guerrilla army and massive urban insurgency was more than Somoza's corrupt and demoralized army could withstand.

At the time of the victory, the guerrilla army grew precipitously. In the final days of the war, many thousands of urban insurgents "joined" the FSLN army by simply "liberating" weapons and uniforms from the thousands of surrendering or fleeing guardsmen. This influx of raw, untrained soldiers was both a blessing and a problem. It allowed the new government to provide police and emergency services from the very start. Indeed, as coauthor Walker traveled through Nicaragua in the week following the victory, he was impressed by the organization, efficiency, and very real courtesy of the relatively untrained young people who were performing police and security functions. Yet there were problems. Whereas most of the veteran members of the FSLN army had been trained not only in military skills but also in the role of the new armed forces and the social mission of the revolution, the new volunteers had not. In the first year after the liberation, therefore, emphasis was placed on weeding out undisciplined riffraff and training the rest to be politically and socially conscious and humane guardians of the revolution. In regular training and during "criticism and self-criticism" sessions held in the evenings, the young men and women of the new armed forces were reminded that, in contrast to the hated National Guard, their role was to act as servants, friends, and protectors of the people.

In the first year, the FSLN's major military concern appears to have been to build a conventional military establishment, with standardized equipment, roughly equivalent to the military institutions of most other Central American countries. However, as noted earlier, the election of Ronald Reagan in November 1980 triggered a new type of military buildup in Nicaragua. Designed not only to contain a constantly growing U.S.-sponsored *contra* army but also to make a U.S. invasion so costly to the invader that it would, they hoped, not take place, this buildup moved in lockstep with the escalating U.S. threat.[7]

In the ensuing years, the Sandinista Armed Forces proved highly successful in containing the *contra* invasion. This was so, in part, because the Sandinista Army and the Sandinista Militias had a keen sense of what they were fighting for and whom they were fighting against. Although Reagan would label the *contras* "Freedom Fighters," their brutal behavior toward civilians made them appear to be little more than a resuscitated version of Somoza's old National Guard. The fact that, as of 1985, forty-six of the forty-eight officers of the Nicaraguan Democratic Forces (FDN—the main *contra* group) were former Somoza National Guard officers did little to dispel that impression.[8]

Although the major functions of the Sandinista Armed Forces were national defense and internal security, they also played a role in political socialization. In undergoing military training and serving in their country's armed forces, hundreds of thousands of men and women of all ages received, at one time or another, additional exposure to the values, principles, and goals of the Sandinista Revolution—perhaps one of the reasons the elite groups were so bitterly opposed to the military draft instituted in 1983.

Although the Sandinistas enjoyed a tremendous political advantage in post-Somoza Nicaragua, they were by no means unopposed. Indeed, they faced tenacious resistance from several quarters—a resistance wielded more by certain interest groups than by formal political parties. The non-Sandinista parties that originated or reemerged during this period lacked leadership, organizational capacity, and, most important, grassroots support. On the right were the Nicaraguan Social Christian party (PSCN), the Social Democratic party (PSD), and the Constitutional Liberal party (PLC). In the center were the Democratic Conservative party (PCD), the Popular Social Christian party (PPSC), and the Independent Liberal party (PLI). To the left of these, and of the Sandinistas, were the Nicaraguan Socialist party (PSN), the Marxist-Leninist Popular Action Movement (MAP-ML), and the Nicaraguan Communist party (PCN). Closely attached to several of the opposition parties were the small labor unions once tolerated by Somoza: the AFL-CIO-oriented Confederation of Labor Unity (CUS) and the Social Christian Confederation of Workers of Nicaragua (CTN).

At first, party opposition came from the right and part of the left, whereas some of the center and left supported the government. The PPSC, the PLI, and the PSN actually joined the FSLN in a pro-government coalition, the Revolutionary Patriotic Front (FPR); and the PCD, while not part of that coalition, furnished one member of the last Junta, Rafael Córdoba Rivas. However, one of the effects of the 1984 electoral campaign was that, although the parties of the right—grouped in something called the Ramiro Sacasa Democratic Coordinating Committee (CDRS, or *la Coordinadora* for short)—abstained in an effort to delegitimize the process, the pro-government coalition disintegrated and each member party, along with the PCD, the MAP-ML, and the PCN, ran their own candidates in opposition to the FSLN. The bitter invective that came out of that campaign made it impossible for the old FPR coalition to ever be resurrected.

The most important opposition, however, came from the conservative hierarchy of the Catholic Church and from the business community. The Catholic Church in Sandinista Nicaragua—never very unified even before the revolution—became badly divided thereafter. On the one hand, a number of lower-level clergy, taking seriously the idea of a preferential option for the poor, accepted posts in the new government (including the Ministries of Culture and Foreign Affairs and the directorship of the 1980 National Literacy Crusade) or continued to work closely with poor communities. At the same time, most of the hierarchy, led by Archbishop Miguel Obando y Bravo, apparently fearing that their authority—*magisterium*—might be undermined by the movement toward participatory democracy within both the church and Nicaraguan society, recoiled from the revolutionary process.

Posters and murals as vehicles of political and social education. A mural (upper left) depicts the popular insurrection while a billboard (lower left) states proudly, "Today the new dawn ceased to be an illusion" (the portraits are of Sandino and Carlos Fonseca). Another billboard (upper right) stresses the virtues of breast-feeding, proclaiming, "Your milk is irreplaceable and it arrives with love." (Photos by coauthor Walker)

Although the government guaranteed freedom of religion and even tried to demonstrate its respect for Nicaraguan religiosity by promoting religious celebrations, inviting a visit by the pope, and retaining "In God We Trust" on newly minted Sandinista coins, Obando and other bishops moved to distance the Catholic Church from the revolution. They attempted unsuccessfully to force all clergy out of public office; they arranged for the removal from the country of many pro-revolutionary foreign clergy and for the reassignment of similarly minded native priests; they denounced popularly oriented church organizations; and eventually they even managed to get many clergy to refuse to conduct burial services for members of the Sandinista Armed Forces killed in clashes with the *contras*. Given the intense religious identification of the Nicaraguan people, the Catholic Church remained an important political factor.

The other important traditional power contender was the private sector. After 1979, its major political instrument was COSEP. The FSLN's decision to preserve a mixed economy in which the bulk of production would remain in the hands of the private sector automatically meant that COSEP and the class it represented retained some political, as well as significant economic, power. This situation created important political strains in revolutionary Nicaragua. Although the government made significant concessions to the moneyed elite that included the provision of reactivation loans, an intermittent effort at dialogue, and the inclusion of COSEP in the Council of State, much of the private sector—convinced from the start that "communism" was just around the corner—was openly hostile in political matters and only grudgingly cooperative in the economic realm. Its political behavior—opposition to the literacy crusade, hostility toward the mass organizations, and insistence on the "depoliticization" of the military— reflected a desire to return Nicaragua to the prerevolutionary status quo.

The 1984 Elections

The system of national government that existed during the first five years was a temporary one, designed simply to carry Nicaragua through a difficult period of transition until more permanent institutions could be devised. Even prior to their victory, the Sandinistas had indicated that their country's governmental institutions would ultimately be based on free elections. In the wake of the Triumph, they talked of holding elections almost immediately. At that point, opposition groups complained that to do so would be unfair given Sandinista popularity in the afterglow of the victory. At the close of the Literacy Crusade in August 1980, the Sandinistas announced that elections would be held in 1985. Then, and over the next three years, the opposition complained that 1985 was too distant and that the Sandinistas were, in fact, betraying their promise to hold elections. This theme was reiterated by candidate, and then president-elect, Ronald Reagan in 1980 and by spokespersons for the new U.S. administration throughout the following three years.

In the meantime, virtually no public notice was given in the United States to the methodical and careful preparations for the promised election then under way in Nicaragua. Commissions were sent to various parts of the world (including Western Europe and the United States) to study party laws and electoral procedures. Following consultation among all parties and groups willing to engage in dialogue, a Parties Law and an Electoral Law were drafted and enacted. In December 1983, the Directorate announced that the election would be moved to 1984, and the following month the exact date (November 4) was set. This time, the Nicaraguan opposition and official Washington decried the fact that the election—still ten months away—was being scheduled too soon. There would be little time, they argued, for the opposition to organize an effective campaign. The whole affair would be a "Soviet-style farce."

In an apparent attempt to make this description of things come true and, hence, to delegitimize the election, the Reagan administration then proceeded to interfere extensively in the Nicaraguan electoral process. As noted in Chapter 3, CIA "asset" Arturo Cruz engaged in a highly publicized cat-and-mouse game in which he went to Nicaragua, held political rallies, and set "conditions" for formal participation, but never actually registered as a candidate in spite of the fact that many of his conditions were met and the deadline for candidate registration was extended twice on his behalf.

Meanwhile U.S. officials in Nicaragua were working feverishly behind the scenes to cajole, counsel, pressure, and, reportedly, bribe the candidates of the six opposition parties that were formally registered in the election to withdraw.[9] Their efforts were not very successful. The PLI presidential candidate, Virgilio Godoy, withdrew too late to be legally removed from the ballot, and last-minute splits within the PCD over the issue of participation only marginally weakened that party's involvement. In the end, the conclusion of impartial and authoritative election observer delegations—such as those sent by the British Parliament and House of Lords, the Irish Parliament, the Dutch Government, the Socialist International (the organization of Western European Social Democratic parties), and the U.S.-based Latin American Studies Association—was that the election had been competitive and meaningful.[10]

These international observers also agreed that the process through which the votes had been cast and counted on election day was beyond reproach. The Nicaraguan electoral law, as previously noted, drew heavily from Western European practices. The government had been given extensive direct technical assistance by members of the Swedish Electoral Commission.

In addition, the Nicaraguan elections clearly benefited from the fact that the unsavory example of the 1984 Salvadoran elections was still fresh in people's minds. In El Salvador, citizens were required by law to vote. Their citizen identification cards, which Salvadorans were required to carry at all times, were stamped at the voting place to indicate that they had, indeed, voted. Furthermore, ballots were individually and sequentially numbered and, like those used in Nicaragua under the Somozas, were translucent so that even when folded they did not ensure a secret vote. Moreover, some voting booths were not fully curtained and all ballot boxes were made of clear acrylic plastic. Finally, there were relatively few voting places. While this fact made for highly filmable scenes of long lines of Salvadorans supposedly registering their faith in the "democratic process," it also caused considerable unnecessary inconvenience, chaos, and numerous irregularities.

In Nicaragua, *all* of these election-day defects were avoided. Voting was not obligatory. There was no stamping of citizen ID cards (Nicaragua had no national system of identification) or any other lasting way of distinguishing between voters and nonvoters. All ballots were identical and featured dark bands across the back of the section in which voters were to mark their "X." All voting places had curtains from floor to ceiling. The ballot boxes were made of wood. And there were 3,892 voting places conveniently located throughout the country. Many Nicaraguans did line up before the polls opened, but for the most part they did not have to wait long after the voting began. The process coauthor Walker witnessed as part of the LASA Observer Delegation (going unescorted, unannounced, and at random to a number of polling places) was orderly and clean.

When asked by the LASA delegation if the United States were not applying a double standard in its evaluation of the 1984 elections in El Salvador and Nicaragua, a U.S. diplomat replied in a pique: "The United States is not obliged to apply the same standard of judgment to a country whose government is avowedly hostile to the U.S. as for a country, like El Salvador, where it is not. These people [the Sandinistas] could bring about a situation in Central America which could pose a threat to U.S. security. That allows us to change our yardstick."[11]

There are some superficially valid criticisms of the Nicaraguan elections, however. First, although censorship of the printed media during the campaign period was drastically reduced, it was not completely eliminated. And there were instances in which angry pro-Sandinista crowds—critics called them *turbas* (mobs)—disrupted opposition political rallies. However, it should be noted that what *was* published in *La Prensa* was bitterly and consistently critical of the Sandinistas and that a half hour on television and forty-five minutes on Sandinista radio were set aside free of charge at prime time every evening during the electoral period for uncensored comment and campaign speeches by opposition parties and candidates. Additional time was also available for purchase. Moreover, the internationally hyped disruptions of opposition meetings by Sandinista *turbas* actually occurred in only "five instances out of some 250 rallies during the campaign period; that is, [they] did not constitute a pattern of activity but [were], rather, the exception."[12]

In the end, as noted earlier, 75 percent of the Nicaraguan electorate chose to vote even though no one was obliged or intimidated to do so; only 6 percent of those who voted spoiled their ballots, although that would have been an excellent way of anonymously registering opposition; and 63 percent of all voters (67 percent of those casting valid ballots) voted Sandinista, even though there were three opposition parties each to the right and the left of the FSLN. By any objective measure, then, the Sandinistas had won a clean, honest, *landslide* victory.

The Elected Revolutionary Government: 1985–1990

The elections gave Nicaragua a president (Daniel Ortega), a vice president (Sergio Ramírez), and a ninety-six-person National (Constituent) Assembly. Inaugurated in January 1985, all elected officials were to hold office for six years unless the Assembly decided otherwise.

The National Assembly had a variety of functions, but clearly the most important was to produce a constitution. Contrary to the conventional wisdom prevailing in the United States, this would not be a matter of simply rubber-stamping an FSLN-prepared document. The people who had designed the

172

Voter education posters produced by the Supreme Electoral Council. The very similar steps for casting a secret ballot are depicted in posters from the 1984 (facing page) and the 1990 (above) electoral periods. A third poster (right) urges voters during the 1990 campaign to "respect the opinions of others." "Nicaragua," it states, "is a country of high ethical and moral values. In the present electoral campaign we should be an example of civic rectitude and respect the country's laws."

electoral law had deliberately selected a Western European system of proportional representation that tended to overrepresent minority parties. In addition, they had included a provision whereby all losing presidential candidates would get seats in the Assembly. The end result was that, while the Sandinistas got sixty-one seats, the opposition parties got a substantial thirty-five (PCD, fourteen; PLI, nine; PPSC, six; PSN, two; PCN, two; MAP-ML, two). This meant that the FSLN had just barely the 60 percent necessary to pass the constitution. Furthermore, the same practical considerations that had caused the Sandinistas to pursue dialogue, feedback, and pluralism during the government of National Reconstruction were very much present as the constitution was being written.

It took a full two years and one of the most rigorous, open, and consultative processes in the history of constitution writing to produce the Nicaraguan Constitution of 1987.[13] For about a year, the National Assembly worked to produce a first draft. Subcommittees—in which minority opposition parties were deliberately overrepresented—were set up to deal with different subject areas. Heated debate developed on a variety of issues. In 1986, an early draft was subjected to a process of domestic and international scrutiny and review. In what was dubbed "the National Consultation" (Consulta Nacional), seventy-eight "open meetings" (*cabildos abiertos*)—organized according to geographical region or interest identification (women, labor, small farmers, Christians, the military, etc.)—were held throughout Nicaragua to elicit feedback. As this process was taking place, large multiparty delegations from the Assembly went to various countries to seek expert advice on the draft constitution. For instance, at a National Conference on the Nicaraguan Constitution (cosponsored by Rutgers University, the City University of New York, the New York University Law School, and others), hundreds of prominent authorities on U.S. constitutional law, human rights, and Nicaraguan affairs organized into workshops on eleven principal themes, meeting for three days to examine and criticize that document.

When all of the comments and suggestions from the national and international consultations were gathered, the original document underwent extensive rewriting and, in January 1987, the final version was formally promulgated. Though it drew heavily on the legal traditions of Western Europe and the United States, the new basic law was also very *nica* in that it was clearly in tune with the social, cultural, and economic characteristics of Nicaragua. For instance, though most Sandinistas had wanted a purely secular document, the constitution that was finally produced bowed to the deep religiosity of the Nicaraguan people by including reference in the Preamble to God (*"DIOS"*) in full capital letters.

Like the U.S. Constitution, that of Nicaragua formalized the system of separation of powers and checks and balances between legislative, executive, and judicial branches, which had been emerging during the government of National Reconstruction. But reflecting its Latin setting, the Nicaraguan Constitution also formalized a fourth coequal governmental body found in many of the region's constitutions, the electoral branch. The Supreme Electoral Council was to have full authority and autonomy in all matters related to the conduct of free periodic elections.

According to the 1987 constitution, general elections were to take place every six years. Since the first had occurred in 1984, the next would come in 1990. Accordingly, the National Assembly now found itself faced with the task of writing new party and electoral laws that would make possible the implementation of that election. By late 1988, the required legislation had been produced and passed. Not unlike the laws that governed the 1984 election, the 1988 parties and electoral laws were among the fairest and most progressive in Latin America. Nevertheless, Washington and a segment of the Nicaraguan opposition maintained, as they had in 1984, that these laws were a blueprint for totalitarianism. Accordingly, anxious to convince the U.S. Congress to end all aid to the *contras* and to ensure that all significant elements of the opposition participate in the 1990 election, the Nicaraguan government agreed to modify the election law in 1989. Among other things, these changes allowed for even more free and uncensored TV and radio time for opposition programming and (something that would never be tolerated in most democracies, including the United States) the foreign financing of participating candidates, parties, and coalitions. Finally, in early August, after a marathon, nationally televised bargaining session, all of the opposition parties agreed not only to participate in the election but also to call for a demobilization of the *contras*.

The *contras* were not disbanded. Indeed, as noted earlier, their presence in Nicaragua was increased during the campaign period. Even so, the election went ahead. The registration of voters was accomplished on four consecutive Sundays in October and the campaign leading to the election of February 25, 1990, took place in the ensuing months. This time Washington would be satisfied with the results and, hence, the process itself.

Groups and Power in the Late 1980s

The outcome of the 1990 elections was less a reflection of growth in the strength and organization of the opposition than it was a product of the decline of certain aspects of Sandinista strength and an attempt by an electorate to bring change. Although the FSLN leadership, even in the late 1980s, could rely on the state apparatus, a powerful military, a segment of the media, and the most powerful party organization in the country, it had gradually lost its ability to mobilize support from an increasingly desperate grassroots base. Some grassroots organizations such as the National Union of Farmers and Ranchers (UNAG) continued to maintain membership and generally to support the FSLN. But others, such as the Sandinista Defense Committees (CDSs) in urban neighborhoods and the National Women's Association, collapsed spectacularly as members became increasingly annoyed with the top-down tasking by an embattled party and state or found themselves so pressed with making a living that they no longer felt they had time for community activities. Attempts by the legendary FSLN *Comandante* Omar Cabezas in 1988 and 1989 to reform, depoliticize, and, hence, resuscitate the CDSs under a new label, the Communal Movement, were to little avail.

Certain opposition-dominated institutions and groups, such as the Catholic Church hierarchy, the opposition daily *La Prensa*, the right-wing business organization COSEP, and Somoza-era labor unions, did act as irritants and instruments of counterrevolutionary propaganda throughout the late 1980s. Apparently financed heavily by the United States through the CIA and the National Endowment for Democracy,[14] each of these did what it could to undermine and discredit the revolutionary government. Church leaders such as Cardinal Miguel Obando y Bravo and Bishop Pablo Antonio Vega denounced the alleged (but essentially undocumented) persecution of religion by the Sandinistas, made seditious statements, and effectively lobbied for aid to the *contras*.[15] In addition to publishing imaginative and often quite irresponsible allegations about the Sandinistas,[16] Violeta Chamorro's *La Prensa* studiously ignored the impact of U.S. economic and military aggression while consistently placing the blame for the country's economic woes squarely on the shoulders of the revolutionary government. Echoing these allegations, COSEP worked tirelessly to prevent *concertación* (negotiation and cooperation) and obstruct economic recovery. And the opposition labor unions promoted strikes, which further aggravated a grave economic crisis.

On occasion, the government struck back by expelling seditious or subversive priests, closing *La Prensa* for more than a year in 1986–1987, and harassing or temporarily arresting some COSEP and opposition union leaders. Under international law, much of this was acceptable for a country under a state of siege. But repressive reaction, however mild or provoked, only tended to confirm Washington's portrayal of the Sandinistas as totalitarian.

Even so, there was practically no growth in the organizational capacity or membership of the opposition parties during this period. In fact, badly fragmented in 1984, the opposition splintered even further during the late 1980s. Each of the major party tendencies—conservative, liberal, social Christian, and communist—split into a variety of warring splinter parties. By 1989, these had been joined by additional new parties such as the Atlantic coast indigenous party Yatama and the Central American Unity Party (PUCA) to bring the total number of opposition microparties to more than twenty. Few of these had an organizational infrastructure that reached much beyond the major cities of the country. In the end, the UNO coalition of fourteen microparties—hastily welded together and micromanaged by the United States in mid-1989—won the 1990 election not because of superior organizational capacity or the grassroots support of a vast party membership but rather because the Nicaraguan people apparently felt that voting for UNO was the only way to bring the U.S. military and economic aggression to an end.

GOVERNMENT AND POLITICS AFTER 1990

How does one characterize the period that had elapsed from the Sandinista defeat in 1990 to the time this was being written in 2010? As described in the previous chapter, a dramatic reversal of Sandinista social policy and a real decline in the human condition of most Nicaraguans took place. Even so, at first at least, due to the governmental institutions created in the 1980s, the country was considerably more democratic, and its citizens markedly freer than in the Somoza era. Politics, though frequently nasty, brutish, and corrupt, were much more competitive than they had been prior to the Sandinista victory of 1979. Eventually, however, reasonable negotiation over political differences morphed into self-seeking pact making as the very institutions of the rule of law created under the Sandinistas were corrupted into mere instruments of the country's two major *caudillos*. Ironically, for anyone familiar with the history of Nicaragua, this was nothing new. There was a certain déjà vu between Ortega's pact making with his weaker adversary and Somoza family pact making with some corrupt Conservatives.

As noted earlier, the nature of the basic democratic institutions created during the Sandinista Revolution was the subject of great debate and bargaining early in the post-Sandinista period. Although both Chamorro and Alemán loathed the Sandinistas, they quickly found that the FSLN controlled a large enough bloc of votes in the legislature and exercised sufficient influence in society that it would be difficult to govern without making deals with them. Consequently, "pacts" became a hallmark of the period.

During the Chamorro administration, much of the deal making and institutional modification seemed reasonable since it expanded consensus on the rules of the game without threatening democratic institutions.[17] Early on, the Supreme Court was expanded to include greater representation for non-Sandinistas. By the mid-1990s, a new military protocol was enacted, bringing that institution under greater civilian control, and a number of constitutional reforms—including a prohibition on the reelection of the president and a strengthening of the legislature's budgetary powers—were implemented. The only major unfortunate institutional modification during this early period was the last-minute tinkering with the membership and rules governing the fourth branch of government, the Supreme Electoral Council (Consejo Supremo Electoral, CSE), which took place just before the 1996 elections. This, as noted earlier, led to dramatic irregularities in vote counting in districts under newly appointed Liberal officials.

The pact making of the Alemán period represented a far greater threat to Nicaragua's infant democratic institutions. Motivated by a desire to protect and promote both personal and party interests, the country's two leading *caudillos*, Ortega and Alemán, met privately in the late 1990s to hammer out a major pact that was passed into law by the FSLN/PLC legislative majority early in 2000. As a result, the Supreme Court, the Office of the Comptroller General, and the Supreme Electoral Council were all packed with FSLN/PLC partisans.

While these maneuvers significantly undermined Nicaragua's democratic institutions, they did not completely destroy them. As we noted, the elections of 2001 and 2006, though designed in advance to favor the two major parties, were relatively clean procedurally. And in 2002, newly inaugurated President Enrique Bolaños was able to use the legal system to pursue Alemán and other individuals in his corrupt administration.

The period from 2007 onward, however, witnessed the further erosion of democratic institutions as Ortega extended his control over the judiciary, electoral commission, and civil society. Municipal governments, once heralded by the FSLN as a hallmark of autonomy, were increasingly under attack as several FSLN and Liberal mayors were dismissed by city councils on specious grounds, giving the FSLN central government greater control over local government.[18]

Governmental Institutions

Odd as it may sound, the Nicaraguan security forces—military and police—were among the most respected public institutions in post-1990 Nicaragua and the last to be tinkered with by that country's politicians. The army constituted one of these pivotal institutions. During the cold war, local security institutions had been used by the United States as an instrument to control Latin American states and societies.[19] Throughout the hemisphere, hundreds of thousands of civilians had been arrested and murdered or disappeared by U.S.-trained military and police establishments in an effort to silence opposition to anticommunist dictatorships.[20] Not surprisingly, the Sandinistas did not want this to happen in Nicaragua after they left power in 1990. Accordingly, there was considerable hard bargaining between them and their opposition over the future of what had been called the Sandinista Army and Sandinista Police. Although the word *Sandinista* was dropped from both titles and the size of the army was drastically reduced, Daniel Ortega's brother Humberto was allowed to stay on as head of that body for several years—thus ensuring that it could not be used as an instrument to repress Sandinistas. In 1994, a new Military Code was hammered out in the National Assembly giving the president more control over the military.

In 2002, the issue of the political neutrality of the military resurfaced. Early that year, some Nicaraguan military personnel began training at the Western Hemisphere Institute for Security Cooperation (WHISC) at Fort Benning, Georgia.[21] Formerly the School of the Americas (SOA), this institution had the dubious reputation of having trained many of Latin

America's worst human rights violators. Revelations in 1997 indicated that at least some of that training involved manuals featuring instructions in the techniques of state-sponsored terror.[22] The new training at WHISC—the first since the Sandinista Revolution had interrupted SOA training of Somoza's infamous National Guard in 1979—worried many Nicaraguans.

Though the training continued, the military's political neutrality and reasonably good human rights behavior did not seem to be significantly affected. Remarkably, both the police and military were still very popular even in the second decade of post-1990 Nicaragua. An opinion poll conducted in 2009 showed that great or moderate confidence in the military had actually grown from 80.7 percent in the first year of the Bolaños administration to 87.9 percent in Ortega's third year. For the National Police the figures were 69.4 percent and 79.4 percent. Granted, this latter jump may have been due in part to Bolaños's 2006 appointment of Aminta Granera, a former Catholic novitiate turned Sandinista guerrilla fighter, as head of the National Police. As of December 2009, she was the most popular public figure in the entire country. Meanwhile, for comparison, approval of the Supreme Court had slumped from 85 percent to 39.8 percent in the same period—more in line with that of other governmental institutions.[23]

Sadly, by 2010, even the integrity of the security forces was under attack by the Ortega government. In July, riot control police forcibly removed ALN mayor Hugo Barquero from the municipal building in Boaco. Barquero, who had been accused of mismanagement, resisted removal from his office for a week after the FSLN and PLC-dominated City Council dismissed him. His removal apparently took place in spite of the fact that Granera, who had been stubbornly independent in other instances, had promised it would not.[24]

Parties

During the Somoza period, political parties had been stunted by the undemocratic character of the system. Even the ruling Liberal party lacked real importance since the Somozas ruled through the military and rigged elections. The leaders of the traditional Conservative party were easily co-opted to provide the appearance of democratic opposition. And third parties such as the Social Christians and Socialists, though occasionally serious in their organizational efforts, stood no chance of winning even a modicum of power. Based on the changes implemented by the Sandinistas in the 1980s, however, party competition in the 1990s and early twenty-first century was much more rigorous. Now, instead of facade "competition" between the traditional Liberals and Conservatives, there was real competition between the Sandinistas (FSLN) and anti-Sandinistas (mainly Liberals). The emergence of this two-party system was part natural and part forced. In major elections, voters tended to desert minor parties to vote pro- or anti-Sandinista. It is not that voters preferred only the two major parties. Indeed, the behavior of Daniel Ortega in clinging to party leadership and in making pacts with Alemán, on the one hand, and Alemán's corruption, on the other, clearly tarnished the images of both parties. However, when the moment of truth came, few voters wanted to "throw away" their vote. In addition, as noted earlier, the emergence of this two-party system was also forced to some extent by changes in electoral laws resulting from the Ortega-Alemán pact of late 1999 that were designed to eliminate third parties.

The end result was something approaching a two-party system featuring the FSLN and the PLC. In one sense, it was rigorously competitive. In another, it was not—since the U.S. government would repeatedly demonstrate its willingness to pressure the Nicaraguan electorate into voting anti-Sandinista. This is not to say that the Sandinistas—with their increasingly unpopular perennial candidate Ortega—did not handicap themselves. However, it is almost certain that overt U.S. threats and pressure went a long way in shaping the electoral outcomes of 1990, 1996, and 2001. The fact that U.S. threats failed in 2006 was due largely to changes in the electoral laws and the schism within the PLC.

Pact making and the resultant two-party system were accompanied by significant changes within the FSLN and PLC, all of which increased the power and prominence of the party *caudillos*—Ortega and Alemán.

Important changes occurred in the FSLN following their loss in the 1990 election—a shock for many in the party. Daniel Ortega emerged as the dominant power within the party, using his popularity at the base to control party congresses—expelling alternative voices or causing them to leave the party. While the FSLN of the 1980s had been governed by a multiperson Directorate that ruled by consensus, the party after 1990 was increasingly run by one *caudillo*, Ortega, and his wife, Rosario Murillo. By the twenty-first century, the vast majority of the original top leadership of the FSLN had left the party. As of 2010, of the original nine on the Directorate, only Ortega, Tomás Borge, and Bayardo Arce were still in the FSLN.

The emergence of the Sandinista Renovation Movement (*Movimiento de Renovacion Sandinista*, or MRS) in 1995 was a direct response to the increasingly autocratic nature of the FSLN. Founded by former vice president Sergio Ramírez, it became the political expression of the anti-pact left and included some of the most prominent faces of *Sandinismo*, including Gioconda Belli, Henry Ruiz, and Dora María Téllez. There were also significant differences over strategy and the role of the FSLN as a revolutionary party in a postconflict context, with Ramírez and others arguing that the left needed to develop an electoral party with broad national appeal. Despite these differences, the MRS maintained an electoral alliance with the FSLN in the 2001 presidential and 2000 and 2004 municipal elections. But in 2005, when former Managua mayor Herty Lewites announced that he would run against Ortega in the FSLN's presidential primary, he was expelled from the party. Instead, Lewites ran as the candidate of the MRS Alliance with another newly formed party of prominent Sandinistas, the Movement to Rescue Sandinismo (Movimento por el Rascate del Sandinismo).[25]

The right also became divided over the pact—especially during the Bolaños administration. His pursuit of Alemán's prosecution forced Bolaños out of the party—and nearly out of office. He formed the Alliance for the Republic (APRE) in 2004 with others from the PLC and PC (Conservative party). In 2005, opponents of Alemán from within the PLC, including Eduardo Montealegre, founded the Nicaraguan Liberal Alliance (ALN). Montealegre was dismissed from the ALN by the CSE over allegations of corruption in the CENI scandal. The electoral alliance between the PLC and Montealegre's new movement *Vamos con Eduardo* in the 2008 municipal elections ended in defeat for Montealegre, some suggested by design.[26] Even from house arrest, Alemán remained the right's most powerful politician and, after his sentence was overturned, the Liberal boss quickly announced his intention to seek the presidency in 2011.

Pact making and increasing corruption had a significant, negative impact on the public perception of parties. Although Nicaraguans remained more engaged in political party life than other Latin Americans,[27] relatively few expressed confidence in the country's political parties. A 2008 survey revealed that Nicaraguans exhibited the third-lowest level of trust in political parties in the Americas, with less than one-quarter expressing trust.[28] As a result, no party could dominate the electoral field outright, although the FSLN had the largest number of sympathizers—about a third of the electorate.[29] This necessitated electoral alliances, such as those described above, for the FSLN and the PLC. These alliances often resulted in strange bedfellows, uniting former enemies to defeat current ones. For example, Yatama, which governed the RAAN from 1990 to 1996, worked with the FSLN in 2002 to reclaim power from the PLC. Yatama then supported Ortega in 2006 in exchange for promises on progress toward regional autonomy.

Groups and Nongovernmental Institutions

Perhaps the brightest aspect to the post-1990 scene was the democratic, constructive role played by institutions and groups independent of both the parties and the government. One of these was the media. Frequently attacked or repressed during the Somoza period and periodically censured under state-of-siege conditions during Sandinista rule, the media were given great freedom after 1990. In this period, a variety of newspapers, radio stations, and TV channels—expressing widely different points of view—vied with each other to catch the public's attention. Sensationalism and heavy-handed political slant were commonplace. But there were also moments of high-quality, professional journalism. True, there were attacks on the media during the Ortega administration.[30] But generally the media still featured vigorous debate about the issues of the day, and politicians and government officials were constantly the objects of close scrutiny and scathing exposés.

The Catholic Church—influential during both the Somoza and Sandinista periods—continued to play a major political role in the two decades after 1990. Though it had challenged Somoza in the 1970s and though some of its lower-level personnel had pursued liberation theology and supported Sandinista programs in the 1980s, by the mid-1980s the church was very much under the control of its conservative leader, Cardinal Miguel Obando y Bravo. During the Chamorro and Alemán administrations, it virtually ran the important Ministry of Education and exercised a rightward pull on public policy in general. In the 1996 and 2001 elections, Cardinal Obando was unabashed in his public support of Alemán and Bolaños. In 2006, however, Cardinal Obando did an abrupt about-face, throwing his support to Ortega after the FSLN pledged to support a ban on therapeutic abortion. That said, much of the rest of the church continued to oppose Ortega.[31]

This period was particularly interesting in that it was a time of an increasingly important role for grassroots associations and domestic and international nongovernmental organization (NGOs). Though these had existed

The Siamese twins. Ortega (right) to Alemán (left), after using the 1999 pact to devastate the country's democratic institutions: "Wait, Fatty, we've left something standing." The pillar left standing is identified as "the independent press." (This cartoon, which also appeared in *La Prensa* on January 19, 2000, is reproduced here with the permission of the cartoonist, Manuel Guíllen.)

under the Somozas and had flourished in the early 1980s under the Sandinistas, they gained new importance in the 1990s.

As noted in Chapter 3, grassroots organizations—representing women, students, labor, agricultural workers, and neighborhood dwellers—that had existed clandestinely or semilegally in the Somoza period were encouraged and supported by the Sandinistas, especially in the early 1980s. Indeed, new organizations, including one representing peasants, came into existence and flourished during that period. But in the late 1980s, war, economic hard times, and excessive "tasking" by the Sandinistas caused many of these groups to atrophy. However, during the conservative restoration, many of these groups regained prominence.[32]

There were several reasons for the resurgence of the grassroots organizations. A major one seems to have been simple necessity: The new governments were essentially indifferent—if not openly hostile—to the interests of the poor majority. Thus, peasants found themselves struggling to protect their access to land; farmworkers fought to protect their interests as the government—pressured by the United States—sought to restore the "rights" of Somoza-era landowners whose land was confiscated during the revolution; women in general organized to confront antifeminist initiatives of the new governments; and unionized workers confronted the negative aspects of neoliberal privatization and the downsizing of government.

Another reason the grassroots organizations were able to rebound was that, with the Sandinistas out of power, they could now become more independent from their former party mentor. The huge peasant organization, the National Union of Farmers and Ranchers (UNAG), had always exercised relative autonomy from the FSLN. Now labor unions, farmworker groups, and women's organizations could do the same. This gave them greater legitimacy and helped them to flourish.

Nongovernmental organizations—national and international—concerned with promoting the welfare of Nicaragua's poor majority had existed from the time of the Somozas. Tolerated through the 1970s, they were wooed and encouraged by the Sandinistas. However, with the neoliberal economic policies of the 1990s and the consequent shrinking role of government in the social realm, the NGOs took on an even greater role in this latter period. The NGOs included numerous domestic and international church organizations, scores of Sandinista-era sister-city groupings, and other philanthropic organizations.

One of the most interesting NGOs was the Institute for Human Promotion (INPRHU), created in 1964. Working with peasants during the Somoza period, it was barely tolerated by the regime. During the Sandinista Revolution, it continued to function, and its founder, Reinaldo Antonio Téfel, became minister of the Nicaraguan Social Security and Welfare Institute (INSSBI). When they lost their jobs after the 1990 election, Téfel and his able vice minister, Ricardo Chavarría, simply moved many of their programs back to INPRHU. Interestingly, much of the international funding that some governments—especially those of the Nordic countries—had been channeling to social projects in Nicaragua through INSSBI was now channeled for the same purposes through INPRHU. Accordingly, by the late 1990s, INPRHU had become the largest NGO in the country.

As noted earlier, the increased importance of grassroots organizations and NGOs in post-Sandinista Nicaragua was dramatically illustrated in the wake of Hurricane Mitch in 1998. Decimated by neoliberal downsizing throughout the 1980s, the government's social service infrastructure was simply incapable of responding to the massive human need created by the disaster. In the end, it was grassroots organizations and NGOs like INPRHU that came to the rescue.

Finally, no discussion of grassroots organizations and NGOs would be complete without some mention of the Citizens Power Councils (CPCs). Created in December 2007, the CPCs were to be locally elected and charged with making proposals to the local governments. If under FSLN leadership, those governments would be obliged to implement CPC proposals.[33] The stated objective—a laudable one, indeed—was to create "direct democracy." However, the fact that President Ortega created the CPCs by decree (November 30, 2007), that the decree violated the Municipalities Law and Civil Participation Law approved in 2003, that it undermined municipal autonomy, and that it placed CPCs under his government's Communication and Citizenship Council coordinated by his wife, Rosario Murillo, belied their nature as either nongovernmental or grassroots.[34]

AN UNCERTAIN FUTURE

As of mid-2010, when this was being written, it was not easy to predict Nicaragua's political future. The Sandinista government of the 1980s had resulted in more democratic institutions and greater grassroots participation. However, corrupt pact making in subsequent years had weakened a number of these institutions, and heavy-handed U.S. interference had strengthened the power of the privileged classes. Despite his anticorruption efforts, Bolaños had been unable to repair damage done to the democratic system in the previous several years. Daniel Ortega's efforts to consolidate power upon his return to office in 2007 was seriously threatening Nicaraguan democracy. The future of this proud little nation was simply very unclear.

NOTES

1. For an examination of the history and activities of this party as of the late 1960s, see Thomas W. Walker, *The Christian Democratic Movement in Nicaragua* (Tucson: University of Arizona Press, 1970).

2. Small wonder that few people in Nicaragua were particularly saddened to hear fourteen months later that Somoza's life of comfortable exile in Paraguay had

ended in a crescendo of bazooka and automatic-weapon fire. The *ajusticiamiento* (bringing to justice) of Somoza had been carried out by a group of Argentine guerrilla fighters who had served as international volunteers in the insurgency in Nicaragua little over a year before. They were apparently acting on their own. See Claribel Alegría and D. J. Flakoll, *Somoza: Expediente Cerrada, La historia de un ajusticiamiento* (Managua: Editorial El Gato Negro, 1993).

3. "Afirma el Comandante Bayardo Arce, 'El Consejo de Estado garantiza el Pluralismo Político,'" *Patria Libre*, vol. 4 (May 1980), p. 22.

4. John A. Booth, "The National Governmental System," in *Nicaragua: The First Five Years*, ed. Thomas W. Walker (New York: Praeger, 1985), p. 39. For more detailed discussion of a number of other topics covered in this section, see (1) Charles Downs, "Local and Regional Government," (2) Luis Héctor Serra, "The Grass-Roots Organizations," (3) Stephen M. Gorman and Thomas W. Walker, "The Armed Forces," (4) Michael Dodson and Laura O'Shaughnessy, "Religion and Politics," and (5) Dennis Gilbert, "The Bourgeoisie," in Walker, ed., *Nicaragua: The First Five Years*, pp. 45–144, 163–182.

5. For a critical examination of the TPAs, see Lawyers Committee for International Human Rights, *Nicaragua: Revolutionary Justice, A Report on Human Rights and the Judicial System* (New York and Washington, D.C.: LCIHR, 1985), pp. 33–93.

6. Comandante Carlos Nuñez Téllez, *Un Pueblo en Armas* (Managua: Secretaría Nacional de Propaganda y Educación Política del FSLN, 1980), p. 26.

7. For details about the Sandinista military, see coauthor Walker's chapter, "The Armed Forces," in *Revolution and Counterrevolution in Nicaragua*, ed. Thomas W. Walker (Boulder, Colo.: Westview Press, 1991).

8. Arms Control and Foreign Policy Caucus, U.S. House of Representatives, "Who Are the Contras?" *Congressional Record*, vol. 131, no. 48 (Daily Edition, April 23, 1985), H2335.

9. Latin American Studies Association, *The Electoral Process in Nicaragua: Domestic and International Influences* (Austin, Texas: LASA, 1984), pp. 30, 31.

10. For the bibliographical information on the European reports, see Note 25 in Chapter 3.

11. LASA, *The Electoral Process*, p. 32.

12. Americas Watch, *Human Rights in Nicaragua: Reagan, Rhetoric, and Reality* (New York: Americas Watch, 1985), p. 62.

13. For a concise description of this process, see the section on the constitution in Andrew A. Reding, "The Evolution of Formal Governmental Institutions," in Walker, ed., *Revolution and Counterrevolution*.

14. In September 1988, Speaker of the House Jim Wright created a furor in the United States by disclosing that antigovernment demonstrations and other activities in Nicaragua were being orchestrated by the CIA and other U.S. agencies. See Susan Bennett, "Wright: CIA Admits Provoking Sandinistas," *Miami Herald*, September 21, 1988, p. 1; and Steven Kinzer, "Wright Attacks Policy," *New York Times*, September 24, 1988. For discussion of National Endowment for Democracy funding of opposition groups in Nicaragua, see Andres Oppenheimer, "U.S. Agency to Send Funds to Anti-Sandinista Groups," *Miami Herald*, July 21, 1988, p. 22A. For a discussion of U.S. funding and manipulation of the Nicaraguan Catholic hierarchy, see Betsy Cohn and Patricia Hynds, "The Manipulation of the Religion Issue," in *Reagan Versus the Sandinistas: The Undeclared War on Nicaragua*, ed. Thomas W. Walker (Boulder, Colo.: Westview Press, 1987), pp. 97–122. For information about similar funding and manipulation of the opposition newspaper, *La Prensa*, see John Spicer Nichols, "*La Prensa:* The CIA Connection," *Columbia Journalism Review*, vol. 27, no. 2 (July–August 1988), pp. 34–35.

15. Cohn and Hynds, "The Manipulation," pp. 97–122.

16. See Angharad Valdivia, "The U.S. Manipulation of Nicaraguan and Other Latin American Media," in Walker, ed., *Revolution and Counterrevolution*.

17. For a good discussion, see Shelley A. McConnell, "Institutional Development," in *Nicaragua Without Illusions: Regime Transition and Structural Adjustment in the 1990s*, ed. Thomas W. Walker (Wilmington, Del.: Scholarly Resources, 1997), pp. 45–63.

18. See Nitlápan-*Envío* team, "The Games We Played During the World Cup," *Envío*, no. 348 (July 2010), and Silvio Prado, "Municipal Autonomy Is More Threatened than Ever," *Envío*, no. 349 (August 2010).

19. For useful insight into the importance the United States placed on the Latin American military establishment as a key instrument to control state and society, see Morris H. Morley, *Washington, Somoza and the Sandinistas: State and Regime in U.S. Policy Towards Nicaragua* (New York: Cambridge University Press, 1994). For an excellent analysis of U.S. manuals used during the cold war in training Latin American military personnel in the techniques of state-sponsored terrorism, see Lisa Haugaard, "How the U.S. Trained Latin America's Military: The Smoking Gun," *Envío*, vol. 16, no. 195 (October 1997), pp. 33–38.

20. Actually, we would calculate that between 400,000 and a half million Latin Americans lost their lives at the hands of U.S.-trained Latin American military establishments and associated death squads. More than 200,000 such killings took place in Guatemala alone.

21. Apparently, thirteen Nicaraguans were to train at Fort Benning in 2002 and nineteen in 2003. From José A. Recio, chief, International Student Division, WHISC, "Fiscal Year 2002 Student Projections" and "Fiscal Year 2003 Student Projections" (photocopied charts).

22. Haugaard, "How the U.S. Trained Latin America's Military."

23. M&R Consultores, Sistema de Monitoreo y Opinion Publica (SISMO), Edicion 23, November 27–December 5, 2009.

24. Carlos Salinas Maldonado, "Jefe policial anulada por 'cuadros' de Ortega en Boaco; Granera en crisis de autoridad," *Confidencial*, July 6, 2010.

25. Members of the Rescate group included Mónica Baltodano and Víctor Hugo Tinoco. See Mónica Baltodano, *Sandinismo, Pactos Democracia y Cambio Revolucionario: Contribuciones al pensamiento politico de la izquierda nicaragüense* (Managua: Mónica Baltodano, 2009).

26. Coauthor Wade interview with Carlos Fernando Chamorro, July 27, 2009; Asier Andrés, "Ortega-Alemán Pact Corners Montealegre," *Central America Report*, no. 3509, February 29, 2008.

27. Margarita Corral, "Participation in Meetings of Political Parties," Americas Barometer Insights: 2009, Latin American Public Opinion Project.

28. Margarita Corral, "(Mis)Trust in Political Parties in Latin America," Americas Barometer Insights: 2008, vol. 2, Latin American Public Opinion Project.

29. "Líderes opositores pierden terreno," *La Prensa*, July 13, 2010.

30. For one, in 2009 Ortega family interest came close to silencing Carlos Fernando Chamorro, its most vocal TV critic and former editor of the Sandinista daily, *Barricada*, by buying the TV channel that aired his popular evening news and commentary programs, *Esta Noche* and *Esta Semana*. But with some difficulty, Chamorro was able to move to another channel daring enough to give him a new platform. From Walker interviews with Chamorro, December 14 and December 17, 2009, and from subsequent e-mail correspondence.

31. Coauthor Wade interview with Marta María Blandón, director of Ipas Central America, July 23, 2009.

32. See Erica Polakoff and Pierre La Ramée, "Grass-Roots Organizations," in Walker, ed., *Nicaragua Without Illusions,* pp. 185–202.

33. Pedro Ortega, "Porque los pueblos mandan y tienen derecho de ser 'Presidente,' CPC para el progreso de Nicaragua," www.elpueblopresidente.com/PODER-CIUDADANO/281107_nicaraguaprogrese.html, November 26, 2007.

34. Nitlapán-*Envío* Team, "How Many Conflicts Will the New 'Direct Democracy' Trigger?" *Envío*, vol. 26, no. 312 (December 2007), pp. 1–9.

8
The International Dimension

In November 1979, as coauthor Walker deplaned at Managua's Augusto César Sandino International Airport on his second visit to Nicaragua since the liberation, he stopped to gaze at a large new sign on the main terminal building: "Welcome to Free Nicaragua." For some international visitors, this greeting may have held little significance. For others, it probably reinforced deep-seated fears and suspicions. But for one who had studied and empathized with the plight of the Nicaraguan people for over a decade, this proud salutation was rich with bittersweet meaning. After four and a half centuries of foreign domination and abuse, the Nicaraguan people had seemingly won the right to proclaim themselves sovereign and independent—a stirring and historic accomplishment. Yet one could not help wondering whether it could last. Could a tiny republic (then barely 2.5 million people) located deep within the geopolitical sphere of influence of one of the world's superpowers actually set an independent course for itself? As it turned out, Nicaragua managed to fend off the reimposition of U.S. hegemony for almost eleven years.

NICARAGUA AS A CLIENT STATE

As the reader probably will have gathered from the historical chapters of this book, real sovereignty was almost a totally new experience for Nicaragua. During its first half century of "independence," Nicaragua had been buffeted by the conflicting commercial and geopolitical interests of the United States and Great Britain. In the latter part of the nineteenth century, the modernizing liberal dictator, José Santos Zelaya, had briefly championed the cause of Nicaraguan and Central American self-determination. The British had been dislodged from the Atlantic territories; the cause of Central American unity had been revived; U.S. overtures for a very concessionary Nicaraguan canal treaty had been rejected; and an effort had been made to diversify the country's international trade relationship in order to reduce dependence on the United States. However, as we saw, the United States eventually reacted to Zelaya's independent attitude—and especially to the possibility that he might let other international interests build a canal that would compete with the newly constructed U.S. waterway at Panama—by conspiring with Zelaya's Conservative opposition and backing them militarily in their effort to overthrow Zelaya and then to stay in power as a minority party.

During the first third of the twentieth century, Nicaragua's tiny privileged elite—Conservative and Liberal alike—came to realize that its narrow class interests could best be pursued through a subservient, symbiotic relationship with the United States. The Conservatives were the first to get the message. They would never have succeeded in their rebellion against the central government in 1909, nor defeated Benjamín Zeledón's nationalist forces in 1912, had it not been for direct U.S. military intervention. Accordingly, they learned to address their foreign protectors in a groveling and obsequious manner. For instance, after Zeledón's defeat, a group of Conservatives of "the highest social, political, and financial standing" sent the local commander of the occupying Marines a message of thanks that was clearly tailored to appeal to the ethnocentric and chauvinistic interpretation of Central American reality prevalent in the United States at that time.

> The lamentable situation of these countries, perturbed by constant uprisings, is all the sadder when we consider their proximity to the great American nation, which, founded on wise institutions and inspired by the spirit of liberty and justice, marches at the head of the destiny of humanity. Thus the presence of the American troops among us marks an era of peace for this Republic because she now has spread over us the protecting influence of her altruistic policy.[1]

The Conservative elite also ingratiated itself to the Americans by taking loans with private U.S. banks, allowing the occupiers to run many aspects of the country's public finances, and giving their protectors almost exactly the type of concessionary canal treaty Zelaya had vehemently rejected as injurious to the national interest. Among other things, the Bryan-Chamorro Treaty of 1916 allowed the United States to corner the rights to a Nicaraguan canal, thus ensuring that the new U.S. waterway through Panama would continue to operate without competition.

By the late 1920s, the Liberal elite also came to realize that its class interests could best be promoted by cultivating a symbiotic relationship with the United States. After the United States blocked one last attempt to remove the Conservatives by force, all of the major Liberal leaders, except Augusto César Sandino, bowed to the inevitable and endorsed the U.S.-sponsored Peace of Tipitapa in May 1927. Having done so, they won the U.S.-sponsored presidential elections of 1928 and 1932.

The behavior of the Liberal and Conservative client governments that nominally ruled Nicaragua during the second U.S. occupation (1926–1933) was obsequiously pro-American. The occupiers continued to play a key role in the financial affairs of the country. The U.S.-trained, -equipped, and -officered "Nicaraguan" National Guard was rapidly developed and expanded as an immediate response to Sandinista "banditry" and as a long-range answer to the problem of ensuring pro-U.S. stability in the region.

One of the clearest examples of the subservient character of these governments can be seen in Nicaragua's docile ratification of the very unfavorable Barcenas Meneses-Esguerra Treaty of 1928. As a result of this treaty, Nicaragua relinquished to Colombia the Providencia and San Andrés islands and certain keys off Nicaragua's Atlantic coast. Though even a cursory glance at a map of the Caribbean would tend to verify Nicaragua's historic right to these territories, Colombia had long maintained a conflicting claim based on rather vague policing authority granted its colonial predecessor by the Spanish crown. While it was certainly not in Nicaragua's interest to relinquish these possessions, the United States benefited in two ways. First, the treaty helped assuage long-simmering Colombian resentment over U.S. connivance and military involvement in the independence of the former Colombian province of Panama in 1903. Then, too, it voided additional Colombian claims that had tended to cloud the validity of certain U.S. rights under the Bryan-Chamorro Treaty.

The Role of the Somozas

While it is clear that Nicaragua's status as a client state had developed long before the Somozas took power, it is also true that Anastasio Somoza García and his two sons did much to refine that undignified relationship. Throughout most of the Somoza period, Nicaraguan and U.S. foreign policy were virtually indistinguishable. As a bitter Anastasio Somoza Debayle remarked shortly after his overthrow: "I stood back to back with the U.S. and gave my ally all the support I could muster. . . . [No] president anywhere supported the policies of the United States more devoutly than I did. . . . No such loyalty existed anywhere."[2]

The relationship was one of mutual benefit. The Somozas tailored their foreign policy to the interests of their international protector, and the United States, in turn, lavished various favors on its client. Throughout the whole affair, the interested parties whose aspirations and needs were consistently ignored were the citizens of Nicaragua. U.S. personnel occasionally may have experienced some queasiness over the nature of the system they were supporting, but as Franklin Delano Roosevelt is said to have remarked at one point, "Somoza might be an S.O.B., but he is *our* S.O.B."

For their part, the Somozas served the perceived foreign-policy interests of the United States in a number of ways. In the United Nations and other international forums, they consistently voted with the United States. They leased military bases to the United States during the Second World War. They allowed Nicaraguan territory to be used as a training and staging area for CIA-sponsored invasions of Guatemala (1954) and Cuba (Bay of Pigs, 1961). They sent Nicaraguan National Guardsmen to aid in the U.S. occupation of the Dominican Republic in 1965. And they even offered to send troops to Korea and Vietnam.

In the late 1960s and early 1970s, the last of the Somozas, Anastasio Somoza Debayle, also served U.S. interests as a surrogate enforcer of stability in Central America. In 1964, early in the Alliance for Progress, the Pentagon persuaded the military dictators of Central America to form the Central American Defense Council (CONDECA) to coordinate the enforcement of stability so that, theoretically, social and economic development could take place. By the late 1960s and early 1970s, the warped nature of dependent economic "development" and the near total absence of beneficial social change led to increased social unrest that, in turn, apparently caused the United States to rely more heavily on brute military control.[3] In these circumstances, Somoza, the dean of Central America's dictators and a rabid anticommunist, naturally became the principal figure in CONDECA. Under his leadership, joint maneuvers were held, guerrilla foci were located and wiped out, and for a while, the status quo was preserved.

Nicaragua under the Somozas also served U.S. economic interests. While it is true that U.S. investments in that country were never very significant from the U.S. point of view, it is also a fact that the generally laissez-faire economic philosophy of the Somozas strayed little, if at all, from that espoused by the developmentalist economists in the State Department. In more concrete terms, Anastasio Somoza Debayle in the early 1970s protected U.S. economic interests at his own country's expense by helping to sabotage Latin American schemes to create coffee and banana cartels to enforce higher commodity prices.

In spite of all this, however, the Somozas were never quite willing to take U.S. "friendship" for granted. They also engaged in an extensive and well-financed propaganda and lobbying campaign in the United States. Millions of dollars were paid to U.S. public relations firms to create a favorable image of their regime among Americans, and full-time professional lobbyists devoted considerable effort manipulating U.S. politicians at all levels.[4] As a result, the Somozas could always count on the fervent support of a large number of U.S. congressmen and senators. Some of these individuals undoubtedly behaved as they did out of honest conviction. However, the subsequent indictment and/or conviction of some prominent members of the so-called Somoza Lobby on charges related to Abscam and other corrupt activities lends credence to long-standing suspicions that more personal and material motivations may have been operative in some cases.

In return for their loyalty, the Somozas received extensive support from the United States. After the beginning of the Alliance for Progress, hundreds of millions of dollars in U.S. loans and grants-in-aid were lavished on Nicaragua, ostensibly to help in various high-sounding social and economic development projects. After the 1972 earthquake, there were additional large infusions of funds destined, supposedly, for relief and reconstruction. In fact, of course, most of the money simply evaporated. Social projects carried out by the Somozas were trivial, most of Managua remained an unreconstructed moonscape, and the positive impact of such economic "development" as did take place fell mainly on the Somozas and a small privileged elite. Yet, since the real purpose of the aid was political rather than social, Washington continued to pour taxpayers' dollars down the Somoza rat hole until the day the dictator was finally ousted.

The remarkable inconsistencies in logic underlying the U.S. aid program for Nicaragua were clearly demonstrated in the spring of 1978 when the beleaguered Somoza dictatorship was sent yet another infusion of funds "to meet basic human needs." By that time, the U.S. aid program was so un-popular among most Nicaraguans that a lengthy in-house debate actually took place in the State Department over the questions of whether to at-tempt to send the aid without a public announcement. Finally, it was de-cided to give the ambassador the go-ahead to announce the aid, as it was felt that, even if secrecy were attempted, someone in Nicaragua would surely leak the information, making the U.S. position even less tenable.[5]

The United States also gave the Nicaraguan National Guard massive assistance, including training, in-country advising, arms, ammunition, and equipment. Indeed, the National Guard was the most heavily U.S.-trained military establishment in Latin America. More members of Somoza's Guard had received military training in the United States or at U.S. bases in the Canal Zone than any other military establishment in Latin America,[6] in-cluding that of Brazil, a country approximately fifty times larger in popula-tion. Virtually all Guard officers were U.S.-trained. In reality, then, there was very little that was either "Nicaraguan" or "national" about the Nicaraguan National Guard.

Finally, the United States gave the Somozas considerable political sup-port. With a few exceptions, U.S. ambassadors to Nicaragua were individu-als of very low professional qualifications who were easily co-opted and manipulated by the family. They tended to act more as agents and cronies of the Somozas than as envoys of the people of the United States to the people of Nicaragua. The two most clear-cut examples are those of Thomas Whelan (1951–1961) and Turner Shelton (1970–1975).

The owner of a grain and potato warehouse and one-time chairman of the Republican party of North Dakota, Whelan received his ambassador-ship during the Truman administration shortly after William Langer, chairman of the Senate Judiciary Committee, threatened to block all ad-ministration legislation until such time as someone from North Dakota, Langer's home state, received an ambassadorship, a post never before held by a North Dakotan.[7] Although he never learned to speak Spanish, Whelan quickly became an intimate of the Somoza family. When Somoza García was gunned down in 1956, Whelan saw to it that the grave condition of the dictator as he lay dying in a hospital in Panama was not immediately made public. In doing so, he gave Luís and Anastasio time to consolidate their control over Nicaragua. Thereafter, he became a second father to the young Somozas. Years later, a former top adviser to Luís commented nostalgically to coauthor Walker that "he was *our* ambassador."[8]

The case of Turner Shelton is certainly no more uplifting than that of Whelan. An undistinguished, about-to-be-retired foreign service officer, Shelton apparently owed his appointment as ambassador to his friendship with, and campaign contributions to, Richard Nixon. Former consul general to Nassau, he had close ties with Bebe Rebozo and Howard Hughes. Indeed, he later arranged for Hughes to set up residence in Managua. Like Whelan, Shelton spoke no Spanish but quickly became an intimate friend of the Somozas. It was he who helped arrange the Somoza-Agüero pact of 1971, which enabled Somoza to retain control of the country beyond his original term of office. At the time of the earthquake, when it became apparent that Somoza's personal guard had been thrown into such temporary disarray that it could no longer protect the dictator, Shelton immediately arranged for six hundred armed U.S. troops to be flown from the Canal Zone and stationed on the grounds of Somoza's residence to "help in the relief effort." Shelton's incredible callousness to the suffering of the quake victims and his initial reluctance to offer his palatial ambassadorial residence as a temporary site to house embassy operations were so scandalous that Secretary of State Henry Kissinger eventually saw fit to rebuke him. Even so, his ultimate removal from Managua was delayed until 1975, apparently the result of active lobbying by his friend Anastasio Somoza.

Somoza and Carter

After the overthrow of Somoza, there was a tendency in the United States either to credit or to blame the administration of Jimmy Carter for consciously promoting the downfall of the Somoza system. Such an assertion is unwarranted. It is highly doubtful that the Carter administration ever desired the overthrow of the Somoza system, much less the coming to power of the FSLN. Though the administration's behavior may have contributed to that outcome, the effect was purely unintended.

When it came to office in 1977, the Carter administration was intent on demonstrating that its much-publicized human rights policy could, indeed, find practical application. Unfortunately, the promotion of human rights by the United States was deemed impractical in many parts of the world for strategic and political reasons. However, this was not the case in Nicaragua. There, it was felt that the United States could push human rights without jeopardizing its strategic or economic interests. Unlike some other Latin American dictators, Somoza was sure to follow orders. Since the administration had been assured that the FSLN guerrilla threat had been crushed by Somoza's counteroffensive of the previous two and a half years, it felt that a rights crusade could be implemented without endangering the stability of the system as a whole.

As it turned out, this perception of Nicaraguan reality was badly flawed. On the one hand, Washington was correct in expecting that Somoza would follow orders. In 1977, the administration was successful in getting him to call off the National Guard's campaign of terror against the peasantry and to lift the state of siege and reinstate limited freedom of the press. On the other hand, Washington made two fundamental errors in judgment. First, it underestimated the popularity and resilience of the Sandinista National Liberation Front. Second, it failed to perceive that an artificial injection of civil and political liberties into a system built on the denial of basic social and economic justice can have a highly destabilizing effect.

The Carter team learned its lesson the hard way. By the end of 1977, it was clear not only that the FSLN had not been wiped out but that it was actually receiving increasingly wide support from important and very vocal civilian groups. Alarmed by this totally unexpected situation, the administration began downplaying its human rights campaign and maneuvering for a peaceful solution that would preserve the National Guard and the old elite while at the same time blocking the FSLN. Accordingly, the human rights report on Nicaragua that the State Department sent to Congress early in 1978 was essentially a whitewash; the administration wanted congressional approval for its economic and military aid packages for that country. In addition, even as the War of Liberation was beginning, U.S. diplomatic personnel were urging Nicaraguans to eschew violence and wait for the next Somoza-run elections in 1981. In the summer of 1978, at the urging of the National Security Council, Carter even went so far as to send Somoza the infamous congratulatory letter regarding the dictator's promises to improve his performance in the area of human rights. Then came the National Palace operation of August 1978 and the massive urban uprising the following month. Extremely worried, the administration promoted an Organization of American States (OAS) effort at mediation in which an attempt was made to get Somoza and representatives of the privileged elite to agree to a solution that would have removed Somoza, preserved the Guard and Somoza's Liberal party, and excluded the broad-based coalition led by the FSLN. Finally, in the summer of 1979, as the FSLN closed in on Managua in its Final Offensive, the United States dropped all pretenses and officially requested that the OAS send a peacekeeping force (à la Dominican Republic, 1965) to Nicaragua. That request, as noted earlier, was unanimously rejected.

In sum, the role of the United States in the downfall of the Somoza system was entirely unwitting. Throughout the process, the most revolutionary outcome ever envisioned by Washington was the creation of what Nicaraguans derisively refer to as "*Somocismo* without Somoza," a political system in which a slightly broader spectrum of traditional privileged elites would have participated in a superficially democratic system under the watchful eye of a cosmetically reorganized National Guard. Not until just before Somoza fell, when it had exhausted all other alternatives, did the Carter administration face reality and begin serious communication with the popularly based Sandinista National Liberation Front.[9]

REVOLUTIONARY NICARAGUA

In an article written before the Final Offensive and subsequently published in the United States at the time of the FSLN victory, Sergio Ramírez, who was to become a central figure in the new governing junta and, later, vice president, made some important statements.

> To think that a new, democratic government in Nicaragua might be hostile to the United States is a perverse fantasy. To think that a new and truly representative Nicaraguan government is going to insist on dignified relations with the more powerful countries . . . is to think correctly. . . . We aspire to dignity, integrity, and international respect. . . . The United States should learn not to fear the ghosts of its past mistakes.[10]

Immediately after the liberation, both the Junta and the Directorate of the FSLN made various efforts to convey to U.S. authorities their "wish to develop the best possible relations and to heal the wounds inflicted as a result of Washington's historical complicity with Somoza."[11] These wounds, of course, were raw and painful. The struggle to overthrow a U.S.-backed dictator and to dismantle his U.S.-trained and -equipped army had cost Nicaragua the lives of approximately 50,000 people, or roughly 2 percent of its then 2.5 million population. In the United States at the time, that would have been equivalent to a loss of 4.5 million people, well over seventy-five times the U.S. death toll in the entire Vietnam conflict. Nevertheless, given

Nicaragua's geopolitical position, its economic dependence on the United States, and the remarkably widespread goodwill of Nicaraguans toward the people of the United States, it was deemed highly important to try to construct good relations with that country. Even in the exuberance of the initial victory, U.S. citizens in Nicaragua were treated courteously. There was no attack on the U.S. Embassy, nor were hostages taken. Normal relations were preserved, and government and FSLN leaders traveled to the United States on goodwill missions. Nicaraguan officials turned out en masse at social affairs held by the U.S. ambassador in Managua. In all, it was hoped "that Nicaraguan-U.S. relations could develop into a model of mutual respect between a revolutionary nation and the dominant power of the western hemisphere."[12]

Though intent on developing good relations with the United States, the new government was equally determined that Nicaragua should never again become subservient to any foreign power. The concepts of self-determination and nonalignment, therefore, became the central principles of Nicaraguan foreign policy. In fewer than two months after the revolutionary victory, Nicaragua joined the Movement of Nonaligned Countries. In doing so, it was expressing solidarity with—and seeking the support of—the peoples and governments of the Third World. It was also implementing ideas that dated back in Nicaraguan history at least to the days of Augusto César Sandino.[13]

Nonalignment, however, was not construed by the members of the movement as a position of meek neutrality. While the Sandinistas were determined that Nicaragua would never again be a client state of any great power or permit its soil to be used for foreign military bases, East or West, it would henceforth take stands on many important issues—especially those of interest to the Third World. Yet, although Nicaragua often voted in the United Nations against the United States and with other revolutionary countries, there were important East-West issues in which its mission either abstained (e.g., Afghanistan and the Soviet downing of a Korean airliner) or sided with the United States against the USSR (e.g., the proposal to send a UN peacekeeping force to Lebanon early in 1984). And in the silly but nonetheless symbolic squabbles over the Olympics, Nicaragua decided to send teams to both the 1980 Olympics in Moscow (which the United States and many Western allies boycotted) *and* its 1984 sequel in Los Angeles (from which the USSR, Cuba, and most of the Socialist Bloc countries were absent). For its part, the FSLN, as a party, pursued friendly relations not only with the Communist parties of the Socialist Bloc but also with the Social Democrats of Western Europe (through the Socialist International), the Liberal International, and the Permanent Conference of Political Parties of Latin America (COPPPAL). As a result of these efforts, Nicaragua avoided the international isolation that had befallen Cuba twenty years earlier. Indeed, in 1982 it was chosen by a large vote to occupy the nonpermanent UN Security Council seat traditionally assigned to a Latin America country.

The Sandinista policy of pursuing diplomatic relations with as many countries as possible regardless of ideology was put into motion immediately following the Triumph. Within a year, the new government had relations with a majority of the countries of the world—over twice as many as under the Somozas. In earlier times there had been no need for much diplomatic infrastructure since Nicaraguan foreign policy, for all practical purposes, had been "made in the USA." After July 1979, however, things changed so rapidly that by August of the following year an official in the Foreign Ministry noted, with obvious pride, that the ministry had been obliged to move to a large complex of buildings in order to house the various "area desks" into which it was now organized, much in the style of any modern foreign ministry.[14]

Of course, there were some problems with this global approach to foreign policy. The U.S. media and the Reagan administration consistently pointed with alarm to Nicaragua's ties with the Socialist Bloc and such radical regimes as those of Libya and Iran. At the same time, however, they generally ignored Nicaraguan success in building good working relations with many other types of countries, including the governments of Western Europe and even some of Latin America's most conservative military dictatorships. To try to counteract this distortion, the Nicaraguans were careful to make sure that most, if not all, high-level trips to Europe included stops in both Eastern Bloc *and* Western European countries. But this effort was often to no avail, as evidenced by Daniel Ortega's carefully balanced trip to Europe in May 1985, which the Reagan administration, the media, and a surprisingly large number of liberals in the U.S. Congress characterized simply as "Ortega's trip to Moscow."

Then, too, the development of relations with the two Chinas initially proved problematic. The People's Republic of China at first insisted that formal ties with the mainland should be contingent on severing Nicaragua's long-standing relations with Taiwan. Eventually, however, although

Nicaragua refused to comply, it was able to develop excellent trade relations with the PRC, which ultimately became a major purchaser of Nicaraguan cotton. Overall, Nicaragua's open approach to foreign relations seemed to produce more benefits than costs.

One of the pillars of Nicaragua's new foreign policy was the continuance and enrichment of relations with Western Europe.[15] The organization of Western Europe social democratic parties, the Socialist International (SI, which in the late 1970s included the ruling parties of West Germany, Sweden, Austria, Denmark, etc.) had been very supportive of the FSLN during the War of Liberation. After the Triumph, as it became increasingly worried about possible future U.S. behavior toward Nicaragua, the SI went so far as to form an International Committee for the Defense of the Nicaraguan Revolution, which included an impressive list of SI leaders (among them former West German Chancellor Willy Brandt). The Government of National Reconstruction built on this support by frequently sending high-level delegations to Europe to explain Nicaraguan positions and to solicit aid and trade.

Nicaraguan relations with Western Europe fluctuated from country to country and from time to time. The United States, especially under Reagan, vigorously pressured its allies to diminish their ties to Nicaragua. And there were changes in European governments that affected relations with the Sandinistas. The coming to power of the Social Christians in Germany in 1982 was a clear loss. On the other hand, that setback was balanced by social democratic victories in France (1981) and Spain (1982).

Overall, however, the relationship with Western Europe was constructive, especially during the early to mid-1980s. Although the United States blocked the transfer of all but a trickle of badly needed arms from Western Europe to Nicaragua, it was forced to listen to European calls for a peaceful settlement and was relatively ineffective in slowing the flow of trade and aid. Indeed, as noted earlier, when the Reagan administration hit Nicaragua with a full trade embargo in May 1985, the Western European countries expressed their disapproval not only by refusing to join but also by immediately offering Nicaragua a total of $198 million in new assistance. And, of course, several Western European countries had earlier played a crucial role not only in verifying the legitimacy of the 1984 electoral process but, perhaps more important, in helping to set it up in the first place.

A more universal approach to diplomacy also implied the pursuit of relations with various Communist countries both within and outside the Socialist Bloc. Logically, Nicaragua's strongest relationship was that with

Cuba: The two countries had strikingly similar historical experiences in having undergone first foreign domination and dictatorship, then a successful guerrilla war, and finally a genuine social revolution in which sweeping programs of social change and national defense had to occur simultaneously. Almost immediately after the Triumph, Nicaragua received a number of Cuban advisers in the areas of health, education, and military training. Moreover, leaders of the two countries exchanged visits. Both before and immediately after the victory, Fidel Castro advised the Nicaraguans to preserve a private sector and retain good relations with the United States. Relations with the rest of the Socialist Bloc also advanced, but at a slower pace. Gradually, diplomatic relations were established or reopened, and agreements for trade and aid were signed.

Although the new Nicaraguan armed forces were pathetically equipped throughout 1979 and 1980, the Sandinistas saw fit to import only relatively small amounts of Socialist Bloc weaponry until well after Ronald Reagan was inaugurated in January 1981. Much effort, at first, was spent in attempting to obtain standardized equipment from less controversial sources—the United States and Western Europe. Eventually, however, when the United States not only refused to sell arms but also blocked the transfer of any significant amount of matériel from sources in Western Europe (an arms agreement with France signed late in 1981 was subsequently killed under intense pressure from Washington),[16] Nicaragua moved ahead with the large-scale procurement of Socialist Bloc weaponry. There was simply no alternative. The importation of such matériel grew as a clear response to the escalating threat from Washington.[17] And each purchase appears to have been carefully thought out with respect to its political implications. For instance, the first standardized equipment received by the Sandinista Militia were obsolete Czech BZ-52 ten-shot rifles—hardly an offensive weapon. The militia was not issued modern AK-47 automatic rifles until 1983, almost two years into the Reagan administration's CIA-directed *contra* invasion. The several dozen Soviet-built tanks that Nicaragua imported shortly after Reagan came to power were old T-54s and T-55s. These were not obtained from the manufacturer but, rather, were sent secondhand from Algeria—an apparent effort to remove any political connotation. Eventually, of course, the rhythm of Socialist Bloc arms procurement picked up as the Contra War accelerated, and repeated deliberate disinformation "leaks" from official sources in Washington indicated that a full-scale U.S. invasion might be in the offing.

Even as of mid-1985, Nicaragua's relationship with the Socialist Bloc was measured and practical. Trade with the bloc stood at about 20 percent of Nicaragua's total. The Soviet Union and other countries were giving some aid, but the USSR, for one, refused to offer the hard-currency support that Nicaragua so badly needed. It had also indicated that it would not intervene militarily in Nicaragua's defense in the event of a U.S. invasion. The USSR *was*, by default, Nicaragua's major arms supplier. But at no time had it given the Sandinista Armed Forces an offensive capability. Nicaragua had almost no air force, little logistical infrastructure, and insufficient fuel-storage capacity to launch a serious invasion against any of its neighbors. And even though the Reagan administration repeatedly stressed the military danger that the Sandinista Armed Forces purportedly posed to neighboring countries, it did so knowing that what it was saying was simply not the truth. Indeed, the Reagan administration was embarrassed in September 1982 when a subcommittee of the House Committee on Intelligence issued a staff report criticizing U.S. intelligence performance in Central America and noting in particular that, while U.S. intelligence services were publicly trumpeting Nicaragua's supposed offensive capabilities and intentions, there had been "classified briefings whose analytical judgments about Nicaragua's intentions were quite distinct from those that appeared implicit in the briefings on the buildup."[18] And the in-house assessment did not change over time. A classified intelligence report prepared in 1984 still contended that "the overall buildup [in Nicaragua] is primarily defense-oriented, and much of the recent effort has been devoted to improving counterinsurgency capabilities."[19] What is more, at no point had the Soviet Union attempted to put its own bases in Nicaragua—as Washington often warned it would. In fact, the Sandinistas had repeatedly stated categorically that they would not allow such a thing.

Socialist Bloc assistance, which peaked in the mid-1980s, declined rapidly thereafter, as the new Soviet leader Mikhail Gorbachev became increasingly interested in improving relations with the United States.[20] By 1989, with the Contra War ostensibly over, the Soviet Union had ceased arms shipments to Nicaragua. But economic assistance had dropped off even earlier. In 1986, Soviet deliveries of oil to Nicaragua fell 40 percent short of the promised amount. Overall, Socialist Bloc assistance declined by over two-thirds that year and would continue to slump gradually thereafter. One economist later commented that "the reduction in Socialist Bloc assistance may be the most important dimension underlying the crisis of 1987 and 1988."[21]

Nicaragua's major foreign policy problem, from the start, had been the United States.[22] As previously noted, the Carter administration had done almost all it could—short of sending troops—to block the Sandinista victory. True, after the Triumph it then tried to make the best of what it perceived to be an unwelcome situation by maintaining relations with Nicaragua, sending emergency relief, continuing nonmilitary aid already "in the pipeline" to Somoza, and proposing an additional $75 million in new aid. However, 1980—an election year—was hardly a convenient time for a weak incumbent president to be designing a rational policy of coexistence with a new revolutionary government in his "own back yard." Hardliners in Congress had a field day with the Nicaraguan aid bill, amending it and holding it up until the second half of 1980. And although a joint report of the State Department and the Pentagon recommended a favorable reply to the Nicaraguan request to help arm its small military establishment,[23] the Carter administration rejected the idea. Such a proposal, however realistic, would have stood scant chance in Congress while certainly subjecting the Democratic incumbent to further charges of being soft on communism. Thus, early in 1980 the Carter administration chose instead to build up the Honduran military while doing nothing to pressure the government of that country to disband groups of *contras* that already were being harbored in training camps in Honduras.

Some things about the Sandinistas were upsetting to Washington. Many of Nicaragua's new leaders were indeed Marxists—a fact they had never made any attempt to hide. They *were* developing relations with Cuba and other Communist countries both within and outside the Socialist Bloc. And the Sandinistas *were* using rhetoric heavily laced with buzz words— "imperialism," "capitalist exploitation," "bourgeoisie," "proletariat," "liberation," "vanguard"—which, though appropriate in their own setting, tended to unnerve U.S. decision makers having little contact with, or understanding of, Central American reality. These same individuals were further alarmed to be told over and over that the new Nicaraguan "national anthem" included a section calling upon Nicaraguans to "fight against the Yankee, the enemy of humanity." In fact, these words were a part not of the national anthem but, rather, of the FSLN battle hymn, which, like all such hymns, is a historical artifact; hence, over time, it could lose its jingoistic import just as the Marine Corps hymn, with its unfriendly reference to Mexico and Tripoli, is now a historical curiosity rather than a cause for offense to Mexicans and Arabs.

But in fairness to the Sandinistas, we must note that they made considerable efforts to remain "respectable" in the eyes of Washington. These efforts were not just superficial gestures. The Sandinistas' prolonged attempt to buy badly needed arms from Western rather than Communist sources was a clear effort to avoid being unduly dependent on the Socialist Bloc. The decisions to pay Somoza's foreign debt, to preserve a mixed economy, to respect religious liberty, to allow almost complete freedom of the press until 1982, to accept U.S. aid in spite of grossly insulting conditions,[24] to create a pluralistic system of temporary government, and to forge ahead to carry out promised elections—all of these and a number of other policies were designed, at least in part, to signal to the West that this was a uniquely Nicaraguan revolution worthy of being given a chance.

Be that as it may, the administration inaugurated in Washington in January 1981 showed scant interest in coexisting with the Sandinistas. There were some initial attempts at negotiation, but these were conducted in a haughty and condescending manner and against a backdrop of bellicose statements from Washington that almost seemed designed to defeat their purpose. In addition to the termination of aid previously frozen by the Carter administration, the new administration suspended the wheat shipments on which the country relied. By late 1981, the CIA-*contra* effort had been given the president's formal approval and, from then on, there was apparently no turning back. U.S. military maneuvers and infrastructural buildup in the area escalated inexorably. By 1984, upward of 15,000 *contras* were harassing the Nicaraguan government.

Throughout Reagan's first term, both sides claimed to be interested in a negotiated settlement. But the sincerity of these claims appears to have been rather one-sided. In the diplomatic exchanges that occurred in the second half of 1981, Nicaragua had proposed the creation of a joint Honduran-Nicaraguan border patrol to prevent illegal movement in either direction across the border. Such an arrangement would have helped address U.S. worries over alleged Nicaraguan arms shipments across Honduran territory to the guerrillas in El Salvador, which was the original excuse for the *contra* aid. The United States not only turned the proposal down but also pressured Honduras, which had initially shown interest in it, to do the same. In early 1982, after Reagan's December 1981 authorization of CIA-*contra* activities against Nicaragua had been leaked to the U.S. press, France, Mexico, and segments of the U.S. Congress began demanding an alternative peaceful solution. Accordingly, in April the National Security Planning Group (consisting of the president and his most trusted foreign-policy advisers) adopted a top-secret but subsequently leaked planning document in which the authors stated: "We continue to have serious difficulties with U.S. public and congressional opinion, which jeopardize our ability to stay the course. International opinion, particularly in Europe and Mexico, continues to work against our policies." Later, under the category of "policy implications," these planners declared that the administration should "step up efforts to co-opt [the] negotiations issue to avoid congressionally mandated negotiations, which would work against our interests."[25]

From then on, the administration was careful to *appear* to be interested in negotiation. A roving ambassador, Richard Stone, was recruited and sent to Central America ostensibly to investigate the possibility of peace. As a conservative former senator from Florida and a former lobbyist for the military regime in Guatemala, Stone hardly seemed the appropriate choice for the job. Surprisingly, Stone took his formal mandate seriously. Nevertheless, in February 1984, after a long period of having been ignored and shunted aside in Reagan administration policy making toward Central America, he resigned and was replaced by an apparently more trustworthy hawk, Harry Shlaudeman. Starting in June 1984, Shlaudeman went through the motions of conducting bilateral peace negotiations with Nicaraguan representative Víctor Hugo Tinoco in Manzanillo, Mexico. Apparently designed largely to make Ronald Reagan's Central America policy appear reasonable during the 1984 campaign, these talks were abruptly and unilaterally terminated by the United States early in 1985.

In 1983, Colombia, Mexico, Panama, and Venezuela began their own search for a peaceful settlement—a search dubbed "the Contadora Process" after the Panamanian island on which the diplomats from the four countries had first met. Both the United States and Nicaragua expressed interest, but it was Nicaragua that, on October 15 of the same year, produced four draft peace treaties they claimed were based on the Contadora Process. Hand-delivered to the State Department by Nicaraguan Foreign Minister Miguel d'Escoto, these proposals were rejected out of hand without discussion. The Contadora Process, however, ground on, and by September 1984 the four Contadora countries, in consultation with the United States and all Central American countries, had produced the Contadora Act, a comprehensive

Nicaraguans under siege. (Upper left) As the Contra War grew and the threat of a U.S. invasion became ever more real, Nicaraguans of all ages and sexes joined the militia and demanded to be armed. (Lower left) Members of the self-defense agricultural communities in the north work with their weapons (in this case, an AK-47) strapped to their shoulders. (Upper right) Urban dwellers dig L-shaped slit trenches in vacant lots and bank patios. (Lower right) Meanwhile, from late 1983 onward, a large segment of the U.S. community in Managua held regular Thursday-morning peace vigils in front of the U.S. Embassy asking their government not to "rescue" them—a reference to the pretext used for the invasion of Grenada. (Photo of the boy with the AK-47 courtesy of J. Harold Molineu; other photos by co-author Walker)

draft peace proposal. Again, the United States had been expressing support of the Contadora Process and "officials from Honduras, Guatemala, El Salvador and Costa Rica [had] indicated their Governments would be willing to sign the treaty."[26] However, after Nicaragua surprised the world by agreeing to sign unconditionally, the United States and its Central American allies did a complete reversal of position, saying that the act (which called for withdrawal of foreign military advisers, a reduction of armaments, etc.) was incomplete and that Nicaragua could not be trusted. El Salvador, Honduras, and Costa Rica, the three Central American countries most closely tied to the United States, then produced a long list of objections to the very document they had originally helped shape. One bewildered State Department official—apparently somewhat "out of the loop"—commented candidly, "The whole point [of the Manzanillo talks] was to get the Nicaraguans to accept the Contadora proposals. Now they have, but we say we are not satisfied. I am not sure if I would blame the Nicaraguans if they were confused."[27]

Discouraged, but not defeated, by these machinations, the Contadora Group enlisted the backing of a "Contadora Support Group," composed of Argentina, Brazil, Peru, and Uruguay. In 1986, the two groups, representing over 80 percent of Latin America's population, produced a second draft treaty that included many of the amendments proposed by U.S. allies in Central America when they rejected the 1984 act. After arduous negotiations, Nicaragua agreed to accept the new document provided the United States, the major promoter of the *contras*, would also sign. Washington refused, arguing in essence that it was not a party to the conflicts.

In 1986, the Iran-Contra scandal broke. Reagan administration officials had been caught in a covert, illegal scheme to sell weapons to Iran—then engaged in a bloody war with Iraq—in return for the release of U.S. hostages in Lebanon. The profits from those sales were to be diverted to the *contras* in Nicaragua for whom Congress had temporarily cut off aid following the passage of the Boland Amendment in late 1982.[28] The scandal plunged U.S. Central American policy into disarray and seeded doubts among Washington's allies in Central America about U.S. ability to continue to fund the *contras*. In this power vacuum, the U.S. client states in Central America began searching more earnestly for avenues for peace. Early in 1987, Costa Rican President Oscar Arias began working on a peace proposal based on the second Contadora draft treaty. Not to be outmaneuvered, and anxious to renew aid to the *contras*, Ronald Reagan enlisted Speaker of the House Jim Wright that August to cosponsor a "peace plan" for Central America—one that, because it contained provisions that were clearly unacceptable to the Sandinistas, would undoubtedly have been rejected by Managua, thus providing the ideal pretext for bipartisan congressional support for renewed *contra* aid.

Given that the Wright-Reagan plan was announced just two days before they were to meet in Esquipulas, Guatemala, to discuss the Arias plan, the five Central American presidents worked with a new sense of urgency to amend, sign, and announce their "Procedure for the Establishment of a Strong and Lasting Peace in Central America" (also known as the Central American Peace Accord, the Esquipulas Accord, and the Arias Peace Plan). With provisions designed to promote national reconciliation, cessation of hostilities, democratization, free elections, cessation of assistance to irregular forces, the nonuse of national territory for irregular forces attacking other states, and international and internal verification, the accord temporarily caught the Reagan administration off balance, won international acclaim, and earned Oscar Arias a Nobel Peace Prize.

As it turned out, though they were supposed to apply to all five Central American countries, only Nicaragua made a serious effort to implement the accords.[29] Though the Contra War continued, the Sandinistas lifted the state of siege, reinstituted freedom of the press, eventually released all political prisoners (including large numbers of convicted National Guard war criminals and *contra* POWs) and proceeded to hold a free and open election in 1990 (as actually provided for in the 1987 Constitution). They even went beyond what was required in the accord by entering into formal face-to-face negotiations with the *contras* in 1988. For its part, the United States sabotaged a 1988 *contra* effort to come to terms with the Sandinistas and continued funding its surrogate army in spite of the fact that the International Verification and Follow-up Commission (formed as part of the accords) would note at one point, "The definitive termination of such assistance is still an indispensable prerequisite for the success of peace efforts and the success of the Procedure as a whole."[30]

Though the Reagan and first Bush administrations had consistently defied world public opinion and the concerted effort of most Latin American countries to achieve peace, their tenacious policy of low-intensity conflict against Nicaragua would eventually pay off. Having watched their government for most of a decade attempt valiantly, but unsuccessfully, to achieve peace while preserving sovereignty, a majority of Nicaraguan voters opted on February 25, 1990, for peace by other means.

NICARAGUA'S POST-SANDINISTA
ROLE IN WORLD AFFAIRS

For all practical purposes, the Chamorro inauguration two months later signaled the reimposition of U.S. hegemony over Nicaragua. Eventually the *contras* were formally demobilized and the economic embargo was quickly terminated, but the recovery aid promised by the United States was woefully inadequate to clean up the economic mess that the low-intensity conflict had created. In addition, much of it was periodically held back as a carrot to guide the new government in U.S.-approved economic and political directions.

Activities in its Managua embassy immediately reflected Washington's determination to reassert control over its wayward satellite. From before the election to the end of the year, the embassy staff grew from one of the smallest in the world to one of the largest. Heading this team as ambassador was Harry Shlaudeman, the tough career diplomat who had represented the United States in the Manzanillo talks five years earlier. Shlaudeman had also played an important role in the reinforcement or reimposition of U.S. hegemony in the Dominican Republic in the 1960s and in Chile in the early 1970s.[31]

Washington enforced its will in several ways. The granting or withholding of direct foreign aid, though trivial given the economic damage the United States had inflicted on Nicaragua, was used to discipline its client. Much more important, the United States—with its controlling interests in key international lending agencies—orchestrated those agencies (the International Monetary Fund, the World Bank, and the Inter-American Development Bank) and other international donors to enforce Washington's vision of neoliberal economic reform in the client country. And finally, as we noted above, at election time, U.S. public officials, from secretary of state on down, made public pronouncements on the evils of the Sandinistas. Accordingly, from 1990 through the first decade of the twenty-first century, a large majority of the Nicaraguan electorate would consistently vote against Washington's favorite bugaboo, Daniel Ortega. His victory in 2006 was not a product of new courage by the Nicaraguan electorate but rather the result of a split in the majority anti-Ortega opposition and recently modified electoral laws allowing a plurality victory.

While the conservative administrations from 1990 to 2007 did occasionally try to exercise independence, they generally submitted to U.S.

wishes. True, Chamorro pursued a policy of internal peace that, of necessity, involved making some accommodations to the most powerful single party in the country, the FSLN. The Chamorro administration also decided to continue as a member of the Nonaligned Movement. And for some time, it resisted U.S. pressure to withdraw the Sandinista government's suit for $17.8 billion in reparations from the United States in connection with the case Nicaragua had won against that superpower in the World Court in 1986. Eventually, however, it did withdraw its very legitimate reparations claim and, on most matters regarding implementation of U.S.-promoted neoliberal economic policy, Chamorro was enthusiastically in step with Washington.

Though as much a neoliberal as his predecessor, Alemán's rampant corruption strained relations with the United States, which canceled his entry visa in 2002. Bolaños, who attended university in the United States, maintained close ties with Washington throughout his administration. His anti-corruption campaign was praised by the George W. Bush administration, which supported him by threatening to suspend aid amid calls for his impeachment. In addition to negotiating CAFTA with the United States, all three administrations worked closely with the IMF and submitted to its socially regressive demands for "reform." With minor exceptions, Nicaragua was once again as subservient to the hemispheric hegemon as it had been under Somoza.

The Ortega government was both openly defiant and curiously submissive to the demands of its old enemy. In addition to joining ALBA (and its new alliance with Venezuela) and reinvigorating relations with Cuba, Ortega sought to expand relations throughout the globe. Shortly after returning to office, Ortega embarked on a tour, sponsored by the Libyan government, of Algeria, Libya, Senegal, Iran, Cuba, and Venezuela.[32] The visits, especially those to Iran and Libya, aroused the ire of U.S. and domestic critics. Ortega briefly—for one day—broke off diplomatic relations with U.S. ally Colombia in 2008 when the Colombian military raided a FARC camp inside the Ecuadorian border. During the 2009 Summit of the Americas, Ortega criticized "expansionist" U.S. policies in the region—both distant past and present—and criticized the continuing blockade of Cuba.[33] Additionally, Ortega was an outspoken critic of the 2009 coup in Honduras, calling for ousted President Manuel Zelaya's reinstatement, denouncing the brief "disappearance" of Honduran foreign Minister Patricia Rodas, and refusing to recognize the newly elected President Lobo. As of August 2010,

Nicaragua was the only Central American country opposed to the readmission of Honduras into the Central American Integration System (SICA).

In addition to Ortega's presence on the international scene, Nicaragua's international profile was enhanced when, in 2008, former Nicaraguan Foreign Minister Miguel D'Escoto was elected president of the UN General Assembly. D'Escoto, who famously won a case against the United States in the International Court of Justice for mining Nicaraguan waters in 1984, remained a vocal critic of U.S. policy.[34]

For its part, Washington was less than receptive to Ortega's rhetoric and politics. As discussed in Chapter 4, the United States openly campaigned against Ortega in the 2001 and 2006 elections and stopped aid following alleged corruption in the 2008 municipal elections. Following the vote that would permit Ortega to seek reelection in 2011, U.S. Ambassador Robert Callahan repeatedly criticized the ruling of Nicaragua's packed Supreme Court.[35]

However, despite all these public displays of discord between the two countries, the Ortega administration pursued certain key economic policies very much in conformity with U.S. wishes. Among other things, it retained Nicaraguan membership in the U.S.-sponsored Central American Free Trade Agreement. And, even more important, it chose to maintain a relationship with the IMF—Washington's major economic enforcer. In fact, the initial three-year agreement negotiated by Ortega differed little from that of his predecessor. Though in conformity with the behavior of all three post-1990 governments, this move, as indicated, was a radical departure from the nationalist and sovereign economic policy of the Sandinistas of the 1980s.

NOTES

1. A letter from sixty-one Nicaraguans to Major S. D. Butler, Granada, October 9, 1912. From folder 5 of the "Personal Papers" of Joseph H. Pendleton in the U.S. Marine Corps Historical Center, Washington, D.C., Naval Yard.

2. Anastasio Somoza and Jack Cox, *Nicaragua Betrayed* (Belmont, Mass.: Western Islands, 1980), pp. 77–78.

3. The shift in emphasis can be seen in a report prepared by Nelson Rockefeller after an official fact-finding visit to Latin America in 1969. Nelson A. Rockefeller, *The Rockefeller Report on the Americas* (Chicago: Quadrangle Books, 1969).

4. Though Somoza lobbying efforts were at least as extensive in the 1970s, the most detailed documentation of this type of activity pertains to the early 1960s. U.S. Congress, Senate Committee on Foreign Relations, *Activities of Nondiplomatic Representatives of Foreign Principals in the United States*, part 2, hearing of March 3, 1963 (Washington, D.C.: U.S. Government Printing Office, 1963).

5. From a conversation coauthor Walker had with an informed source in the State Department in April 1978.

6. Richard Millett, *The Guardians of the Dynasty* (Maryknoll, N.Y.: Orbis Press, 1977), p. 252.

7. See Albert M. Colegrove, "Nicaragua: Another Cuba?" *The Nation*, July 1, 1961, pp. 6–9; and Roland Young, *The American Congress* (New York: Harper, 1958), p. 201.

8. Walker interview with Pedro Quintanilla, vice minister of labor and education during the presidency of Luís Somoza, in his home in Managua on July 23, 1967.

9. For an excellent and more detailed examination of U.S. policy during the Sandinista insurrection, see William M. LeoGrande, "The Revolution in Nicaragua," *Foreign Affairs*, vol. 58, no. 1 (Fall 1979), pp. 28–50.

10. Sergio Ramírez, "What the Sandinistas Want," *Caribbean Review*, vol. 7, no. 3 (Summer 1979), pp. 50, 51.

11. Alejandro Bendaña, "The Foreign Policy of the Nicaraguan Revolution," in *Nicaragua in Revolution*, ed. Thomas W. Walker (New York: Praeger, 1982), p. 326.

12. Ibid.

13. For more information on Sandinista involvement in the Nonaligned Movement, see Waltraud Queiser Morales and Harry E. Vanden, "Relations with the Nonaligned Movement," in *Nicaragua: The First Five Years*, ed. Thomas W. Walker (New York: Praeger, 1985), pp. 167–184; and Robert Armstrong, "Nicaragua: Sovereignty and Non-Alignment," in *NACLA Report on the Americas*, vol. 19, no. 3 (May–June 1985), pp. 15–21.

14. From a lengthy conversation coauthor Walker had with Carlos Chamorro Coronel, chief of staff of the Ministry of Foreign Relations, in Managua, August 1980.

15. For more detailed information about this subject, see Nadia Malley, "Relations with Western Europe and the Socialist International," in Walker, ed., *Nicaragua: The First Five Years*, pp. 485–498; and Robert Matthews, "The Limits of Friendship: Nicaragua and the West," *NACLA Report on the Americas*, vol. 19, no. 3 (May–June 1985), pp. 22–32.

16. Matthews, "The Limits of Friendship," pp. 29–30.

17. This is the conclusion drawn by Theodore Schwab and Harold Sims in "Relations with the Communist States," in Walker, ed., *Nicaragua: The First Five Years*, p. 161.

18. Staff Report, Subcommittee on Oversight and Evaluation, Permanent Select Committee on Intelligence, *U.S. Intelligence Performance on Central America: Achievements and Selected Instances of Concern*, September 12, 1982, mimeographed, p. 43.

19. Clifford Drauss and Robert S. Greenberger, "Despite Fears of U.S., Soviet Aid to Nicaragua Appears to Be Limited," *Wall Street Journal*, April 3, 1985, p. 1.

20. Post–cold war research in previously closed Soviet materials shows that the Soviets at this time were clearly quite cautious and hesitant in their relations with Nicaragua. They were not intent, as the Reagan administration claimed, on building a beachhead in Central America. See Danuta Paszyn, *The Soviet Attitude to Political and Social Change in Central America, 1979–1990: Case Studies on Nicaragua, El Salvador, and Guatemala* (New York: St. Martin's Press, in association with the School of Slavonic and East European Studies, University of London, 2000).

21. Michael E. Conroy, "The Political Economy of the 1990 Nicaraguan Elections," a paper presented at the Coloquio sobre las Crisis Económicas del Siglo XX, Universidad Complutense de Madrid, April 17–19, 1990.

22. For information about the U.S.-Nicaraguan relationship, see Matthews, "The Limits of Friendship"; William M. LeoGrande, "The United States and Nicaragua," in Walker, ed., *Nicaragua: The First Five Years*, pp. 425–446; and Thomas W. Walker, "Nicaragua-U.S. Friction: The First Four Years, 1979–1983," in *The Central American Crisis: Sources of Conflict and the Failure of U.S. Policy*, ed. Kenneth M. Coleman and George C. Herring (Wilmington, Del.: Scholarly Resources, 1985), pp. 157–189.

23. Extracts from State Department and Pentagon, *Congressional Presentation Document*, Security Assistance Programs, FY 1981, as reproduced in Matthews, "The Limits of Friendship," p. 24.

24. By law, none of the $75 million was to go to health and education programs in which Cubans were involved (i.e., most health and education programs). Of the money, 1 percent was to be spent on publicly advertising that the United States had given it.

25. "National Security Council Document on Policy in Central America," *New York Times*, April 7, 1983.

26. Stephen Kinzer, "Nicaraguans Say They Would Sign Proposed Treaty," *New York Times*, September 23, 1984, p. 20.

27. Philip Taubman, "U.S. Reported to Fear Sandinista Publicity Coup," *New York Times*, September 24, 1984, p. A12.

28. In addition to being unpopular among congressional Democrats, public opinion polls at the time indicated little popular support for such activities in Nicaragua.

29. For details, see Latin American Studies Association, *Extraordinary Opportunities and New Risks: Final Report of the LASA Commission on Compliance with the Central American Peace Accords* (Pittsburgh: LASA, 1988); and William Goodfellow and James Morrell, "From Contadora to Esquipulas to Sapoá and Beyond," in *Revolution and Counterrevolution in Nicaragua*, ed. Thomas W. Walker (Boulder, Colo.: Westview Press, 1991).

30. From a leaked document titled, "Comments, Observations, and Conclusions of the International Verification and Follow-up Commission," available in *Perspectives on War and Peace in Central America*, ed. Sung Ho Kim and Thomas W. Walker (Athens, Ohio: Papers in International Studies, Ohio University Press), pp. 53, 54.

31. Kent Norsworthy with Tom Barry, *Nicaragua: A Country Guide* (Albuquerque, N.M.: Inter-Hemispheric Education Resource Center, 1990), p. 155.

32. "Ortega's 'Ideology Tour' Draws Fire," *Central America Report*, no. 3425 (June 29, 2007).

33. Tim Rogers, "Ortega Leads Anti-U.S. Critique at Latin American Food Summit," *Christian Science Monitor*, May 9, 2008, www.csmonitor.com/World/Americas/2008/0509/p04s02-woam.html.

34. Barbara Crossette, "Father D'Escoto's United Nations," *The Nation*, October 29, 2008, www.thenation.com/article/father-descotos-united-nations.

35. "Nicaraguans Protest Remarks by U.S. Envoy," *New York Times*, October 30, 2009.

Annotated Sources in English

BOOKS

Americas Watch. *Human Rights in Nicaragua: Reagan, Rhetoric and Reality.* New York: Americas Watch, 1985.

> Written by one of the world's major human rights monitoring organizations, this report highlights the gap between fact and rhetoric in the Reagan administration's charges concerning alleged human rights violations in Sandinista Nicaragua. Its conclusions are in conformity with evidence presented in the reports of other major human rights monitoring organizations such as Amnesty International and the Organization of American States Inter-American Commission on Human Rights.

Anderson, Leslie E., and Lawrence C. Dodd. *Learning Democracy: Citizen Engagement and Electoral Choice in Nicaragua, 1990–2001.* Chicago: University of Chicago Press, 2005.

> Using surveys from 1990, 1996, and 2001, the authors offer a thoughtful assessment of voter choice and voting behavior after the revolution.

Arnove, Robert F. *Education as Contested Terrain: Nicaragua, 1979–1993.* Boulder, Colo.: Westview Press, 1994.

> Based on extensive research in Nicaragua from 1980 onward, this book provides an authoritative and valuable overview of the nature and role of education during the Sandinista period and of the reversal of Sandinista innovations after 1990.

Babb, Florence E. *After Revolution: Mapping Gender and Cultural Politics in Neoliberal Nicaragua*. Austin: University of Texas Press, 2001.

Based on solid research in post-Sandinista Nicaragua, this volume examines gender relations in a time of transition and great stress.

Belli, Gioconda. *The Country Under My Skin: A Memoir of Love and War*. New York: Anchor, 2003.

A memoir about personal and national liberation written by one of the revolution's most important poets.

Booth, John A. *The End and the Beginning: The Nicaraguan Revolution,* 2nd ed. Boulder, Colo.: Westview Press, 1985.

One of the best overall studies of Nicaragua through the mid-1980s. Particularly useful for its examination of the historical and sociopolitical backdrop to the revolution.

Borge, Tomás. *The Patient Impatience: From Boyhood to Guerrilla, A Personal Narrative of Nicaragua's Struggle for Liberation*. Willimantic, Conn.: Curbstone Press, 1992.

A guerrilla testimonial by one of the three founding fathers of the FSLN and a central figure in both the revolutionary government and the rapidly fragmenting FSLN of the post-Sandinista period

Burns, E. Bradford. *Patriarchs and Folk: The Emergence of Nicaragua, 1798–1858*. Cambridge, Mass.: Harvard University Press, 1991.

Written by one of our most insightful Latin Americanist historians, this volume fills an important gap in the English-language literature about Nicaragua.

Butler, Judy, David R. Dye, and Jack Spence. *Democracy and Its Discontents: Nicaraguans Face the Election*. Boston: Hemisphere Initiatives, 1996.

A very careful study of the 1996 elections.

Cabestrero, Teófilo. *Blood of the Innocent: Victims of the Contras' War in Nicaragua*. Maryknoll, N.Y.: Orbis Books, 1985.

A leading specialist on the theology of liberation and a priest working closely with Nicaragua's poor, Cabestrero describes the stark human consequences of the Contra War.

————. *Ministers of God, Ministers of the People.* Maryknoll, N.Y.: Orbis Books, 1983.

> A glimpse at three Roman Catholic priests (Fernando Cardenal, Miguel D'Escoto, and Ernesto Cardenal) who served as ministers in the Sandinista government. Brief introductory sections are followed by more lengthy direct quotations from the three priests.

Cabezas, Omar. *Fire from the Mountain: The Making of a Sandinista.* New York: Crown, 1985.

> An earthy, irreverent, humorous, yet tender and intimate first-person account of anti-Somoza and guerrilla activities in the late 1960s and early 1970s.

Cardenal, Ernesto. *The Gospel in Solentiname.* 4 vols. Maryknoll, N.Y.: Orbis Books, 1976.

> Translation of conversations concerning the meaning of the Gospel, which Cardenal conducted with his followers in the community of Solentiname.

[Central Intelligence Agency]. *Psychological Operations in Guerrilla Warfare.* New York: Vintage Books, 1985.

> Discovered by a member of Witness for Peace and disclosed by U.S. media in 1984, this controversial document, prepared in 1983 by the U.S. Central Intelligence Agency, was designed to instruct the U.S.-backed *contras* fighting the Sandinistas in the techniques of guerrilla war, including assassination, misinformation, and so on. The manual is accompanied by a historical introduction by Joanne Omang (*Washington Post*) and an epilogue by Aryeh Neier (Americas Watch).

Chamorro, Violeta Barrios de. *Dreams of the Heart: The Autobiography of President Violeta Barrios de Chamorro of Nicaragua.* New York: Simon & Schuster, 1996.

> Widow of martyred newspaper editor Pedro Joaquín Chamorro, Violeta Chamorro served as president of the republic from 1990 to 1997.

Close, David. *Nicaragua: The Chamorro Years.* Boulder, Colo.: Lynne Rienner, 1999.

> A solid overview of the first post-Sandinista administration.

Close, David, and Kalowatie Deonandan. *Undoing Democracy: The Politics of Electoral Caudillismo.* Lanham, Md.: Lexington Books, 2004.

> The most important scholarly examination of the pacts and their role in weakening Nicaraguan democracy.

Collins, Joseph. *Nicaragua: What Difference Could a Revolution Make? Food and Farming in the New Nicaragua,* 3rd ed., rev. San Francisco: Institute for Food and Development Policy, 1986.

>A beautifully written and informative study of the Sandinista Revolution focusing on agrarian reform and food policy.

Craven, David. *Art and Revolution in Latin America, 1910–1990.* New Haven, Conn.: Yale University Press, 2002.

>This book on art and revolution gives significant coverage to governmental cultural policy and the explosion of artistic expression during the Sandinista Revolution in Nicaragua.

Dickey, Christopher. *With the Contras: A Reporter in the Wilds of Nicaragua.* New York: Simon & Schuster, 1985.

>A close-up look at the *contras* by a *Washington Post* reporter who interviewed and made a brief foray with them inside Nicaragua.

Diederich, Bernard. *Somoza: And the Legacy of U.S. Involvement in Central America.* New York: E. P. Dutton, 1981.

>A journalistic but nonetheless quite solid examination of the Somoza era by *Time*'s Mexico City bureau chief. Particularly rich in its coverage of events during the final years of the dictatorship.

Dodson, Michael, and Laura Nuzzi O'Shaughnessy. *Nicaragua's Other Revolution: Religious Faith and Political Struggle.* Chapel Hill: University of North Carolina Press, 1990.

>An overview of the history and conflicting roles of religion in the Nicaraguan Revolution, this book makes a valuable contribution by setting the church-state and intra-church debates against the backdrop of conflicting models of democracy.

Donahue, John M. *The Nicaraguan Revolution in Health: From Somoza to the Sandinistas.* South Hadley, Mass.: Bergin and Garvey, 1986.

>Written by a U.S. scholar with considerable field experience in his subject, this is an important study of health policy in Nicaragua in the mid-1980s.

Dore, Elizabeth. *Myths of Modernity: Peonage and Patriarchy in Nicaragua.* Durham, N.C.: Duke University Press, 2006.

>A fascinating piece of feminist scholarship that dissects the debt-peonage system that results from the country's coffee economy, which Dore argues was organized according to patriarchal rather than capitalist principles.

Edmisten, Patricia Taylor. *Nicaragua Divided:* La Prensa *and the Chamorro Legacy.* Pensacola: University of West Florida Press, 1990.

An occasionally factually flawed and somewhat naive and romantic portrayal of the role of *La Prensa* and the Chamorro family in Nicaraguan politics, this short study nevertheless is of merit in that it presents some data about its important subject that are not readily available elsewhere.

Enriquez, Laura J. *Agrarian Reform and Class Consciousness in Nicaragua.* Gainesville: University Press of Florida, 1997.

Based on her intensive study of two Sandinista agrarian reform projects in the Masay area, the author attempts to shed light on why peasant beneficiaries voted against the Sandinistas in 1990 and which types of peasants were most/ least receptive to the revolution.

————. *Harvesting Change: Labor and Agrarian Reform in Nicaragua, 1979–1990.* Chapel Hill: University of North Carolina Press, 1991.

An important examination of the contradictions inherent in carrying out agrarian reform in an agro-export-oriented economy.

Everingham, Mark. *Revolution and the Multiclass Coalition in Nicaragua.* Pittsburgh: University of Pittsburgh Press, 1996.

Based on extensive interviews in Nicaragua, this excellent study explains why many Nicaraguan capitalists formed alliances with the FSLN insurgents in the two decades leading up to the overthrow of the Somoza regime.

Garfield, Richard, and Glean Williams. *Health and Revolution: The Nicaraguan Experience.* London: Oxfam, 1989.

A study of revolutionary health policy based on considerable observation and investigation in Nicaragua.

Gilbert, Dennis. *Sandinistas: The Party and the Revolution.* New York: Basil Blackwood, 1988.

A solid study and critique of the FSLN as a party and as the central force in the government in the 1980s.

Giraldi, Giulio. *Faith and Revolution in Nicaragua: Convergence and Contradictions.* Maryknoll, N.Y.: Orbis Books, 1989.

An Italian scholar examines the contradictions, tensions, and possibilities flowing out of the convergence of Marxism and Christianity in the Nicaraguan Revolution.

Gobat, Michel. *Confronting the American Dream: Nicaragua Under U.S. Imperial Rule.* Durham, N.C.: Duke University Press, 2006.

> A critical examination of the role of the United States in early twentieth-century Nicaragua and the transformation of elites into opponents of U.S. power.

Gould, Jeffrey L. *To Die in This Way: Nicaraguan Indians and the Myth of Mestizaje, 1880–1965.* Durham, N.C.: Duke University Press, 1998.

> An authoritative examination of the pressures applied from the nineteenth century though the 1960s by Hispanic Nicaraguan society to force various indigenous communities to become part of the national society and economy.

———. *To Lead as Equals: Rural Protest and Political Consciousness in Chinandega, Nicaragua, 1912–1979.* Chapel Hill: University of North Carolina Press, 1990.

> A very solid piece of research into the history of the peasant movement up to the time of the Sandinista victory, this book features a skillful use of oral history.

Gutman, Roy. *Banana Diplomacy: The Making of American Policy in Nicaragua, 1981–1987.* New York: Simon & Schuster, 1988.

> Written by a former State Department employee turned *Newsday* national security correspondent, this is a well-documented, meticulously researched critique of the formulation of U.S. foreign policy toward Nicaragua during most of the Reagan period.

Hale, Charles R. *Resistance and Contradiction: Miskitu Indians and the Nicaraguan State, 1894–1987.* Stanford, Calif.: Stanford University Press, 1994.

> An anthropologist and leading specialist on the indigenous peoples of the Atlantic coast of Nicaragua, Hale reconstructs the history of normally rocky coast-state relations from the point at which Nicaragua asserted its dominion over the *Costa* through the Somoza period to the period of conflict, negotiation, and accord under the Sandinistas.

Helms, Mary W. *Asang: Adaptations to Culture Contact in a Miskitu Community.* Gainesville: University of Florida Press, 1971.

> A solid ethnographic study of a Miskito community in northeastern Nicaragua.

Hirshon, Sheryl, with Judy Butler. *And Also Teach Them to Read.* Westport, Conn.: Lawrence Hill, 1983.

> A personal account of the activities of twenty-five rural literacy *brigadistas* during the 1980 Literacy Crusade. The author, a teacher from Oregon, served as their group leader.

Hodges, Donald C. *Intellectual Foundations of the Nicaraguan Revolution.* Austin: University of Texas Press, 1986.

> An excellent study of the roots of Sandinismo by one of the leading U.S. authorities on the left in Latin America.

Horton, Lynn. *Peasants in Arms: War and Peace in the Mountains of Nicaragua, 1979–1994.* Athens: Ohio University Center for International Studies, 1998.

> Based on extensive field research in the region, this study examines and explains the involvement of peasants in northern Nicaragua in revolutionary and counterrevolutionary struggle.

Hoyt, Katherine. *The Many Faces of Sandinista Democracy.* Athens: Ohio University Center for International Studies, 1997.

> An excellent study of Sandinista democracy, which had a rich participatory aspect even before it became formally electoral and representative.

Isbester, Katherine. *Still Fighting: The Nicaraguan Women's Movement, 1977–2000.* Pittsburgh: University of Pittsburgh Press, 2001.

> By tracing the history of the women's movement in Nicaragua, the author makes a valuable contribution to the literature on social movements in general and the women's struggle in particular.

Jones, Adam. *Beyond the Barricades: Nicaragua and the Struggle for the Sandinista Press, 1979–1998.* Athens: Ohio University Press, 2002.

> A thoughtful and original analysis of the role of *Barricada*, the official newspaper of the FSLN, from the time of the revolution until it closed in 1998.

Kamman, William. *A Search for Stability: U.S. Diplomacy Toward Nicaragua, 1925–1933.* Notre Dame, Ind.: University of Notre Dame Press, 1968.

> A thorough and useful study of an extremely important period of U.S.-Nicaraguan relations.

Kampwirth, Karen. *Women and Guerrilla Movements: Nicaragua, El Salvador, Chiapas, and Cuba.* University Park: Pennsylvania State University Press, 2002.

> Using interviews with more than two hundred female guerrilla participants, Kampwirth looks at how women came to be guerrillas and how their experience changed their lives and impacted their societies.

Kinzer, Stephen, and Merilee Grindle. *Blood of Brothers: Life and War in Nica-ragua.* Cambridge, Mass.: David Rockefeller Center for Latin American Studies, 2007.

> The Nicaraguan Revolution from the point of view of the *New York Times* reporter in Nicaragua who, throughout the 1980s, was responsible for "making the news fit" for that mainstream U.S. publication.

Kirk, John M. *Politics and the Catholic Church in Nicaragua.* Gainesville: University of Florida Press, 1992.

> A solid study of the internal politics of the Nicaraguan Catholic Church during the Sandinista government.

Kornbluh, Peter. *Nicaragua: The Price of Intervention.* Washington, D.C.: Institute for Policy Studies, 1987.

> Covers various aspects of U.S. intervention in Nicaragua, including the Contra War, direct CIA activity, economic strangulation, and military encirclement.

Lake, Anthony. *Somoza Falling.* Boston: Houghton Mifflin, 1989.

> Lake, who was a State Department official at the time of Somoza's decline, describes the failure of U.S. policy making in the years immediately preceding the overthrow of the Somoza dictatorship.

Lancaster, Roger N. *Life Is Hard: Machismo, Danger, and the Intimacy of Power in Nicaragua.* Berkeley: University of California Press, 1992.

> This beautiful ethnography was researched in the late 1980s in a poor neighborhood in Managua as the Nicaraguan Revolution was slowly being suffocated by the U.S.-sponsored low-intensity war.

———. *Thanks to God and the Revolution: Popular Religion and Class Consciousness in the New Nicaragua.* New York: Columbia University Press, 1988.

> This excellent, anthropologically based study of the role of religion in the Nicaraguan Revolution innovates by going beyond the conventional wisdom to demonstrate that the revolutionary role of many poor Nicaraguan Catholics can be traced to centuries-old anti-elitist characteristics in local folk religiosity.

Latin American Studies Association. *Electoral Democracy Under International Pressure: The Report of the Latin American Studies Association Commission to Observe the 1990 Nicaraguan Elections.* Pittsburgh: LASA, 1990.

In the fall of 1989 and the winter of 1990, a team of LASA observers made repeated field trips to Nicaragua to study not only the election itself but also the background conditions and campaign leading up to it. This report is based on those meticulous observations. This and the three LASA reports listed below are available through the LASA Secretariat, William Pitt Union, Room 946, University of Pittsburgh, Pittsburgh, Penn. 13260.

————. *The Electoral Process in Nicaragua: Domestic and International Influences: The Report of the Latin American Studies Delegation to Observe the Election of November 4, 1984.* Austin, Texas: LASA, 1984.

A lengthy and careful study of the 1984 elections and the background conditions leading up to them. LASA's conclusion that this was a relatively fair and meaningful election was corroborated by delegations sent by the British and Irish parliaments as well as the Dutch government. Lengthy excerpts from the LASA report can be found in Rosset and Vandermeer, *Nicaragua, Unfinished Revolution: The New Nicaragua Reader*, pp. 73–107.

————. *Extraordinary Opportunities and New Risks: Final Report of the LASA Commission on Compliance with the Central American Peace Accord.* Pittsburgh: LASA, 1988.

Another LASA team observer effort, this is a careful examination of the implementation of the 1987 peace accords as of early 1988.

————. *Peace and Autonomy on the Atlantic Coast of Nicaragua: A Report of the LASA Task Force on Human Rights and Academic Freedom.* Pittsburgh: LASA, 1986.

A careful team study of the human rights situation and efforts to achieve peace on the Atlantic coast of Nicaragua as of 1986.

Lethander, Richard Walter Oscar. *The Economy of Nicaragua.* Ph.D. dissertation, Duke University, 1968.

A substantial but quite traditional examination of the Nicaraguan economic system in the mid-1960s. This and the other dissertations mentioned in this section are available for purchase in photostatic copies or microfilm from University Microfilms International, 300 N. Zeeb Road, Ann Arbor, Mich. 48106.

Macaulay, Neill. *The Sandino Affair.* Chicago: Quadrangle Books, 1967.

A sound and scholarly study of the guerrilla war led by Augusto C. Sandino against occupying U.S. forces in the late 1920s and early 1930s.

Martinez Cuenca, Alejandro. *Sandinista Economics in Practice: An Insider's Critical Reflections.* Boston: South End Press, 1992.

> Minister of economic planning during the Sandinista government, Martinez Cuenca offers a frank appraisal of that government's economic problems and the role the Sandinistas themselves played in them.

Méndez, Jennifer Bickham. *From the Revolution to the Maquiladoras: Gender, Labor, and Globalization in Nicaragua.* Durham, N.C.: Duke University Press, 2005.

> An important look at the women's labor movement and the challenges of organizing in free trade zones in the new global era.

Merrill, Tim L., et al., eds. *Nicaragua: A Country Study.* Washington, D.C.: U.S. Department of the Army, 1994.

> Like the Army's country study of Nicaragua produced in 1982 (see Rudolph, below), this one contains much useful information but stays carefully within the narrow bounds of Washington, D.C., "conventional wisdom." The chapters on history and politics, for instance, completely ignore the massive U.S. manipulation of the 1990 elections.

Mijeski, Kenneth J., ed. *The Nicaraguan Constitution of 1987: English Translation and Commentary.* Athens, Ohio: Monographs in International Studies, Latin America Series no. 17, 1991.

> After a historical introduction by the editor, this important volume presents the complete text of the 1987 Nicaraguan constitution followed by lengthy analysis and commentary by a variety of supporters and detractors.

Miller, Valerie. *Between Struggle and Hope: The Nicaraguan Literacy Crusade.* Boulder, Colo.: Westview Press, 1985.

> An intimate and moving, yet scholarly examination of Nicaragua's 1980 Literacy Crusade by a North American scholar who served as an international adviser in that ambitious program.

Millett, Richard. *The Guardians of the Dynasty: A History of the U.S.-Created Guardia Nacional de Nicaragua and the Somoza Family.* Maryknoll, N.Y.: Orbis Books, 1977.

> A scholarly, historical study of the creation of the National Guard, the rise and reign of the Somozas, and the role played in all of this by the United States.

Morley, Morris H. *Washington, Somoza and the Sandinistas: State and Regime in U.S. Policy Towards Nicaragua, 1969–1981.* New York: Cambridge University Press, 1994.

An excellent study of U.S. policy toward Nicaragua under the last Somoza administration and during the first two years of the Sandinista Revolution. Very insightful in its explanation of the fundamentals of U.S. foreign policy toward Nicaragua and, indeed, Latin America in general.

Mulligan, Joseph E. *The Nicaraguan Church and the Revolution.* Kansas City, Mo.: Sheed & Ward, 1991.

Written by a Jesuit priest who moved to Nicaragua in 1986, this is yet another solid contribution to the surprisingly large body of literature on church and revolution in Nicaragua.

Nietschmann, Bernard. *Between Land and Water: The Subsistence Ecology of the Miskito Indians, Eastern Nicaragua.* New York: Seminar Press, 1973.

Like the Helms monograph, this, too, is a very sound study of a Miskito community, the turtle-fishing village of Tasbapauni.

Norsworthy, Kent, with Tom Barry. *Nicaragua: A Country Guide.* Albuquerque, N.M.: Inter-Hemispheric Education Resource Center, 1990.

This overview of Nicaragua provides a wealth of information about contemporary politics in that country. It is an excellent resource for those interested in the early period of transition from the Sandinista administration to UNO rule.

Pastor, Robert. *Not Condemned to Repetition: The U.S. and Nicaragua,* 2nd ed. Princeton, N.J.: Princeton University Press, 2002.

A criticism of Reagan administration policy in Nicaragua by a principal actor in the Carter administration policy toward that country.

Paszyn, Danuta. *The Soviet Attitude to Political and Social Change in Central America, 1979–1990: Case Studies on Nicaragua, El Salvador, and Guatemala.* New York: St. Martin's Press, in association with the School of Slavonic and East European Studies, University of London, 2000.

Using recently released Soviet documents unavailable during the cold war, the author lays to rest the U.S. government's argument in the 1980s that the conflicts in Central America were little more than a manifestation of "Soviet expansionism." To the contrary, Paszyn, whose best coverage is of the Nicaraguan aspect, shows that the Soviet Union was a very reluctant and restrained actor in its policy toward that country.

Pezzullo, Lawrence. *At the Fall of Somoza.* Pittsburgh: University of Pittsburgh Press, 1993.

The personal observations of the career diplomat who served as U.S. ambassador to Nicaragua at the time of the fall of Somoza and the beginning of the revolutionary government.

Prevost, Gary, and Harry E. Vanden, eds. *The Undermining of the Sandinista Revolution*. New York: St. Martin's Press, 1997.

A fine edited volume that examines the forces that contributed to the demise of the Sandinista Revolution. Though principal responsibility is placed on the United States, Sandinista errors and domestic causes are also cited.

Radell, David Richard. *An Historical Geography of Western Nicaragua: The Spheres of Influence of León, Granada, and Managua, 1519–1965*. Ph.D. dissertation, University of California, Berkeley, 1969.

A very good historical study of major regions of western Nicaragua.

Randall, Margaret. *Sandino's Daughters: Testimonies of Nicaraguan Women in Struggle*. Vancouver and Toronto: New Star Books, 1981.

A series of interviews with some of the most important women in the Nicaraguan Revolution.

Reyes, Reynaldo, and J. K. Wilson. *Rafaga: The Life Story of a Nicaraguan Miskito Comandante*. Norman: University of Oklahoma Press, 1992.

The biography of an important *contra* commander, who at first fought against and later made peace with the Sandinista Revolution.

Robinson, William I. *A Faustian Bargain: U.S. Intervention in the Nicaraguan Elections and American Foreign Policy in the Post–Cold War Era*. Boulder, Colo.: Westview Press, 1992.

A solid exposé of the truly massive covert/overt U.S. involvement in the Nicaraguan elections of 1990.

Ruchwarger, Gary. *People in Power: Forging a Grassroots Democracy in Nicaragua*. Granby, Mass.: Bergin and Garvey, 1987.

An excellent examination of the role of grassroots organizations in the creation of what the Sandinistas called "participatory" democracy.

Rudolph, James D., ed. *Nicaragua: A Country Study*. Washington, D.C.: Government Printing Office, 1982.

Produced under contract with the U.S. government, this volume is in the tradition and format of the old Area Handbook series (see Ryan et al., 1970).

However, it is a solid and useful study, and remarkably, much of what is said in it contradicts the negative picture that the Reagan administration was trying to paint of Nicaragua.

Ryan, John Morris, et al. *Area Handbook on Nicaragua.* Washington, D.C.: U.S. Government Printing Office, 1970.

Though written for the U.S. government and concerned in part with "order and internal security" under the Somoza system, this study contains much valuable information about a variety of subjects pertaining to Nicaragua.

Ryan, Phil. *The Fall and Rise of the Market in Sandinista Nicaragua.* Montreal: McGill-Queens University Press, 1995.

Though sympathetic to the Sandinista Revolution, the author shows how FSLN mistakes—often driven by ideological considerations—contributed to economic failure in the 1980s.

Selser, Gregorio. *Sandino.* New York: Monthly Review Press, 1981.

A translation by Cedric Belfrage of Selser's excellent two-volume Spanish-language work, *Sandino, General de hombres libres* (Buenos Aires: Editorial Triángulo, 1958). Contains many of Sandino's writings.

Snarr, Neil, and associates. *Sandinista Nicaragua: An Annotated Bibliography with Analytical Introductions* (Part 1: Revolution, Religion and Social Policy, and Part 2: Economy, Politics and Foreign Policy). Ann Arbor, Mich.: Pierian Press, 1989, 1990.

Excellent, comprehensive annotated bibliographies that cover nearly the entire span of the Sandinista Revolution.

Solaún, Mairicio. *U.S. Intervention and Regime Change in Nicaragua.* Omaha: University of Nebraska Press, 2005.

An interesting look at patterns and cycles of U.S. intervention in Nicaragua during the Somoza years by the U.S. ambassador to Nicaragua from 1977 to 1979.

Somoza, Anastasio, and Jack Cox. *Nicaragua Betrayed.* Belmont, Mass.: Western Islands, 1980.

Somoza's side of the story, of interest not so much as a reliable source of information but, rather, as a historical curiosity.

Spalding, Rose J., ed. *Capitalists and Revolution in Nicaragua: Opposition and Accommodation, 1979–1993.* Chapel Hill: University of North Carolina Press, 1994.

Based on extensive in-country research and interviews, this is the best available study of Nicaragua's capitalist class during and just after the Sandinista period.

————. *The Political Economy of Revolutionary Nicaragua.* Boston: Allen and Unwin, 1987.

In this fine study, a team of scholars examines the political economy of the Nicaraguan Revolution in the context of the revolution's domestic and international constraints.

Spoor, Max. *The State and Domestic Agricultural Markets in Nicaragua: Opposition and Accommodation, 1979–1993.* New York: St. Martin's Press, 1995.

Based on considerable research in Nicaragua, this study examines errors in Sandinista agricultural policy and compares them with policy under Chamorro, which the author feels was also flawed.

Strachan, Harry Wallace. *The Role of Business Groups in Economic Development: The Case of Nicaragua.* D.B.A. dissertation, Harvard University, 1972.

A traditional but very useful examination of the major business groups in the Nicaraguan economic system in the late 1960s.

Vanden, Harry E. *Democracy and Socialism in Sandinista Nicaragua.* Boulder, Colo.: Lynne Rienner Publishers, 1993.

A very useful study based on extensive field research and observation throughout the revolutionary period.

Vanderlaan, Mary B. *Revolution and Foreign Policy in Nicaragua.* Boulder, Colo.: Westview Press, 1986.

A solid and detailed analysis of Nicaraguan foreign policy under the Sandinistas, appropriately set against the background of domestic and international constraints.

Vilas, Carlos. *State, Class, and Ethnicity in Nicaragua: Capitalist Modernization and Revolutionary Change on the Atlantic Coast.* Boulder, Colo.: Westview Press, 1989.

A study of the problems of the Atlantic coast during the Sandinista Revolution by one of the world's leading authorities on the subject.

————. *The Sandinista Revolution.* New York: Monthly Review Press, 1985.

An Argentine scholar who lived in Nicaragua from 1980 onward, Vilas provides an insightful class analysis of the insurrection and the revolutionary system that emerged after the Triumph.

Walker, Thomas W. *The Christian Democratic Movement in Nicaragua.* Tucson: University of Arizona Press, 1970.

This brief study of the Christian Democratic, or Social Christian, movement in Nicaragua examines party and related interest-group organization and activity during the heyday of the Christian Democratic opposition in the 1960s.

————, ed. *Nicaragua: The First Five Years.* New York: Praeger, 1985.

A product of the field research of more than thirty scholars, this book systematically examines the Nicaraguan Revolution through its first half-decade in power. Its twenty-five chapters focus on a variety of topics under four main headings: power and interests, economic policy, social policy, and the international dimension. An epilogue contains a condensed version of the LASA report on the 1984 elections.

————, ed. *Nicaragua in Revolution.* New York: Praeger, 1982.

Similar in concept to *Nicaragua: The First Five Years,* this earlier volume concentrates on the first year and a half of revolutionary rule. In addition, it features a three-chapter section dealing with the insurrection.

————, ed. *Nicaragua Without Illusions: Regime Transition and Structural Adjustment in the 1990s.* Wilmington, Del.: Scholarly Resources, 1997.

Representing the work of nineteen specialists, this volume provides a comprehensive overview of Nicaragua during the administration of Violeta Barrios de Chamorro. Its chapters are divided under three headings: the international setting, the new order, and groups and institutions.

————, ed. *Reagan versus the Sandinistas: The Undeclared War on Nicaragua.* Boulder, Colo.: Westview Press, 1987.

Also utilizing a team approach, this book provides a comprehensive examination of the most massive action, short of direct U.S. invasion, ever mounted by the United States against a foreign government. In addition to dealing with obvious topics such as the contra invasion, military encirclement, and economic destabilization, it examines disinformation, the "patriotic agenda" in the U.S. media, radio-TV penetration of Nicaragua, and the implications of Reagan's Nicaragua policy for international law and world order.

————, ed. *Revolution and Counterrevolution in Nicaragua.* Boulder, Colo.: Westview Press, 1991.

An international team of eighteen specialists systematically examines all important aspects of both the Sandinista Revolution and the U.S.-orchestrated counterrevolution that brought it to an end. Each chapter covers its subject from its historical beginning to the inauguration of the U.S.-sponsored candidate, Violeta Barrios de Chamorro, in 1990.

Walker, (General) William. *The War in Nicaragua*. Tucson: University of Arizona Press, 1985.

A personal account of "the first American invasion of Central America," by William Walker, the U.S. adventurer who briefly imposed himself as president of Nicaragua in the 1850s.

Walter, Knut. *The Regime of Anastasio Somoza, 1936–1956*. Chapel Hill: University of North Carolina Press, 1998.

Meticulously researched in Nicaragua for well over a decade, this is the best study yet of the first member of the Somoza dynasty.

Webb, Gary. *Dark Alliance: The CIA, the Contras, and the Crack Cocaine Explosion*. New York: Seven Stories Press, 1998.

This book, which alleges a connection among the CIA, the *contras*, and an upsurge in cocaine use in Los Angeles, comes out of a series of articles by Webb in the *San Jose Mercury News*. Though the articles were roundly criticized by the mainstream U.S. media, the book is well documented. In addition, it has considerable surface plausibility since this would not be the first time that the CIA had used drug money to finance a secret operation (e.g., CIA operations in Laos during the Vietnam War).

Whisnant, David E. *Rascally Signs in Sacred Places: The Politics of Culture in Nicaragua*. Chapel Hill: University of North Carolina Press, 1995.

A massive and well-researched examination of Nicaraguan culture and its interplay with politics.

Williams, Philip J. *The Catholic Church and Politics in Nicaragua and Costa Rica*. Pittsburgh: University of Pittsburgh Press, 1989.

Though looking at the role of the church in the rather dissimilar political settings of Costa Rica and Nicaragua, Williams shows, nevertheless, that the church hierarchy in both countries has acted to obstruct the movements for social change out of apparent fear that such movements threaten the teaching authority and influence of its ancient institution.

Wright, Bruce E. *Theory in the Practice of the Nicaraguan Revolution*. Athens: Ohio University Center for International Studies, 1995.

Appearing on *Choice Magazine*'s list of "Outstanding Academic Books" for 1995, this volume masterfully demonstrates how the Sandinista concept of

Socialist revolution evolved over time to accommodate changing reality in Nicaragua.

Zimmerman, Matilde. *Sandinista: Carlos Fonseca and the Nicaraguan Revolution.* Durham, N.C.: Duke University Press, 2000.

This well-researched book focuses on the most important, yet often mis-understood, figures in the FSLN insurgency of the 1960s and 1970s.

PERIODICALS

Clearly the most useful and scholarly English language periodical devoted to Nicaragua is *Envío* (English edition). Published monthly by the Instituto Histórico Centroamericano in Managua, it is reproduced and distributed in the United States ($40 per subscription) by the Central American Historical Institute, Intercultural Center, Room 307, Georgetown University, Washington, D.C. 20057.

Index